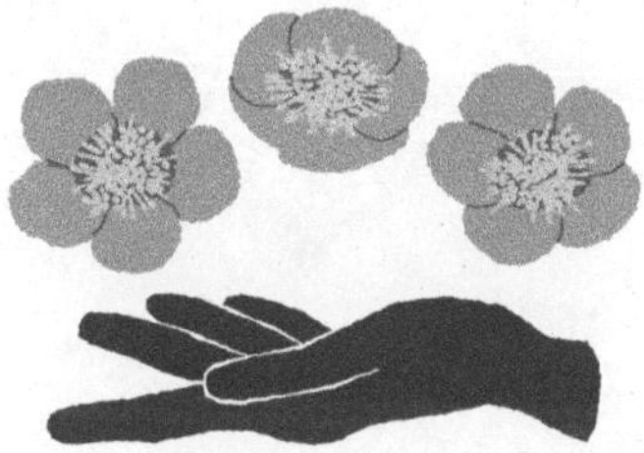

SPARE THE CHILD

Ending Childhood Corporal Punishment

AILSA M. WATKINSON

University of Regina Press

Printed and bound in Canada. The text of this book is printed on 100% post-consumer recycled paper with earth-friendly vegetable-based inks.

Cover design: Evan Marnoch
Interior layout design: John van der Woude, JVDW Designs
Copyeditor: Rachel Ironstone
Indexer: Jess Herdman

Library and Archives Canada Cataloguing in Publication

Title: Spare the child : ending childhood corporal punishment / Ailsa M. Watkinson.
Names: Watkinson, Ailsa M., author
Description: Includes bibliographical references and index.
Identifiers: Canadiana (print) 20250270129 | Canadiana (ebook) 20250270153 | ISBN 9781779401045 (softcover) | ISBN 9781779401052 (hardcover) | ISBN 9781779401069 (EPUB) | ISBN 9781779401076 (PDF)
Subjects: LCSH: Corporal punishment of children—Law and legislation—Canada.
Classification: LCC KE3515.W38 2026 | LCC KF3735.W38 2026 kfmod | DDC 346.7101/7—dc23

10 9 8 7 6 5 4 3 2 1

U OF R PRESS

University of Regina Press, University of Regina
Regina, Saskatchewan, Canada, S4S 0A2
TEL: (306) 585-4758 FAX: (306) 585-4699
WEB: www.uofrpress.ca

We acknowledge the support of the Canada Council for the Arts for our publishing program. We acknowledge the financial support of the Government of Canada. / Nous reconnaissons l'appui financier du gouvernement du Canada. This publication was made possible with support from Creative Saskatchewan's Book Publishing Production Grant Program.

Canada Council for the Arts Conseil des Arts du Canada
Canada
creative SASKATCHEWAN

For Jake and Emma

This book is dedicated to all children and to those who work to improve their lives by protecting them from cruelty and violence and by enabling the provision and enjoyment of a child's rights to justice, equality, and care as promised in the United Nations *Convention on the Rights of the Child.*

CONTENTS

ACKNOWLEDGEMENTS

I wish to extend my heartfelt thanks to all who have contributed to my book. This includes reviewers, researchers, the publisher, colleagues, family, and friends. Thank you to those who were meticulous in their reviews and offered tangible suggestions to strengthen the manuscript. Thank you to the committed professionals and researchers whose works have inspired me and informed and shaped this book. Thank you to the University of Regina Press and their professional and supportive staff, including my acquisition editor, Rachel F. Stapleton, and my managing editor, Shannon Parr. Their expertise and encouragement have been invaluable. Finally, I want to thank my family, colleagues, and friends for their support and encouragement throughout this journey, and thank you to my friend the poet Rita Bouvier for entrusting her poem "remembering Charlie" to this book.

A NOTE ON TERMINOLOGY

Throughout this book, I use the term *Indigenous* to include the First Peoples of Canada—Inuit, Métis, and First Nations. Other terms such as *First Nations, Indian, Métis, Inuit,* and *Aboriginal Peoples* appear as recorded by others.

The terms *corporal punishment, child physical punishment, spanking,* and *smacking* are used interchangeably, depending on the terms used in research or quotes. The United Nations' definition of corporal punishment includes these terms. In my own writings, I use the terms *corporal punishment* and *child physical punishment* interchangeably. I do not use the word *spanking* when describing child physical punishment as I consider the word a euphemistic cover for all the harm and brutality that can hide behind it.

DEFINITIONS

Anti-social behaviour: Aggressive actions against siblings, parents, and others such as hitting, bullying, verbal abuse, and threats.

Assault: The *Criminal Code of Canada* defines assault as follows:

s. 265 (1) A person commits an assault when

(a) without the consent of another person, he applies force intentionally to that other person, directly or indirectly;

(b) he attempts or threatens, by an act or a gesture, to apply force to another person, if he has, or causes that other person to believe on reasonable grounds that he has, present ability to effect his purpose; or

(c) while openly wearing or carrying a weapon or an imitation thereof, he accosts or impedes another person or begs.

Child maltreatment: Causing harm and injury through physical abuse, sexual abuse, emotional abuse, physical and emotional neglect, and exposure to intimate partner violence. At this time, child physical punishment that does not cause harm or injury does not meet the standard of maltreatment.

Child physical abuse: Classified as a form of child maltreatment, child physical abuse currently differs from child physical punishment in that it implies physical harm or injury.

Child physical punishment: Used interchangeably with *corporal punishment*. Includes such actions as spanking, smacking, hitting, and physical force. The act of hitting a child as a means of discipline, including actions that do not cause injury or harm.

Corporal or physical punishment: Defined by the United Nations Committee on the Rights of the Child as

> any punishment in which physical force is used and intended to cause some degree of pain or discomfort, however light. Most involves hitting ("smacking," "slapping," "spanking") children, with the hand or with an implement—whip, stick, belt, shoe, wooden spoon, etc. But it can also involve, for example, kicking, shaking or throwing children, scratching, pinching, burning, scalding or forced ingestion (for example, washing children's mouths out with soap or forcing them to swallow hot spices).

The phrase is synonymous with the terms *child physical punishment* and *physical force*, and the words *hitting*, *smacking*, and *spanking*, and these terms are used interchangeably throughout this book.

Defence: A legal provision to negate what otherwise might be a crime, such as an assault.

Indigenous Peoples: Includes First Nations, Inuit, and Métis peoples in Canada.

Positive discipline: Non-violent, solution-focused, and respectful guidance based on the child's age and development. The focus is on verbal interactions—explaining to a child why something is wrong, providing clear and firm age-appropriate rules, being consistent in what is considered appropriate behaviour, providing structure and predictability bolstered by a warm and involved family environment.

Spanking: Hitting a child twice on the buttocks with an open hand. However, this term is often used euphemistically to describe severe hitting.

Trauma-informed care (TIC): TIC explicitly acknowledges and makes a deliberate attempt to understand the impact of traumatic events such as adverse childhood experiences (ACEs). It can be incorporated in many professional practices to support the health-care needs of clients within a safe environment. The focus is on "what happened to you?" rather than "what's wrong with you?"

Violence: Behaviour involving threats and/or physical force to harm or intimidate another.

ACRONYMS

ACEs: adverse childhood experiences
CFCYL: Canadian Foundation for Children, Youth and the Law
CRC: United Nations *Convention on the Rights of the Child*
TRC: Truth and Reconciliation Commission
UN: United Nations
UNICEF: United Nations Children's Fund (formerly the United Nations International Children's Emergency Fund)

PREFACE

> *In their mission to civilize and Christianize, the school staff relied on corporal punishment to discipline their students.... The [Truth and Reconciliation] Commission believes that corporal punishment is a relic of a discredited past and has no place in Canadian schools or homes.* ***We call upon the government of Canada to repeal Section 43 of the Criminal Code of Canada.***[1]

During the summer of 1994, the American Peterson family were holidaying in Canada. The parents, David and Paula, along with their children, Rachel (five years old) and William (almost two), were celebrating Paula's birthday at an Ontario restaurant. At some point, David and the children left the restaurant to collect a gift for Paula that was in the car. The children were in the back seat and, as noted by the Ontario Provincial Court judge, "almost immediately, young Rachel started to misbehave. She started fighting with her brother"[2] and pushed him out of the open car door. When William attempted to climb back in, Rachel slammed the door of the car on her brother's fingers. He screamed. David pulled Rachel out of the car, placed her across the trunk of the car, and administered a "bare bottom spanking." The event was witnessed by a number of people, one of whom called the

---

1 Truth and Reconciliation Commission of Canada (TRC), *Honouring the Truth, Reconciling for the Future*, 144–45. Emphasis added.

2 *R. v. Peterson*, [1995], 98 CCC (3d) 253 (Ont. CJ (Prov. Div.)), at ¶ 8.

police, and Mr. Peterson was charged with assaulting Rachel. The story hit newspapers across the country.

I read the news reports at the time and knew that the chances of Mr. Peterson being convicted of assault were slim to none. The reason being that parents, teachers, and others acting in the place of parents are provided with a defence within the *Criminal Code of Canada*. Section 43 is one of several defences within the *Criminal Code* that permits the use of force in specific incidences. Section 43 excuses those who use physical force on children for the purpose of correction, making children the only group of people specifically mentioned in the *Criminal Code* upon whom corporal punishment can be used. It states the following:

> Every school teacher, parent or person standing in the place of the parent is justified in using force by way of correction toward the pupil or child, as the case may be, who is under his care, if the force does not exceed what is reasonable under the circumstances.[3]

Mr. Peterson was successful in using section 43 as his defence. The Ontario Provincial Court ruled that the physical punishment he meted out upon his five-year-old daughter was "reasonable under the circumstances," and thus the assault charge against him was dismissed.[4]

I had written previously about child physical punishment, calling for an end to its use as a form of discipline and seeking the repeal of s. 43 of the *Criminal Code*.[5] The Peterson case spurred me on to apply the law—the *Canadian Charter of Rights and Freedoms*—in my challenge of s. 43. The *Charter* challenge argued that s. 43 of the *Criminal Code of Canada* violated the equality rights of children under the *Charter* (s. 15) as well as their right to "security of the person" (s. 7), and that corporal punishment is a form of "cruel and unusual treatment" (s. 12). The case, carried forward by the Canadian Foundation for Children, Youth and the Law, was eventually heard by the Supreme Court of Canada, which issued its decision in

---

3 *Criminal Code of Canada*, RSC 1985, c. C-46.

4 *R. v. Peterson*, [1995], 98 CCC (3d) 253 (Ont. CJ (Prov. Div.)).

5 Watkinson, "Corporal Punishment: Apply the Charter," 15; Watkinson, "Children Still Unprotected from Violence," A11.

January 2004, and upheld s. 43 of the *Criminal Code*,[6] while clarifying the limits of its scope.

The focus of this book, informed by critical theory, comes from a children's rights perspective and advocates for the right of children to a caring and non-violent upbringing. The book traces the historical, legal, and common law justifications for using physical force on children and critically examines the legal process involved in using the *Canadian Charter of Rights and Freedoms*[7] and international human rights documents, specifically the United Nations *Convention on the Rights of the Child*,[8] as a means of promoting change to common social practices. The analysis focuses in large part on the legal attempt to transform the inequitable status of children to individuals endowed with rights.[9].

The debate and subsequent Supreme Court challenge were seen by some as promoting the rights of children as autonomous beings. Others saw it as a threat to parental authority and autonomy, to religious values, and to family values. They represent a conflict between the characterization of the oppression and domination of children on the one hand and the need to protect and enhance parental authority to raise children as they see fit on the other. It is a conflict that calls upon the authority of human rights laws, religious teachings, custom, social science, common law, and "common sense."

This book explores and records the history of corporal punishment in Canada, the assumptions supporting its use, the justification for banning the use of corporal punishment on some citizens but not others, the legal arguments used in the *Charter* challenge, the evidence presented, and the final outcome and parents' understanding of the Supreme Court decision and the implications it has for them. Finally, it highlights the effectiveness of human rights laws in bringing about social transformation.

---

6 *Canadian Foundation for Children, Youth and the Law v. Canada (Attorney General)*, [2004] 1 SCR 76.

7 *Canadian Charter of Rights and Freedoms*, as enacted by *Canada Act, 1982*, (UK), 1982 C.11. See appendix A.

8 *Convention on the Rights of the Child*, (1989), UN Doc. A/RES/44/25 (1989). See appendix B.

9 Price Cohen et al., "The UN *Convention on the Rights of the Child*," 216; Turner and Finkelhor, "Corporal Punishment as a Stressor Among Youth," 155.

SECTIONS AND CHAPTERS

Section I

Chapter 1 provides a historical account of the social and legal status of childhood and the development and iterations of s. 43 of Canada's *Criminal Code* throughout its history. It considers the legacy of European colonization, religion, and ideology in the acceptance and justification of child physical punishment.

Chapter 2 explores the disruption within Indigenous families brought about by colonialism. Prior to European colonization, Indigenous children were raised, educated, and nurtured within their homes and communities and upon the land. Early colonizers recorded that physical punishment was not a form of discipline. Indigenous familial connections were abruptly disrupted by the establishment of residential schools. Residential school history is highlighted in this chapter to illustrate the colonial influence on the spread of child physical punishment and lack of regard for children—racialized children in particular. The chapter explores the findings of the Truth and Reconciliation Commission and their call to repeal s. 43, while outlining the intergenerational harm residential schools has caused Indigenous people and families.

Chapter 3 reviews the development of child welfare and the lack of awareness of child physical punishment as a form of child maltreatment. The historical account moves into the twenty-first century with an exploration of the move toward children's rights as outlined in Canada's *Charter of Rights and Freedoms*[10] and the United Nations *Convention on the Rights of the Child*.[11]

Section II

Section II focuses on the legal challenge to section 43, including the arguments in the case, the decision, and the aftermath. The legal process undertaken to challenge s. 43 of Canada's *Criminal Code* is discussed in chapter 4, detailing the arguments for and against the challenge. The chapter describes the legal challenge, the role of the *Charter of Rights and*

---

10 *Canadian Charter of Rights and Freedoms*, as enacted by *Canada Act, 1982*, (UK), 1982 C.11.

11 *Convention on the Rights of the Child*, (1989), UN Doc. A/RES/44/25 (1989).

Freedoms, the UN *Convention on the Rights of the Child*, international human rights laws, social science research, and the roles and positions of the intervenors in the case.

Chapter 5 reviews and critically analyzes the Canadian Supreme Court's ruling, in a 6–3 split decision, that s. 43 is constitutional—a ruling that rejected all arguments put forward challenging its constitutionality. While the Supreme Court refused to find s. 43 unconstitutional, it developed limits on the use of s. 43, referred to as the "zone of risk."

Chapter 6 discusses the aftermath of the Supreme Court's decision regarding the public's knowledge of the case and the limitations it placed on the use of child physical punishment. It also reviews the application of the limits to child welfare cases and subsequent legal cases dealing with child physical punishment.

Section III

Chapter 7 takes an in-depth look at current research, which consistently shows the harm associated with child physical punishment. Social science evidence demonstrates that child physical punishment has negative long-term social, emotional, and developmental outcomes. The evidence has grown exponentially since the 2004 Supreme Court decision. This evidence lends further support to the human rights obligation to end child physical punishment.

The final chapter contemplates where we go from here. It explores the possibility of instigating a new challenge to s. 43 of the *Criminal Code of Canada*, considering recent Supreme Court decisions that have opened the door to revisiting previous *Charter* cases found constitutional. It also examines the experiences of other countries that have done away with their equivalent of s. 43 and provides alternatives to the fear of "criminalizing" parents who use corporal punishment on their children. It discusses other means of working with children to guide their behaviour and actions that do not include physical punishment. Chapter 8 also discusses the implications of the Supreme Court decision for parents, child protection workers, teachers, police, religious leaders, health-care professionals, children's advocates, and policy-makers and concludes with recommendations for change.

SECTION ONE

1

A BRIEF HISTORY OF CHILDHOOD CORPORAL PUNISHMENT

It is difficult, if not impossible, to make anyone, child or adult, realize the justice of a flogging. To the contrary, flogging is almost certain to arouse in the individual who is punished, whatever be the nature of his offence, a feeling of injustice.[1]

LEGAL STATUS OF CORPORAL PUNISHMENT

CHILDHOOD, ACCORDING TO SEVENTEENTH-CENTURY FRENCH cleric Pierre de Bérulle, "is the most vile and abject state of human nature, after that of death."[2] American law professor Susan Bitensky describes childhood as moving "in dark shadows that loom large with fear and pain."[3] I argue that these shadows are cast by adults with the backing of legal authority and power to use corporal punishment on young children, all in the name of discipline.

1 Ryley Scott, *The History of Corporal Punishment*, 244.
2 Heywood, *A History of Childhood*, 9, citing Pierre de Bérulle.
3 Bitensky, *Corporal Punishment of Children*, xiii.

Children, like adults, value their personal safety. As adults, we object to and are insulted by slaps and blows to the body. Yet, even though our sense of outrage and shock over intrusions into our personal security is at times visceral, we do not as easily acknowledge the same reaction in children. Such an inability to empathize with children is a curious fact, particularly since we all were children once. Why is it, then, that corporal punishment is still permitted and in fact is a legal entitlement in many jurisdictions, including Canada?

Corporal or physical punishment[4] is defined by the United Nations Committee on the Rights of the Child as

> any punishment in which physical force is used and intended to cause some degree of pain or discomfort, however light. Most involves hitting ("smacking," "slapping," "spanking") children, with the hand or with an implement—whip, stick, belt, shoe, wooden spoon, etc. But it can also involve, for example, kicking, shaking or throwing children, scratching, pinching, burning, scalding or forced ingestion (for example, washing children's mouths out with soap or forcing them to swallow hot spices).[5]

At the same time, it is considered a violation of Canada's *Criminal Code* to apply force upon another without their consent—such force is considered an assault. Section 265 of the *Criminal Code of Canada* states that a person commits an assault when they apply force to another without their consent, threatens to apply force to another, or impedes a person while carrying a weapon.[6] However, there are times and circumstances in which using force

---

4 The terms *corporal punishment*, *child physical punishment*, *spanking*, and *smacking* are used variably in research and quotes. The UN's definition of corporal punishment also includes these terms. In my own writing, I use the phrases *corporal punishment* and *child physical punishment* interchangeably.

I do not use the word *spanking* when describing child physical punishment as I consider it a euphemistic cover for all the harm and brutality that can hide behind it. Its origins come from the German word "*spakkern*, *spenkern* used in reference to horses"—that is, the breaking of horses. McGillivray and Durrant, "Child Corporal Punishment," 177; Brown et al., "Spank, Slap or Hit?," 1.

5 UNCRC, *General Comment No. 8.*; Pinheiro, *World Report on Violence Against Children.*

6 *Criminal Code of Canada*, RSC 1985, c. C-46, s. 265 (1) states: "A person commits an assault when: (a) without the consent of another person, he applies force...

on another person is justified, and the *Criminal Code* provides defences that can be applied to justify such actions. For example, s. 37 allows the use of force to defend oneself and others under one's protection as long as the force used is no more than is necessary; s. 38 provides a defence for those who use force to protect their property as long as no bodily harm is caused to the trespasser; and s. 45 protects those who perform skilled and careful surgical operations for the benefit of a patient. Section 43 is another defence, one available to parents, teachers, and others standing in their place who use force to correct a child's behaviour. The section provides protection to only one professional group—teachers. Others who work with children, including daycare workers, social workers, coaches, camp counsellors, religious leaders, and nurses, are not included. If needed, as noted above, there are other defences that these professionals can use to protect themselves from charges of assault when the force they use on children is for their care and protection. Courts have recognized the duty of care parents and teachers have to children and students in their charge. This includes providing nurturing care that may involve restraint such as putting a child in a car seat or preventing them from running onto the street. These are considered acts of care and protection of the child and as such parents who engage in them can be protected from possible criminal repercussions.[7]

Section 43 of the *Criminal Code of Canada* states:

> Every schoolteacher, parent or person standing in the place of the parent is justified in using force by way of correction toward the pupil or child, as the case may be, who is under his care, if the force does not exceed what is reasonable under the circumstances.[8]

This section has been part of Canada's *Criminal Code* since 1892. The only change made to the original section has been the elimination of other

...intentionally to that other person, directly or indirectly; (b) he attempts or threatens, by an act or a gesture, to apply force to another person, if he has, or causes that other person to believe on reasonable grounds that he has, present ability to effect his purpose; or (c) while openly wearing or carrying a weapon or an imitation thereof, he accosts or impedes another person or begs."

7 Milne, *A Brief Submitted to the Standing Committee on Justice*; Ensom, "Submission to the Standing Committee."

8 *Criminal Code of Canada*, RSC 1985, c. C-46, s. 43.

identified groups upon whom corporal punishment could, at one time, be administered. Those originally included were sailors, apprentices, and prisoners. In 2001, s. 446 of the *Criminal Code* was amended to provide stiffer penalties to those who "willfully cause pain to an animal." As Anne McGillivray points out, there is no defence of moderate correction in training animals.[9] Technically, this amendment could mean an owner could not tug on his dog's leash without fear of criminal sanctions. The chances of the owner being prosecuted for such an act are minimal, if they exist at all. But if there is no defence for owners of animals who wilfully cause pain, suffering, or injury—and there should not be—why provide a legal defence for those who cause pain, suffering, or injury to children? Today, the defence available to those who were entitled to use physical punishment on sailors, apprentices, prisoners, wives, or animals is gone. The only remaining group left vulnerable to physical punishment is one of the most vulnerable groups among us: children.

George Ryley Scott, in his historical treatise on corporal punishment, states that there is no information on when or where the use of "flogging" or physical force as a form of punishment came from. He describes the practice as being as old as civilization itself.[10] Physical punishment has been referred to as "soul murder," an experience that "transcends physical sensation."[11] Susan Bitensky notes that corporal punishment has been part of social behaviour for so long that intergenerational norms sanctioning its use have bolstered the assumption that spanking children is a beneficial parental practice.[12] Anne McGillivray, Canadian legal scholar and champion in the battle to end the physical punishment of children, notes it has been used throughout history by "judges over convicts, wardens over prisoners, fathers over children, schoolmasters over pupils, masters over apprentices, husbands over wives, householders over servants, slave-holders over slaves."[13]

---

9 McGillivray, "Child Physical Assault," 133.

10 Ryley Scott, *The History of Corporal Punishment*, 244.

11 Alice Miller describes physical punishment as a "deep humiliation, intimidation, destruction of dignity, loss or power, and torment." Miller, *For Your Own Good*, 223–24. cited in Bitensky, *Corporal Punishment of Children*, xiv.

12 Bitensky, *Corporal Punishment of Children*, xvi.

13 McGillivray, "Child Physical Assault," 137.

The Greek philosopher Aristotle (circa 360 BCE) considered children as on par with animals, and while he acknowledged that people in authority could be very cruel to children, he sanctioned the use of corporal punishment to instill virtuous behaviour.[14] In ancient Roman times corporal punishment was considered "the grossest form of invasion and hence a deep humiliation."[15] It was used as a means of delineating status. Children were considered equal in status to slaves who were owned by the father/master, and thus they were expected to be subservient. McGillivray states this status "was made apparent and incontestable through their legal susceptibility to corporal punishment."[16] Slaves were to be broken, and whippings were a device to "impress upon slaves that they were slaves."[17] Children were to be made ready to obey, and corporal punishment was used to train and teach them. The Roman magisterial powers of *pater familias* gave fathers the legal right to administer their own form of "justice." This could include whipping children and slaves as well as banishment, abandonment of newborns, and even execution.[18]

In 365 CE, the practice of patriarchal enforcement was specifically limited by the Roman Emperors Valentinian and Valens. They advised the Senate that the "correction" of relatives was restricted to minors but prohibited "extremely severe castigation."[19] So the emperors determined that paternal authority could be used to correct the error of youth, but no correction was to be too harsh, which may have meant no floggings or worse.[20] This was, as McGillivray notes, the introduction of the principle of "reasonable correction of children by force."[21] It in fact limited the seemingly unfettered scope of corporal punishment by fathers on their children, a decree of sorts that did not stand the test of time.

---

14 Turner, *Something to Cry About.*

15 Saller, *Patriarchy, Property and Death*, 136.

16 McGillivray, "'He'll Learn It on His Body,'" 200.

17 Saller, *Patriarchy, Property and Death*, 134.

18 McGillivray, "'He'll Learn It on His Body,'" 200; Radbill, "Children in a World of Violence."

19 McGillivray, "'He'll Learn It on His Body,'" 201.

20 McGillivray, "'He'll Learn It on His Body,'" 201; McGillivray, "Nowhere to Stand," 57.

21 McGillivray, "'He'll Learn It on His Body,'" 201.

CHRISTIANITY AND CORPORAL PUNISHMENT

The role of Christianity, historically and currently, in sustaining the use of corporal punishment on children has been significant. The Old Testament, which according to Ryley Scott "ranks as the greatest catalogue of acts of cruelty and persecution that a sadistic god ever reveled in,"[22] illustrates the widespread practice of whipping or flogging as a means of punishing all forms of misdemeanours. Moses proposed up to forty strokes be given, depending on the nature of the offence.[23] The idea of beating specifically children emerged with St. Augustine (354–430 CE), who in his *Confessions* "reflected that in the sight of God 'no man is free from sin, not even a child who has lived only one day on earth.'"[24] As noted by one literary historian, "the Augustinian position 'brought down upon the child the great weight of Christian dogma.'"[25] Augustine taught that the head of the household "had the duty to apply the whip to misbehaving members of the house 'for their benefit.... For just as it is not an act of kindness to help a man when the effect is to make him lose a greater good, so it is not a blameless act to spare a man, when by doing so you let him fall into a greater sin.'"[26] He preached that the father "who denies discipline is cruel....When a father beats his son, he loves him."[27] This notion carried on through the Protestant Reformation. According to early Christian teachings, children were born in sin inherited from Adam's original sin in the Garden of Eden. The idea of original sin also brought with it the notion that a good beating would help expunge the devil from the child. "The argument in favor of the whip to save sinning children from damnation had a long history in later Christian Europe."[28] It is seen by some to be "an act of love."[29]

Proponents rely on selective readings from the Bible to justify the use of corporal punishment on children. Solomon is quoted in this regard: "Do

---

22 Ryley Scott, *The History of Corporal Punishment*, 33.

23 Ryley Scott, *The History of Corporal Punishment*, 34, citing Deut. 25:1–3.

24 Heywood, *A History of Childhood*, 33.

25 Heywood, *A History of Childhood*, 33; Lyman, "Barbarism and Religion."

26 Saller, *Patriarchy, Property and Death*, 145–46.

27 Saller, *Patriarchy, Property and Death*, 146.

28 Saller, *Patriarchy, Property and Death*, 146; Morrow, "What Do We Do with Proverbs?," 91.

29 Straus and Donnelly, *Beating the Devil Out of Them*, 15.

not withhold discipline from a boy; take the stick to him and save him from death. If you take the stick to him yourself, you will preserve him from the jaws of death."[30] This led eventually to the maxim "spare the rod and spoil the child."[31]

However, scholars point out that the prevalent view of the virtue of child corporal punishment did not align with the teachings of Jesus. Philip Greven, in his book exploring the religious roots of physical punishment on children, comments that

> Jesus never once spoke a word recorded in any gospel that can be interpreted as advocating physical assaults against children or urging the infliction of painful punishments on any child. Yet so much pain has been inflicted on so many children for so many centuries in the name of Jesus Christ![32]

The supposed inherent evil of children was eventually challenged around the sixteenth century, with the counterview of the innocent child in need of kind and nurturing interactions.[33] Seventeenth-century philosopher John Locke described a child as a *tabula rasa*, wax to be moulded, or a blank slate. He promoted treating children kindly, yet at another time he approved the whipping of a child and warned parents against "humoring and cuckolding" little children. He noted with approval "an example of a

---

30 Prov. 23:13–14. There are other quotations from Proverbs that are relied on to justify the physical punishment of children. See, for example, the following: "Rod and reprimand impart wisdom, but a boy who runs wild brings shame on his mother" (Prov. 29:15); or "Correct your son, and he will be a comfort to you and bring you delights of every kind" (Prov. 29:17).

31 The maxim is not a direct quote from the Bible, but comes from what is described as a sado-masochistic seventeenth-century satire entitled *Hudibras* by Samuel Butler:

> If matrimony and hanging go
> By dest'ny, why not whipping too?
> What med'cine else can cure the fits
> Of lovers when they lose their wits?
> Love is a boy by poets stil'd;
> Then spare the rod and spoil the child (Part II Canto I)

32 Greven, *Spare the Child*, 219.

33 Donnelly, "Putting Corporal Punishment of Children," 45; Pollock, *Forgotten Children.*

'prudent and kind mother' who whipped her infant daughter eight times in one morning to master her stubbornness. Had she stopped at the seventh, he commented, 'she had spoiled the child for ever.'"[34]

Jean-Jacques Rousseau, an eighteenth-century philosopher, identified children as destined for the spiritual and moral life, thus requiring nurturing and careful training.[35] Nineteenth-century writers such as Victor Hugo, creator of Cosette, the abused young child in *Les Misérables*, and Charles Dickens, whose pen created David Copperfield and other waifs, aroused feelings of compassion and empathy for children.[36] However, that empathy did not extend to ending the use of corporal punishment on children, a practice that ultimately became well entrenched in law, providing parents, teachers, and others acting in the place of a parent with a legal defence to charges of assault.

THE LEGAL DEFENCE OF CORPORAL PUNISHMENT

Blackstone, a judge and legal scholar, summarized the history of the defence of corporal punishment in his 1770 *Commentaries on the Laws of England*. He documented that moderate chastisement was a power belonging to the father to "lawfully correct his child being under age, in a reasonable manner for this is for the benefit of his education."[37] McGillivray describes the shift in focus from what was a limitation of a father's chastisement of his child to chastisement being a "right": "thus what began as a child protection measure under Roman law progressively became an excuse (motive denying *mens rea* in assault), a virtue, a prerogative, a right and a justification."[38] The criminal law defence to adult assaults on children continues to influence the law in Canada and other colonized countries to this day.

Approximately twenty-five years after Canada became a country the legal defence of correction was codified together with other common law defences in Canada's first *Criminal Code*. At that time, the *Criminal Code* also allowed for the use of physical force on sailors, apprentices, and

34 Heywood, *A History of Childhood*, 99, citing Locke; Archard, *Children*, chapter 1.
35 Donnelly, "Putting Corporal Punishment of Children," 45.
36. Radbill, "Children in a World of Violence."
37 McGillivray, "'He'll Learn It on His Body,'" 452–53.
38 McGillivray, "'He'll Learn It on His Body,'" 202.

prisoners. The 1892 *Criminal Code of Canada* stated at s. 55 under the heading "Protection of Persons in Authority,"

> It is lawful for every parent, or person in the place of a parent, schoolmaster or master, to use force by way of correction towards any child, pupil or apprentice under his care provided that such force is reasonable under the circumstances.

The section was revised in 1953, but no major changes were made regarding the protection of children. The terms *master* and *apprentice* were removed from the section at this time. Other minor word changes were made along the way, but the defence as it appears currently under s. 43 of the *Criminal Code of Canada* has endured for 1,600 years.[39]

Today, a law that had its genesis in 364 CE, morphed slightly through the ages, was transcribed into English common law, and transported to Canada and other colonized countries still holds sway over the lives and rights of children. The law sets a tone, an environmental climate, that permeates all attempts to keep children safe and healthy.

IDEOLOGY AND CORPORAL PUNISHMENT

Researchers and academics from a variety of disciplines have attempted to identify why some individuals prefer the use of child physical punishment over other forms of discipline. Various theories abound based on personality types, ideology, socio-economic status, political leanings, religious beliefs, and other variables.[40]

In their investigations, Ellison and Bradshaw ponder whether the "culture wars" that dichotomize socio-political ideology also shape attitudes toward corporal punishment. Earlier findings showed a "robust" association between fundamentalist and evangelical Protestant religions

---

39 The use of corporal punishment on prisoners and sailors was removed from the *Criminal Code* in 1972 and 2001, respectively. "Slave holding and the bearing of slaves had been banned in the British Empire for six decades (prior to 1892). Beating wives and servants was not condoned by the common law in England and Canada after the 1860s." McGillivray, "Child Physical Assault," 133.

40 Garbarino, "Corporal Punishment in Ecological Perspective."

and support for child corporal punishment.[41] Using data from the 1998 National Opinion Research Center General Social Survey that included a set of items on religious beliefs and attitudes toward corporal punishment, they found that conservative Protestant beliefs are still a strong predictor of support for child physical punishment, as is socio-political conservatism. They report that "persons who identify themselves as politically conservative are more prone to approve of corporal punishment than their more moderate and liberal counterparts."[42] This stance mirrors conservative support for so-called traditional family values and "antipathy toward intervention in the domain of family life by government agencies or liberal advocacy groups."[43]

A current example of this ideology in practice involves a conservative Christian church that runs its own school. In the summer of 2022, eighteen former students of the Christian Centre Academy in Saskatoon, later known as the Legacy Christian Academy and later Valour Academy, filed charges with the police over allegations of abuse carried out at the school,[44] saying they were subjected to sexual, physical, spiritual, and emotional abuse as students.[45] The physical abuse involved the use of wooden paddles sold at the church store along with a book describing how parents are to punish their children.[46] Members of the girls' senior 2003 volleyball team were severely beaten with a wooden paddle by male school staff after being accused of whispering during a Sunday church service. The following Monday, the girls were lined up and, according to their account, were "yelled at by the director, the principal and their female coach."[47] Then the girls were taken, one at a time, into a room where two male staff members beat each one with the wooden implement, which according to the team captain, looked to be the size of a canoe paddle. The girls were injured,

---

41 Ellison and Bradshaw, "Religious Beliefs," 320; Morrow, "What Do We Do with Proverbs?," 91.

42 Ellison and Bradshaw, "Religious Beliefs," 335.

43 Ellison and Bradshaw, "Religious Beliefs," 335.

44 Warick, "Exorcisms, Violent Discipline"; Warick, "List of Students Alleging Abuse."

45 Legacy Christian Academy changed its name to Valour Academy at the beginning of the 2024–25 school year; negative publicity surrounding its name is speculated to be the reason. Wickstrom, "Name Change Cannot Erase."

46 Warick, "Abuse Allegations from Students."

47 Warick, "Exorcisms, Violent Discipline."

crying, and sustained bruising that, for some, extended from their buttocks to their knees and lasted for days. The political and ideological overlap within this school was such that students had been required to canvass for conservative politicians on school time.[48]

There is a commonality among those who support the use of child physical punishment and their socio-political conservative views and religious beliefs. Alternatively, there is a commonality among the socio-political liberal view and secular stance that generally views corporal punishment of children with suspicion if not abhorrence.

The so-called culture wars clearly emphasize the conservative and liberal distinction over issues such as abortion, same sex marriage, school curriculum, evolution, and creationism.[49] But also included in this list of culture-war topics are the dichotomist views on child physical punishment. The variances in values—socio-political, religious ideologies—play out in the debate over the morality and efficacy of child physical punishment and the entitlement of the child to claim rights.

---

48 Warick, "Abuse Allegations from Students." Currently, a number of former employees of the Christian Centre Academy (subsequently known as the Legacy Christian Academy and now Valour Academy) have been charged with a total of thirty-four criminal offences, including assault with a weapon and sexual assault. At the time of writing, a former director of the Christian school has been found guilty of nine counts of assault with a weapon. He denied ever paddling a student, which he has referred to as "scriptural punishment" (McAdam, "Olubobokun Denies Paddling Nine Students"). The judge in the case said she did "not believe Mr. Olubobkun's testimony" (Joel-Hanson, "John Olubobokun Guilty of Assaulting"). Another former staff member pled guilty to sexually assaulting and exploiting a teenaged student (Latimer, "Sask. Christian School Coach Who Sexually Exploited"). See also *His Majesty the King v. Aaron Travis Benneweis*, E-File Name: 2024-01-18SCPBenneweisA Saskatoon, SK (January 18, 2024). A former principal was found guilty of assault with a weapon (McAdam, "Former Christian School Principal Convicted"). In 2023, a staff member was charged with assault with a weapon when she hit a seven-year-old boy on his head with a baton. Her assault charge was withdrawn after she completed mediation (McAdam, "Assault Charges Withdrawn"). Other criminal charges against former staff are yet to be heard.

The former students have also filed a civil suit against former employees of the Mile Two Church (subsequently renamed Encounter Church) and Legacy Christian Academy seeking damages for sexual, physical, spiritual, and emotional abuse. For updates, see https://scharfsteinlaw.com/class-action/.

49 Davison Hunter, *Culture Wars*, chapter 4.

CHILDREN AND HUMAN RIGHTS

In 1982, Canada's *Charter of Rights and Freedoms*[50] came into effect. It guarantees all citizens, including children, fundamental rights and freedoms, including the right to security of their person (s. 7), the right to be free from cruel and unusual punishment (s. 12), and equality rights (s. 15). Seven years later, Canada took the lead in ratifying the United Nations *Convention on the Rights of the Child* (CRC).[51] The CRC affirms that children are endowed with inherent rights, including the right to freedom from physical punishment (articles 3, 19, 28, and 37). Paulo S. Pinheiro, author of the United Nations 2006 *World Report on Violence Against Children*, said the CRC "signals clearly that children are holders of human rights and acknowledges their distinct legal personality and evolving capacities."[52] All member states of the UN (except the United States) have now ratified the CRC. This means that they are obliged to fulfill the rights as outlined in it and to report on their progress in giving effect to these rights every five years. The United Nations Committee on the Rights of the Child, the body mandated with monitoring the progress of the CRC, reviews each state's submission on a five- to six-year rotation and issues a report. A common call of the UN Committee on the Rights of the Child has been to eliminate the use of corporal punishment on children in all its settings.

CONCLUSION

Currently in Canada, parents, teachers, and others who act in the place of parents can physically assault children. Hitting, spanking, smacking, and other forms of assault on children have been permitted within Canada's

50 *Canadian Charter of Rights and Freedoms.* See appendix A for full text.

51 *Convention on the Rights of the Child.* Each member state's progress in implementing the CRC is monitored by the Committee on the Rights of the Child, a body of experts elected by United Nations States parties. The Committee will, at times, issue explanatory documents referred to as General Comments, giving clearer meanings to various articles in the CRC. States must submit periodic reports every five years for the Committee to examine. The Committee examines each report and addresses its concerns and recommendations to the State party in the form of "concluding observations." See appendix B for full text.

52 Pinheiro, *World Report on Violence Against Children*, 33.

Criminal Code since 1892. The permission comes from a legal defence within the *Criminal Code of Canada*, s. 43, which states,

> Every schoolteacher, parent or person standing in the place of the parent is justified in using force by way of correction toward the pupil or child, as the case may be, who is under his care, if the force does not exceed what is reasonable under the circumstances.[53]

In 1892, when the original defence to charges of assault was established, sailors, apprentices, and prisoners were also included in the list of those upon whom physical punishment could be administered. Today, the s. 43 defence is available only to parents and teachers who use physical force to punish children, effectively making the physical assault of a child legal.

Despite the promise of and expansion of children's rights within the *Canadian Charter of Rights and Freedoms*,[54] the United Nations *Convention on the Right of the Child*,[55] and numerous attempts to repeal s. 43,[56] nothing of any significance has changed.[57] Meanwhile, as of 2025, sixty-seven countries worldwide have done away with their equivalent of s. 43—but not Canada.[58]

---

53 *Criminal Code of Canada*, RSC 1985, c. C-46, s. 43.

54 *Canadian Charter of Rights and Freedoms.*

55 *Convention on the Rights of the Child.*

56 For an update on attempts to repeal s. 43 over the years, see Durrant and Ensom, *Joint Statement on Physical Punishment of Children and Youth*, and CHEO, "Joint Statement."

57 Limits were imposed on the scope of s. 43 in 2004 by the Supreme Court of Canada; see section 2 for a full discussion. See also *Canadian Foundation for Children, Youth and the Law v. Canada (Attorney General)*, [2004] 1 SCR 76.

58 The following states have prohibited the use of child physical punishment in all settings: Albania, Andorra, Argentina, Austria, Benin, Bolivia, Brazil, Bulgaria, Cabo Verde, Colombia, Congo, Costa Rica, Croatia, Cyprus, Denmark, Estonia, France, Georgia, Germany, Greece, Guinea, Honduras, Hungary, Iceland, Ireland, Israel, Japan, Kenya, Kosovo, Latvia, Liechtenstein, Lithuania, Luxembourg, Malta, Macedonia, Mauritius, Moldova, Mongolia, Montenegro, Nepal, Netherlands, New Zealand, Nicaragua, Norway, Paraguay, Peru, Poland, Portugal, Romania, San Marino, Seychelles, Slovenia, South Africa, South Korea, South Sudan, Spain, Sweden, Tajikistan, Togo, Tunisia, Turkmenistan, Ukraine, Uruguay, Venezuela, and Zambia. For updates on the list of countries that prohibit corporal punishment in all settings, including the home, see End Corporal Punishment, "Global Progress Towards Prohibiting All Corporal Punishment," May 2023,...

…http://endcorporalpunishment.org/wp-content/uploads/legality-tables/Global-progress-table-commitment.pdf; and the international organization End Corporal Punishment, now hosted by the World Health Organization.

2

COLONIALISM, DISRUPTION, AND INDIGENOUS CHILDHOOD

Charlie is gone, he died.
lonesome. his aunt said:
he died because of school.

he was malnourished—
his body physically beaten
and psychologically abused—
forbidden to speak Cree.
there is nothing much else to say.
"sorry" doesn't take the pain away.

no one told his mother why.
she wanted to know why
school couldn't be offered
close to his home and family.

he always wanted to be home.
he had a burgundy sweater
he loved.
he had two dogs.
he was twelve.[1]

1 Bouvier, "remembering Charlie," 50.

INDIGENOUS CHILDHOOD AND CORPORAL PUNISHMENT

IT HAS BEEN CONSERVATIVELY ESTIMATED THAT THE NUMBER OF original Indigenous inhabitants at the time of European contact in what is now Canada was around 500,000.[2] They were not a homogenous group but rather members of many different Indigenous nations spread across the continent.[3] Prior to colonization, Indigenous children were raised, educated, and nurtured within their homes, their communities, and upon the land.

One common practice among Indigenous communities that differed markedly from the European colonizers was the treatment of children. A Cree word for children, *awasisak*, translates to mean "glowing sacred flames" that must be protected, nurtured, and loved.[4] Early European settlers recorded that physical punishment was not a form of discipline among First Peoples. The explorer David Thompson (1770–1857) made mention of the child-rearing practices of the Cree, saying in part that they were brought up with "great care and tenderness."[5] Around the early eighteenth century, Jesuit priest Father Lafitau wrote about his observations of Cree child-rearing practices:

> They let them (their children) do everything they like when they are very young, under the pretext that they are not yet at an age of reason and that, when they reach those years, they will follow the light (of reason) and correct themselves... no one moreover would dare strike or punish them... which indicates that in methods of bringing up children, gentleness is more efficacious than punishment.[6]

One colonial official described such tenderness as "foolish" and something that "prevents them from discipling the children and forming their

---

2 Royal Commission on Aboriginal Peoples (RCAP), *Report of the Royal Commission: Looking Forward, Looking Back*, 13–14.
3 RCAP, *Report of the Royal Commission: Looking Forward, Looking Back*, 13–14.
4 McAdam, *Nationhood Interrupted*, 92.
5 Smandych and McGillivray, "Images of Aboriginal Childhood," 246.
6 Smandych and McGillivray, "Images of Aboriginal Childhood," 242.

character."[7] The notion of discipline, as a means of developing the child's character, was evident within Indigenous communities, but not in the usual ways that Europeans recognized. Cree children, according to one twentieth-century ethnographer, "were never beaten and rarely reprimanded."[8] Anthropologist Richard Condon described the Copper Inuit in Northern Canada around the beginning of the twentieth century as rarely if ever using corporal punishment, describing the children as having a great deal of freedom. A misbehaving child "might be teased or briefly chastised, but adults will rarely use verbal threats or physical punishment," Condon writes. "In fact, if a child ignores initial reprimands, parents will just ignore the child."[9] Similar child-raising techniques were observed by anthropologist Diamond Jenness during his field work with the Copper Inuit from 1913 to 1916.[10] Methods of discipline included storytelling to demonstrate behaviour that was considered appropriate. Miller wrote that proper behaviour among Inuit children "was instilled by indirect and non-coercive means, in striking contrast to European child-rearing techniques... discipline was more often administered by ridicule and warning than with blows and deprivation."[11]

The colonial officer mentioned earlier also asserted that overindulgence prevented Indigenous children from receiving a "proper education."[12] What this official considered proper education is unclear, but this must not leave the impression that Indigenous children did not receive an education. Theirs was an encompassing educational environment, one that was ever present within their daily lives. While there were many different and varied Indigenous communities endowed with their own traditions, there were several consistencies underlying their educational and child development practices. Though pre-contact education did not include anything resembling an institutional approach, there existed a process infused with spirituality and an emphasis on instruction that focused on the three *Ls*: looking, listening, and learning.[13]

7 Moogk, "Les Petits Sauvages," 36.
8 Mandelbaum, *The Plains Cree*, 143.
9 Ember and Ember, "Explaining Corporal Punishment of Children," 610.
10 Ember and Ember, "Explaining Corporal Punishment of Children," 610.
11 Miller, *Shingwauk's Vision*, 18.
12 Moogk, "Les Petits Sauvages," 36.
13 Miller, *Shingwauk's Vision*, 16.

Smandych and McGillivray recount the story of Reverand William Cockran (1796–1865), a Red River missionary who actively sought out children for his mission school, motivated to "save their souls." They note that Cockran's "punitive pedagogical style and his frequent recommendations that 'children must be systematically broken, normally by corporal punishment' would have been a profound shock to aboriginal and perhaps country born children."[14] But, as will be discussed further in this chapter, Indigenous childhood changed inextricably when "European images of appropriate child-rearing was experienced by subsequent generations of aboriginal children whose parents were convinced or forced to send them to government funded mission and residential schools."[15]

Upon first contact, it is reported that the Europeans and Indigenous people initially worked together. The Europeans relied heavily on the expertise of the original people. But by the early 1800s, once the country was being infused by European immigrants and the fur trade collapsed, the apparent usefulness of Indigenous people faded.[16] The "Indian" became a "liability" to those settlers who were attempting to clear the land to make their "tidy farms."[17] The solution to this "problem" was to "get rid of the Indian problem"[18] in as peaceful a manner as possible by relocating them onto reserves, outlawing their cultural practices, controlling their livelihood and movements, and establishing residential schools.[19]

COLONIZATION AND RESIDENTIAL SCHOOLS

Residential schools were designed as a means to assimilate Indigenous people into Canadian civil and religious ways.[20] Indigenous children were separated from their families, their communities, their language, and their spiritual connections, disrupting the parents' and communities' ability to protect, nurture, and love their children. Assimilation efforts placed the

14 Smandych and McGillivray, "Images of Aboriginal Childhood," 251–52.
15 Smandych and McGillivray, "Images of Aboriginal Childhood," 251–52.
16 Miller, *Shingwauk's Vision*, 62.
17 Miller, *Shingwauk's Vision*, 62.
18 Milloy, *A National Crime*, 46.
19 RCAP, *Report of the Royal Commission: Looking Forward, Looking Back*, 42–43.
20 TRC, *Honouring the Truth, Reconciling for the Future.*

children into "a world hostile to identity, traditional beliefs and language."[21] This world had an atmosphere imbued with violence.[22]

The Truth and Reconciliation Commission (TRC) highlights the racism evident in the establishment of the residential schools, describing it as a system "based on an assumption that European civilization and Christian religions were superior to Aboriginal culture, which was seen as being savage and brutal."[23] The intersections of racism, ageism (power imbalance), and religion created the "perfect storms" that brought residential schools and corporal punishment upon the lives of Indigenous people.[24]

In 1493 Pope Alexander VI issued the Doctrine of Discovery,[25] which "promoted the idea that Christians enjoy a moral and legal right to dominate Indigenous Peoples and to invade and seize any lands populated by non-Christians."[26] The doctrine was justified on a contested interpretation of the Bible in which Jesus directs his followers "to go and make disciples of all nations."[27] The doctrine bestowed on European explorers the divine freedom to claim lands that were occupied by non-Christians. Manuel and Derrickson describe the Doctrine of Discovery as racist and a "legal fig leaf... to cover naked thievery."[28] The doctrine fed and reinforced the view of the inferiority of Indigenous people, bolstering the self-justifying hierarchy that authorized colonizers to claim ownership of lands occupied by Indigenous Peoples and Christianize them. The Doctrine of Discovery remains the legal justification for the taking of Indigenous land.[29]

The TRC issued Call to Action 45, calling upon the Government of Canada to "repudiate concepts used to justify European sovereignty over

21 RCAP, *Report of the Royal Commission: Looking Forward, Looking Back*, 349.

22 RCAP, *Report of the Royal Commission: Looking Forward, Looking Back*, 349.

23 TRC, *Honouring the Truth, Reconciling for the Future*, 4.

24 Michaelson, "Lies That Have Shaped Us," 51.

25 The Doctrine of Discovery was used to justify the colonization of the Americas and African countries by European states in exchange for converting the Indigenous inhabitants to Christianity; see TRC, *Honouring the Truth, Reconciling for the Future*, 191–200.

26 Michaelson, "Lies That Have Shaped Us," 52–53.

27 Mat. 28:18–20.

28 Manuel and Grand Chief Derrickson, *Unsettling Canada*, 3.

29 Manuel and Grand Chief Derrickson, *Unsettling Canada*, 108; TRC, *Honouring the Truth, Reconciling for the Future*, 191–200.

Indigenous land and peoples such as the Doctrine of Discovery and *terra nullius*." This Call to Action fuelled heavy lobbying of the Vatican and Pope Francis by Indigenous leaders. On March 30, 2023, the Vatican issued a press release repudiating the doctrine:

> In no uncertain terms, the Church's magisterium upholds the respect due to every human being. The Catholic Church therefore repudiates those concepts that fail to recognize the inherent human rights of Indigenous peoples, including what has become known as the legal and political "Doctrine of Discovery."[30]

The colonization of Canada, New Zealand, and Australia by the British brought with it Christian teachings imbued with notions of obedience, submission, and discipline. Christian teachings that laid clear the hierarchy of family relations have supported the view that children are to be obedient and submit to the authority of adults. This is based on the belief that children are born inherently sinful and need to learn obedience to show their submission to God, as discussed in chapter 1.[31] Michaelson notes that "this kind of thinking about the relationship between obedience and sin has informed at least some of the accepted social and cultural norms related to the 'discipline' of children in churches today."[32]

Colonization by the English expanded the prevalence of child physical punishment throughout the world. The use of corporal punishment and the laws legitimizing its use in colonized nations has, according to South African legal policy specialist Sonia Vohito, "its origins in legal frameworks imposed during the colonial era."[33] Ember and Ember found that the presence of a long-standing alien colonizing power predicts the prevalent use of corporal punishment.[34]

Alexander Nicholson, an Australian family court judge notes,

30 Winfield, "Indigenous Leaders Hope."
31 Michaelson, "Lies That Have Shaped Us," 54.
32 Michaelson, "Lies That Have Shaped Us," 54.
33 Vohito, "Africa," 67.
34 Ember and Ember, "Explaining Corporal Punishment of Children," 609–19, 615–16.

> Flogging and physical punishment have played a significant role in the history of countries colonized by England, such as the United States, Canada, Australia, and New Zealand....
>
> The British brought flogging with them to the countries that they colonized. The discipline of the then British Army and Navy was heavily dependent upon flogging and it was a common method of punishment for crime and for controlling prisoners. Beating was also considered an acceptable means of disciplining women, at least until the end of the 19th century, and contemporary literature records the merciless beating of children.[35]

The traditional child-rearing practices of Indigenous families were disrupted by the move to assimilate Indigenous people into Canadian society with the establishment of residential schools. Indigenous children, McAdam writes, are born with four gifts: emotion (nurtured by healthy kinships), mental health (nurtured by language, culture, laws, and Indigenous knowledge), physical health (nurtured by healthy food, clean water, and activities), and spiritual connection to the Creator (the life giver).[36] These gifts were severed in every way. The children were separated from their parents and communities and sent to a world that was hostile to their identity, health, traditional beliefs, and language.[37]

The education of Indigenous people was a promise of the treaties signed during the 1870s between some of the Indigenous nations and the British Crown. However, as Miller notes, though it "is clear that it was the Natives who proposed the inclusion of guarantees of schooling in the treaties... they likely had day schools in mind."[38] But day schools would do little to meet the objective of assimilation, which became the official policy of Canada's first prime minister, John A. Macdonald, since they would allow students to return home in the evenings. According to the influential Davin Report of 1879,[39] removing children from their community was essential as "'the

35 Nicholson, "Choose to Hug, Not Hit," 15.

36 McAdam, *Nationhood Interrupted*, 29–30.

37 RCAP, *Report of the Royal Commission: Looking Forward, Looking Back*, 13–14 and 349.

38 Miller, *Shingwauk's Vision*, 98.

39 Nicholas Flood Davin (1843–1901), a journalist and former Tory candidate, compiled the *Report on Industrial Schools for Indians and Half-Breeds* (the so-called Davin Report) on such schools already established in the United States and their...

influence of the wigwam was stronger than that of the [day] school,' and [children were to] be 'kept constantly within the circle of civilized conditions'—the residential school—where they would receive the 'care of a mother' and an education that would fit them for a life in a modernizing Canada."[40] The Davin Report argued that the child who attended day school also "'learned little and what little he learned soon forgot while his tastes [were] formed at home, and his inherent aversion to toil [was] in no way combated.'"[41]

Following the Davin Report, the federal government, with the active support of Catholic, Methodist, Anglican, and Presbyterian churches, established the assimilation directive of off-reserve residential schools. The policy of assimilation began to take shape "through evangelism, education and agriculture... because more coercive methods of achieving the 'Euthanasia of savage communities' were inimical, expensive and politically dangerous."[42] In this way it synchronized an important goal of British imperialism that influenced the colonization of Indigenous populations around the world, including the New Zealand Māori and the Australian Aborigines.[43]

In a speech to the House of Commons in 1883, Prime Minister Macdonald justified the government's residential school policy, saying,

> When the school is on the reserve the child lives with its parents, who are savages; he is surrounded by savages, and though he may learn to read and write, his habits and training and mode of thought are Indian. He is simply a savage who can read and write. It has been strongly pressed on myself, as the head of the Department, that Indian children should be withdrawn as much as possible from the parental influence, and the only way to do that would be to put them in central training industrial schools where they will acquire the habits and modes of thought of white men.[44]

...application to the Northwest Territories.

40 RCAP, *Report of the Royal Commission: Looking Forward, Looking Back*, 309. However, later studies showed that, "as a general rule, at no time in the history of the system did the schools produce the well-educated graduates that were the prerequisite for... the original scheme" (319).

41 Milloy, *A National Crime*, 26, citing the Davin Report of 1879.

42 Miller, *Shingwauk's Vision*, 75.

43 Milloy, *A National Crime*, 42.

44 TRC, *Honouring the Truth, Reconciling for the Future*, 2.

The focus of the assimilation policy was on the young—as adults were considered "the old unimprovable people."[45] The Royal Commission on Aboriginal Peoples reported that "it would be through residential education, more than any other method, that 'the solution of that problem, designated "the Indian question" would probably be effected.'"[46] Only by removing the children from the "deleterious home influences" could their potential be realized.[47] Lawrence Vankoughnet, deputy superintendent general of Indian Affairs under John A. Macdonald, reported to the prime minister that Indian children "'followed the terrible example set them by their parents' and thus became 'as depraved as themselves not withstanding all the instructions given them at a day school.'"[48] In 1912, the archbishop of St. Boniface, in a letter to the minister of Indian Affairs, wrote that the children must be "caught young to be saved from what is on the whole the degenerating influence of their home environment."[49] It was well understood that Indigenous children received a good education from their parents and Elders, and yet, the decision was made that in order to "kill the Indian in him and save the man,"[50] residential schools, aimed at the young, were to be instituted across the country.

Missionary pressure aimed at the federal government and coming from the Anglicans, Roman Catholics, Methodists, and Presbyterians played a major role in the administration of the schools and helped to bring about an amendment to the *Indian Act* making it compulsory for Indigenous children to attend residential schools.[51] Official records rarely mentioned Métis children, but according to the Royal Commission

45 RCAP, *Report of the Royal Commission: Looking Forward, Looking Back*, 338, citing Reverend E.F. Wilson, founder of the Shingwauk Indian Residential School.

46 RCAP, *Report of the Royal Commission: Looking Forward, Looking Back*, 334, citing from the 1890 Annual Report of the Department of Indian Affairs.

47 RCAP, *Report of the Royal Commission: Looking Forward, Looking Back*, 338, quoting from the 1889 Annual Report of the Department of Indian Affairs.

48 Milloy, *A National Crime*, 26, citing INAC File 1/25-1Vol. 15, L. Vankoughnet to Sir John A. Macdonald (August 26, 1887).

49 Milloy, *A National Crime*, 26, citing INAC File 1/25-1Vol. 15, L. Vankoughnet to Sir John A. Macdonald (August 26, 1887).

50 Milloy, *A National Crime*, 27, citing David Nock, *A Victorian Missionary and Canadian Indian Policy*.

51 Milloy, *A National Crime*, 26; TRC, *Honouring the Truth, Reconciling for the Future*.

on Aboriginal People "they were nevertheless there and were treated the same as all the children were."[52]

In 1920, the federal government amended the *Indian Act* to make attendance in residential schools compulsory for all Indigenous children seven to fifteen years old, furthering the policy of assimilation. The changes to the *Indian Act* also included provisions for enforcement officers and penalties for non-compliance, including fines and imprisonment.[53] Deputy Minister of Indian Affairs Duncan Campbell Scott, whose tenure within the federal government spanned thirty years, said at the time, "I want to get rid of the Indian problem,... our objective is to continue until there is not a single Indian in Canada that has not been absorbed into the body politic, and there is no Indian question, and no Indian Department."[54] By 1931, over eighty residential schools had been established across Canada; the last residential school closed in the late 1990s in Saskatchewan. It is estimated that 150,000 Indigenous, Métis, and Inuit students attended residential schools.[55]

Many of the children entering the residential school system had never been away from their families and had never been subjected to physical punishment. The children were taken "from parents and relatives 'who had never struck a child in their lives'"[56] and placed into the hands of what appeared to be an uncaring state. The children were prohibited from speaking their own language, cultural and spiritual practices were forbidden, and their families were disrupted. Residential schooling has been described as "an integral part of a conscious policy of cultural genocide."[57]

LIFE IN RESIDENTIAL SCHOOLS

From the mid-1800s to the 1970s, "up to a third of all aboriginal children were confined to the schools, many for the majority of their childhoods."[58] In his historical accounting of the residential school system, Milloy writes that "it is clear that the schools have been, arguably, the most damaging of

52 RCAP, *Report of the Royal Commission: Looking Forward, Looking Back*, 311.
53 Milloy, *A National Crime*, 70–71.
54 Milloy, *A National Crime*, 46.
55 TRC, *Honouring the Truth, Reconciling for the Future*, 3.
56 Manuel and Posluns, *The Fourth World*, 67.
57 TRC, *Honouring the Truth, Reconciling for the Future*, 55.
58 Fournier and Crey, *Stolen from Our Embrace*, 50.

the many elements of Canada's colonization of this land's original peoples and, as their consequences still affect the lives of Aboriginal people today, they remain so."[59]

Obedience was demanded by "shame, whippings and harsh denial—contaminating the traditional aboriginal child rearing tradition of modeling behaviour and never hitting a child."[60] And while Duncan Campbell Scott was repeatedly warned of the abuse in the schools, he and his department did nothing to stop it. Even when confronted with the high incidence of child runaways, a clear indicator of abuse,[61] Scott did nothing. Children died as a result, many from abuse, disease, lack of food, inadequate shelter, and exposure to cruel winter weather. The entire system was intolerable:

> All too often, "wards of the Department" [students] were overworked, underfed, badly clothed, housed in unsanitary quarters, beaten with whips, rods and fist, chained and shackled, bound hand and foot, locked in closets, basements and bathrooms, and had their heads shaved or hair closely cropped.[62]

Milloy describes residential schools as often sites of struggle that lacked "sensitivity to the children's hunger, ill-kempt look and illness, and often... pushed the application of discipline over the line into physical abuse and transformed what was to be a culture of care into one of violence."[63] Physical punishment was excessive and condoned by Deputy Superintendent General Vankoughnet, who stated that "obedience to rules and good behavior should be enforced by means including corporal punishment."[64] In 1895, an Indian agent who was concerned about the physical maltreatment of a runaway student recommended to Indian Affairs that the teacher who struck the student be dismissed and charges laid. The agent said, "[the principal's] actions in this and other cases would not be tolerated

---

59 Milloy, *A National Crime*, xiv.

60 Fournier and Crey, *Stolen from Our Embrace*, 63.

61 RCAP, *Report of the Royal Commission: Looking Forward, Looking Back*, 365–76; Rubin Stiffman, "Physical and Sexual Abuse in Runaway Youths," 417; TRC, *Honouring the Truth, Reconciling for the Future*, 103.

62 Milloy, *A National Crime*, 154–55.

63 Milloy, *A National Crime*, 129.

64 RCAP, *Report of the Royal Commission: Looking Forward, Looking Back*, 350.

in a white school for a single day in any part of Canada."[65] Indian Affairs did nothing. Personal stories of those who attended residential schools recounted their shock at the violent nature of the discipline they and others received.[66] The TRC concluded that the lack of any limits opened the door "early to an appalling level of physical and sexual abuse of students, and it remained open throughout the existence of the system."[67]

Residential schools were staffed by willing mission workers and their religious institutions. This arrangement sidestepped cooperation with the provincial education systems and the oversight they may have provided. Thus, as one writer notes, "the interests of church and state merged in a marriage of convenience that was to endure more than a century: the churches could harvest souls at government funded schools while meeting the shared mandate to eradicate all that was Indian in the children."[68] There was an additional problem with this arrangement, that being "the quality of those employees."[69] Some senior staff at the time remarked "that the schools were a dumping ground for less-competent church staff."[70]

Indigenous children were schooled in hard labour, and they were poorly fed, leading them to suffer from hunger and malnutrition. The facilities themselves were teeming with tuberculosis and other diseases foreign to the children's physical systems.[71] The buildings were not designed for harsh winters and were "erected on very primitive plans."[72] The costs were deadly. There are no concrete numbers associated with deaths of children in residential schools due in large part to incomplete record keeping. However, it seems clear that the death toll among Indigenous children in residential schools was far higher "than [deaths] experienced by members of the general Canadian population."[73]

---

65 TRC, *Honouring the Truth, Reconciling for the Future*, 101.

66 TRC, *Honouring the Truth, Reconciling for the Future*, 101.

67 TRC, *Honouring the Truth, Reconciling for the Future*, 105. The abuse many of the students suffered while attending residential schools is described by former students in the TRC's *Final Report* and in Miller, *Shingwauk's Vision*.

68 Fournier and Crey, *Stolen from Our Embrace*, 53–54.

69 Milloy, *A National Crime*, 131.

70 Milloy, *A National Crime*, 131.

71 Daschuk, *Clearing the Plains*.

72 Milloy, *A National Crime*, 78.

73 TRC, *Honouring the Truth, Reconciling for the Future*, 92; see also 90–99.

Dr. Peter Bryce (1853–1932), the chief medical officer with the Department of Indian Affairs (1904–14), tried to warn the government about the high rates of illness and death among Indigenous children at residential schools.[74] He was ignored. In 1922, Dr. Bryce published a study entitled "The Story of a National Crime: An Appeal for Justice to the Indians of Canada." As a result, he was "forced out of public service and children continued to suffer, and many died, due to government neglect."[75]

The TRC estimated that between 1941 and 1945, the death rate among residential school students was 4.9 times that of the general population.[76] Overall, the TRC stated that six thousand or more Indigenous children may have died due to abuse and neglect in residential schools.[77] In Duck Lake, Saskatchewan, for example, the Indian agent estimated that 50 percent of the children in the residential schools died.[78] Duncan Campbell Scott callously responded by pointing out that "fifty percent of the children who passed through the schools did not live to benefit from the education which they had received therein."[79]

In the spring of 2021, signs of 215 unmarked graves were discovered on the grounds of the Kamloops Indian Residential School.[80] The grounds were believed to be the burial place of Indigenous children who attended the residential school. The findings sent shock waves across the country and led to the search for and discovery of other possible unmarked graves on the sites of former residential schools.[81]

---

74 Stefanovich, "Doctor Who Blew Whistle."

75 Stefanovich, "Doctor Who Blew Whistle." This quotation is written on a plaque placed outside the company that published Dr. Peter Bryce's research paper when no one else would. Cindy Blackstock, executive director of the First Nations Child & Family Caring Society, has led the way in exposing and crediting the advocacy work of Dr. Bryce. In October 2024, Dr. Bryce was recognized as a person of national historic significance for his work in advancing public health practices and the alarms he raised about residential schools.

76 TRC, *Honouring the Truth, Reconciling for the Future*, 92.

77 TRC, *Honouring the Truth, Reconciling for the Future*, Calls to Action 71–76. In 2021, Justice Murray Sinclair estimated that the total number of missing children could exceed ten thousand.

78 Milloy, *A National Crime*, 78.

79 Milloy, *A National Crime*, 51.

80 Dickson and Watson, "Remains of 215 Children Found."

81 Eneas, "Sask. First Nation Announces."

According to the National Centre for Truth and Reconciliation, at least 4,100 children died in residential schools, based on death records of First Nations, Inuit, and Métis children,[82] but it is unknown as of the time of writing just how many of the sites believed to be unmarked graves contain the bodies of Indigenous children who were not accounted for. The TRC warned at the time of the release of their report that there were many unreported deaths of Indigenous children in residential schools who were likely buried in unmarked burial sites.[83]

THE RESIDENTIAL SCHOOLS SETTLEMENT AGREEMENT

The legacy of residential schools continues to take its toll on Indigenous people. Decades later the effects are manifested in many ways, including fractured family ties, high suicide rates, alcohol and drug use, poverty, and violence.[84] Phil Fontaine, a former National Chief of the Assembly of First Nations, attended residential schools in Manitoba. He became one of the first high-profile Indigenous leaders to talk publicly about his own experiences of sexual, physical, and emotional abuse and their consequences.[85]

Stories of the extent of the abuse perpetrated by the guardians of the residential schools started to surface in the later 1980s. Survivors eventually organized and brought forward a class action suit against the Government of Canada, the largest class action suit ever filed in the country. The suit sought, among other things, restitution for the sexual and physical abuse and other wrongful acts suffered by the children in Indian residential

82 National Centre for Truth and Reconciliation and the Indian Residential School History and Dialogue Centre at UBC, "Concerted National Action Overdue for All the Children Who Never Came Home from Residential Schools," Joint News Release, June 2, 2021, https://nctr.ca/concerted-national-action-overdue-for-all-the-children-who-never-came-home-from-residential-schools/.

83 TRC, *Honouring the Truth, Reconciling for the Future*, 258–63.

84 See, for example, TRC, *Honouring the Truth, Reconciling for the Future.* In addition, these concerns have been raised many times by various United Nations committee reports; see Committee on the Rights of the Child, "Sixty First Session"; UN Human Rights Commission, "Concluding Observations on the Sixth Periodic Report of Canada," CCPR/C/CAN/6, August 13, 2015, https://docs.un.org/en/CCPR/C/CAN/CO/6 (see recommendations 8, 9, and 18).

85 Fournier and Crey, *Stolen from Our Embrace*, 72.

schools. The case was settled out of court through discussions with former students, organizations representing Indigenous Peoples, the churches involved, and the federal government. The Indian Residential Schools Settlement Agreement included five components to the settlement including the establishment of the Truth and Reconciliation Commission.

THE TRUTH AND RECONCILIATION COMMISSION

The TRC was established in 2008, and it moved across Canada, listening to and recording the stories of thousands of Indigenous residential school survivors. In 2015 the TRC released its report on the impact of residential schooling on Indigenous children and their families. The preface to the summary of the *Final Report* begins thus:

> Canada's residential school system for Aboriginal children was an education system in name only for much of its existence. These residential schools were created for the purpose of separating Aboriginal children from their families, in order to minimize and weaken family ties and cultural linkages, and to indoctrinate children into a new culture—the culture of the legally dominant Euro-Christian Canadian society, led by Canada's first prime minister, Sir John A. Macdonald. The schools were in existence for well over 100 years, and many successive generations of children from the same communities and families endured the experience of them. That experience was hidden for most of Canada's history, until Survivors of the system were finally able to find the strength, courage, and support to bring their experiences to light in several thousand court cases that ultimately led to the largest class-action lawsuit in Canada's history.[86]

Former Prime Minister Stephen Harper stood in the House of Commons on June 11, 2008, to acknowledge these findings and apologize on behalf of the Government of Canada and all Canadians for the damage caused by the Indian residential schools.[87] He said we now know that the

86 TRC, *Honouring the Truth, Reconciling for the Future*, v.
87 The Right Honourable Stephen Harper, "Statement of Apology to Former...

policy of assimilation was wrong and had a profound and negative impact on the culture, heritage, and language of the Indigenous Peoples. Prime Minister Harper acknowledged that many children were abused emotionally, physically, and sexually within the residential schools and that many had died. He acknowledged the intergenerational trauma of residential schools, which "contributed to social problems that continue to exist in many communities today." He said, "We now recognize that, in separating children from their families, we undermined the ability of many to adequately parent their own children and sowed the seeds for generations to follow, and we apologize for having done this."[88]

The Truth and Reconciliation Commission of Canada made note of the social problems that exist in Indigenous communities and called for more understanding of the interplay between the intergenerational legacy of residential schools, racism, poverty, violence, and substance use.[89] As a means of rectifying these ills, the TRC put forward ninety-four Calls to Action to address the systemic nature of racism found in the justice, healthcare, education, and child welfare systems in order to seek reconciliation through government and community action.[90]

Call to Action 6 addresses the issue of child physical punishment, which was such a traumatic part of residential schooling. Call to Action 6 calls "upon the Government of Canada to repeal Section 43 of the

---

...Students of Indian Residential Schools," Government of Canada, June 11, 2008, https://www.rcaanc-cirnac.gc.ca/eng/1100100015644/1571589171655.

88 Harper, "Statement of Apology."

89 TRC, *Honouring the Truth, Reconciling for the Future*, 144, 174; Tait, *Fetal Alcohol Syndrome*; Douglas A. Brownridge et al., "Child Maltreatment and Intimate Partner Violence Among Indigenous and Non-Indigenous Canadians," *Journal of Family Violence*, 32, no. 6 (2017): 607–19.

90 As of 2022 only thirteen of the ninety-four Calls to Action have been implemented. Yellowhead Institute, an Indigenous-led think tank, has been monitoring the "glacial pace" of progress and states that it will take until 2065 to complete all the Calls to Action. Kelly Geraldine Malone, "Progress on Indigenous Reconciliation Calls to Action Going at 'Glacial Pace': Report," *CBC News*, December 16, 2022, https://www.cbc.ca/news/canada/north/yellowhead-trc-calls-to-action-update-1.6689314. In 2023, the Yellowhead Institute said it would no longer publish an annual tracking report because nothing more has been completed over the past year. Allessia Passafiume (Dec. 21, 2023, "Yellowhead Institute to no longer report on TRC call to Action Canada's National Observer," https://www.nationalobserver.com/2023/12/21/news/yellowhead-institute-report-trc-calls-action.

Criminal Code of Canada."[91] The TRC detailed the physical abuse meted out on Indigenous students, something the law permitted in order "to 'civilize' and Christianize" them.[92] The TRC noted that while physical punishment is used less frequently now, it is still legal. They said, "The Commission believes that corporal punishment is a relic of a discredited past and has no place in Canadian schools or homes."[93]

The fact that the TRC pointed specifically to s. 43 of the *Criminal Code* is significant. As noted in the TRC's *Final Report*, many of the dysfunctions evident in the lives of Indigenous individuals and families can be traced to their maltreatment in residential schools. Childhood experiences of trauma are carried into adulthood and manifest themselves in substance misuse and what the TRC has identified as contributors to violence, abuse, family dysfunction, and poverty.[94]

Many of the involved Canadian churches have issued apologies for the role they played in the establishment and administration of residential schools. In 1986, the United Church of Canada (uniting the Methodist, Presbyterian, and Congregational churches) was the first to apologize, followed by the Anglican Church (1993), the Presbyterian Church of Canada (1994), and the Oblates of Mary Immaculate (2001).[95] The most notable outlier was the Roman Catholic Church. Call to Action 58 called upon the pope to issue an apology.

Seven years after the TRC issued its call for the pope to apologize for the church's involvement in residential schools, Pope Francis travelled to Canada to deliver an apology.[96] He apologized for the members of the Catholic Church who promoted Canada's "devastating" policy of residential schools, which created the "disastrous error" and "deplorable evil of residential schools."[97] He said, in part, "I am here because the first step of my penitential pilgrimage among you is that of again asking forgiveness, of

91 Section 43 permits the use of physical punishment on children. It is the only form of child maltreatment that is legally sanctioned.

92 TRC, *Honouring the Truth, Reconciling for the Future*, 144.

93 TRC, *Honouring the Truth, Reconciling for the Future*, 144.

94 TRC, *Honouring the Truth, Reconciling for the Future*, 174. See chapter 7 for a full discussion of the research into the harms associated with child physical punishment.

95 Michaelson, "Lies That Have Shaped Us," 57.

96 Canadian Press, "'I Am Deeply Sorry.'"

97 CBC News, "Pope Francis Apologizes"; Canadian Press, "'I Am Deeply Sorry.'"

telling you once more that I am deeply sorry. Sorry for the ways in which, regrettably, many Christians supported the colonizing mentality of the powers that oppressed the Indigenous Peoples."[98]

In response to the TRC's call for the repeal of s. 43, a group of community, Indigenous, and religious leaders came together to generate a Christian theological response.[99] They called upon Christian churches to seek the repeal of s. 43, recognize the wounds of colonization, and increase awareness in communities on the impact of violence.[100]

CONCLUSION

The establishment of residential schools was a central element in the colonial process of assimilation, which has been described as *cultural genocide*.[101] Residential schools were in existence for over a hundred years. The last one, Gordon's Indian Residential School in Punnichy, Saskatchewan, closed in 1996.

McAdam posits that Indigenous nationhood is tied inextricably to land (mother earth), language (a sacred gift from parent to a child), and culture (a way of living). And while the various Indigenous nations are diverse, land, language, and culture are common variables to their nationhood. These variables were interrupted by the removal of vast numbers of Indigenous children from their land, prohibiting them from speaking their language and practicing their culture through spiritual customs and livelihood.[102]

There was violence in residential schools spurred on by the intersectionality of race, ageism, and religion in the quest to civilize and Christianize the Indigenous population. British colonial hubris, fortified by the Doctrine of Discovery and Christian doctrine, disrupted traditional child-rearing practices of Indigenous communities.[103] The result was an atmosphere of unimaginable physical, emotional, spiritual, and cultural pain. The Government of Canada estimates that "thousands of First Nations, Inuit and

98 Canadian Press, "'I Am Deeply Sorry.'"
99 MacDonald et al., "A Christian Theological Statement," 11; Young, "'On Sparing the Rod,'" 209.
100 MacDonald et al, "A Christian Theological Statement," 12.
101 TRC, *Honouring the Truth, Reconciling for the Future*, 1.
102 McAdam, *Nationhood Interrupted*, 24–25.
103 Michaelson, "Lies That Have Shaped Us," 52.

Métis children never returned home from residential schools. Many were buried in gravesites that are unrecorded, unmarked and unprotected."[104]

Those who survived residential school, along with their families, have lived with its legacy of family dysfunction, poverty, racism, addiction, violence, and child welfare involvement.[105] An understanding of the legacy of colonialism, residential schools, and violence brings into focus the need to confront history and the resulting systemic legal and social barriers to the well-being of Indigenous people in Canada and elsewhere.

---

104 See, Crown-Indigenous Relations and Northern Affairs Canada, "The Government of Canada and the National Centre for Truth and Reconciliation Announce the New National Advisory Committee on Residential Schools Missing Children and Unmarked Burials," Government of Canada, July 20, 2022, https://www.canada.ca/en/crown-indigenous-relations-northern-affairs/news/2022/07/the-government-of-canada-and-the-national-centre-for-truth-and-reconciliation-announce-the-new-national-advisory-committee-on-residential-schools-m.html. See also Truth and Reconciliation Community Bobcaygeon, "Information on Missing Children from Indian Residential Schools," https://trcbobcaygeon.org/buried-children-at-residential-schools/; Murray Mandryk, "Unrepentant, Unmoved," *Saskatoon Star Phoenix*, April 26, 2022, A6.

105 TRC, *Honouring the Truth, Reconciling for the Future*, 178n21. See also Calls to Action 1–5; Fallon et al., "Denouncing the Continued Overrepresentation of First Nations Children."

3

CHILD WELFARE

In stark contradiction to States' human rights obligations and children's developmental needs, much violence against children remains legal, State-authorised and socially approved.[1]

CHILD PROTECTION

IN 1873, NINE-YEAR-OLD MARY ELLEN WILSON[2] OF NEW YORK City was found tied to a bed. She had endured daily beatings at the hands of her adoptive mother for as long as she could remember. At the time, there were no child protection mechanisms in place to assist her, even though there was a New York–based Society for the Prevention of Cruelty to Animals. Legally, children were the chattel of their parents, and what went on in the home was the business of the adults. The case of Mary Ellen garnered a great deal of attention and culminated in the establishment of the New York Society for the Prevention of Cruelty to Children in 1875. It was the first child protection agency in the world.[3]

Historically, children, along with wives and slaves, have been considered the property of the family patriarch; they belong in the private zone ruled

---

1 Pinheiro, *World Report on Violence Against Children*, 3.

2 Mary Ellen Wilson is sometimes referred to as Mary Ellen McCormack, which became her name after she was adopted by Thomas and Mary McCormack.

3 New York Society for the Prevention of Cruelty to Children, "About the NYSPCC."

by the "father." Thus, government involvement in the family has been and is limited. Governments are reluctant to interfere in matters of the family.

The first Canadian law designed to protect children was passed in Ontario in 1893.[4] The Ontario *Children's Protection Act*[5] provided for the care and protection of neglected and dependent children. It became a model for other provinces drafting similar legislation.[6] Children's Aid Societies (CAS) developed alongside child protection legislation, replacing the charitable work previously done by religious groups and other volunteer organizations.[7] However the CAS organizations were poorly funded and, in many cases, run by volunteers, leading to widespread criticism of the CAS across the country as being "weak links in the realization of professional and 'scientific' child care."[8]

In 1928, social worker Charlotte Whitton was invited to conduct a study on the CAS child welfare system in Manitoba. A Royal Commission of Inquiry resulted from an investigative newspaper article outlining the situation in the province's children's homes. Whitton was outspoken in her condemnation, exposing the deplorable conditions the children were living in while under the protection of the Manitoba Children's Aid Society. Her report called for an increase in government funding and a more efficient administration of child welfare to determine, first and foremost, "what children are or are not wards, and where they are [in the child welfare system]."[9] The current system was in disarray with children being unaccounted for and too many living in appalling conditions. Whitton is credited with shifting child welfare from a philanthropic endeavour to one that is supported through legislation by professional staff guided by "a new set of socially informed theories and assumptions of prevention... and a re-examination of the family's needs and responsibilities."[10]

Early child protection legislation was, however, particularly focused on neglect, which was evident by the listing of issues that would come to the

---

4 Bala et al., eds., *Canadian Child Welfare Law.*

5 *Children's Protection Act*, S.O. 1893, c. 45.

6 Child protection acts were passed in Manitoba in 1898 and in Saskatchewan and Alberta in 1909.

7 Dornstauder and Macknak, "100 Years of Child Welfare in Saskatchewan," 2.

8 Rooke and Schnell, *Discarding the Asylum*, 284.

9 Rooke and Schnell, *Discarding the Asylum*, 285.

10 Rooke and Schnell, *Discarding the Asylum*, 338.

attention of child protection workers. In Saskatchewan, for example, the 1908 *Children's Protection Act*[11] identified such things as "child begging" or "association with thieves and vagrants" as evidence of a child in need of protection.[12] A fear of social upheaval was raised by the idea of poor and destitute children.[13] It does not appear that much attention was being paid to the physical abuse of children. Dornstauder and Macknak, in their survey of child welfare in Saskatchewan, show that over the span of four years beginning in 1923, eighty-five cases of "cruelty of parents" were brought to the attention of the Saskatchewan Bureau of Child Protection.[14] Those numbers decreased to thirty, ten, and sixteen in the following three years.[15] These numbers are markedly smaller than all remaining categories, of which there were nine in total. The other eight categories dealt specifically with issues of neglect and included immoral surroundings, illegitimate children, and deceased parents. At the time, child physical abuse was not considered a problem; it was, after all, part of the everyday parenting arsenal and euphemistically referred to as discipline.

In 1962, American pediatrician H.C. Kempe identified, for the first time, the "battered-child syndrome."[16] Kempe, along with other scholars, published what has become a seminal journal article providing evidence that children were being battered. The article caught the attention of doctors and politicians as the evidence of a battered child was supported with X-rays and diagnostic criteria.[17] The authors began their article expressing concern that acknowledgement of the syndrome by therapists, counsellors, and physicians was rare.[18]

11 The stated purpose of Saskatchewan's *Children's Protection Act* of 1908 was "to encourage and assist in the organization and establishment in various parts of the province of societies for the protection of children from neglect or cruelty, and for the due care of neglected and abandoned children in temporary homes or shelters and the placing of such children in properly selected foster homes."

12 Dornstauder and Macknak, "100 Years of Child Welfare in Saskatchewan," 5.

13 Bagnell, *The Little Immigrants.*

14 The Bureau was established alongside the new *Child Protection Act* of 1908. It was the forerunner to the Saskatchewan Ministry of Social Services.

15 Dornstauder and Macknak, "100 Years of Child Welfare in Saskatchewan," 10.

16 Kempe et al., "The Battered-Child Syndrome," 17.

17 Straus and Douglas, "Research on Spanking by Parents," 18.

18 Straus and Douglas, "Research on Spanking by Parents," 18.

CHILD WELFARE

Today, each Canadian province and territory has its own legislation that deals with child welfare and protection.[19] Indigenous child welfare is the responsibility of the federal government as outlined in the *Indian Act*.[20] In the 1950s, there was a move to apply provincial and territorial child welfare legislation to Indigenous people on reserves. Currently, provincial and territorial child welfare legislation applies to almost all Indigenous people living on and off reserves.[21] Researchers point out that "the legacy of colonialism, discrimination and structural inequalities experienced by First Nations"[22] has resulted in the involvement of a disproportionate number of Indigenous children in the child welfare system. For example, First Nations children aged fifteen years and under were 3.6 times more likely to be the subject of a child maltreatment investigation than non-Indigenous children and 17.2 times more likely to be placed in out-of-home care.[23] In response to what was seen as the failings of the child welfare system, First Nations communities began providing their own child welfare services with funding from the federal government. In 2019 the government passed Bill C-92, *An Act Respecting First Nations, Inuit and Métis Children, Youth and Families*, which acknowledges the right of Indigenous communities to create their own policies and laws concerning child welfare.[24] Bill

---

19 Tonmyr et al., "Does Mandatory Reporting Legislation Increase with Child Protection?" For legislative details, see Canadian Child Welfare Research Portal online, https://cwrp.ca/policy-legislation.

20 *Indian Act*, RSC, (1985), c I-5.

21 Fallon et al., "Denouncing the Continued Overrepresentation of First Nations Children."

22 Fallon et al., "Denouncing the Continued Overrepresentation of First Nations Children," 14.

23 Fallon et al., "Denouncing the Continued Overrepresentation of First Nations Children," 12. The history of colonialism and the effects on child welfare funding and services was the focus of a decades-long Canadian human rights investigation. Darren Major and Olivia Stefanovich, "Judge Approves Historic $23B First Nations Child Welfare Compensation Agreement," *CBC News*, October 24, 2023, https://www.cbc.ca/news/politics/judge-approves-23-billion-first-nations-child-welfare-agreement-1.7006351. Cindy Blackstock, executive director of the First Nations Child & Family Caring Society, began this challenge on behalf of Indigenous children in 2007. Stefanovich, "Doctor Who Blew Whistle."

24 Fryer and Tiedemann, "Bill C-92."

C-92 establishes national "minimum standards" in the services offered to Indigenous children and their families and takes into consideration "the need to ensure cultural continuity, to prioritize placement of children with family members, and to notify families and communities of measures involving Indigenous children."[25] Currently there are more than 120 Indigenous Child and Family Services across Canada.

A report examining child maltreatment investigations in Ontario in 2018 compared the involvement of Black children to white children in the child welfare system (aged from birth to fifteen years).[26] The report found that Black children were disproportionately overrepresented in the system. The overall population of Black children in Ontario is 7 percent, but they represent almost 14 percent of children in the child welfare system, while white children in Ontario make up 60.3 percent of the population and 55.4 percent of children in the system. They also found that Black children were 2.2 times more likely to be investigated by child welfare than were white children. Maltreatment investigations into Black children were 16 percent more likely to be substantiated but 21 percent less likely to be transferred to services.[27] Black communities are concerned about these findings and, like Indigenous communities, are seeking alternative procedures and structures that take into account the impact these communities face due to their history of colonization, discrimination, and structural inequalities.[28]

In Saskatchewan, the legislation that deals with child protection is the *Child and Family Services Act*.[29] Legislation for each province and territory is accompanied by regulations and protocols. The common benchmark used in child physical abuse cases investigated by child protection agencies is limited to those cases that provide evidence of physical injury or demonstrable harm. In other words, as the laws are written currently, children are not protected from physical assault unless there is evidence of physical

---

25 Fallon et al., "Denouncing the Continued Overrepresentation of First Nations Children," 16.

26 Bonnie and Facey, *Ontario Incidence Study*.

27 Bonnie and Facey, *Ontario Incidence Study*, 7–8.

28 Antwi-Boasiako et al., "Understanding the Overrepresentation of Black Children," 1; Watkinson and Rock, "A Comparative Study," 192. See also Sansone et al., *Understanding the Effects of Corporal Punishment on Children, Families and Communities*, 32–34; Vittrup, *Children's Assessments of Corporal Punishment*.

29 *Child and Family Services Act*, RSS 1989–90, c. C-7.2

injury or harm. The 2019 Saskatchewan Child Abuse Protocol defines physical abuse as "all actions resulting in non-accidental physical injury or harm. This may include non-accidental injury, cruel or excessive corporal punishment (which may or may not cause physical injury), threats of physical harm, dangerous behavior towards a child or in immediate proximity to the child (e.g. throwing objects, use of weapons)."[30]

The Child Abuse Protocol uses adjectives such as *excessive* and *cruel* with regards to corporal punishment, which circumvents the human rights question of whether child physical punishment, no matter the severity, is still to be permitted. The benchmarks used in child protection legislation across the country, with the exception of Quebec, continue to imply that physical punishment of children is acceptable.

CHILD MALTREATMENT

Since 1998, the Public Health Agency of Canada has collected information on child maltreatment in Canada with the purpose of providing up-to-date information on the scope and conditions leading to child abuse and neglect. During that time, four comprehensive reports, referred to as the *Canadian Incidence Study of Reported Child Abuse and Neglect* (CIS) have been issued.[31] The reports have accumulated statistics, with the assistance of child welfare agencies across Canada, on child maltreatment.

Child maltreatment is defined as "the harm, or risk of harm, that a child or youth may experience while in the care of a person they trust or depend on, including a parent, sibling, other relative, teacher, caregiver or guardian."[32] It includes physical abuse, sexual abuse, neglect, emotional maltreatment, and exposure to intimate partner violence.[33] Physical abuse, a form of child maltreatment, is comprised of various forms of punishment: shaking, pushing, grabbing or throwing, hitting with a hand, punching, kicking, biting, hitting with an object, choking, poisoning, stabbing, and

30 *Saskatchewan Provincial Child Abuse Protocol*, 8.

31 Trocmé and Wolfe, *Child Maltreatment in Canada*; Trocmé et al., *Canadian Incidence Study—2003*; Trocmé et al., *Canadian Incidence Study—2008*; Fallon et al., "Denouncing the Continued Overrepresentation of First Nations Children."

32 Munn et al., *Child Maltreatment in Canada: Overview Paper*, 1.

33 Trocmé et al., *Canadian Incidence Study: Final Report.*

"other physical abuse."[34] The maltreatment definition of physical abuse is consistent with the definition of corporal punishment as defined by the United Nation *Convention on the Rights of the Child* and discussed earlier in chapter 1.

Child physical punishment is a form of child maltreatment. However, there is a great deal of ambiguity between what is known as child physical punishment and child physical abuse. The question for some seems to be, Where do we draw the line? First, we need to ask why we would try to "draw a line" with regards to child physical punishment in the first place, since there is no line drawn in cases of child sex abuse or wife battery. Furthermore, drawing a line is impossible considering such important variables as a child's age, their development level, and the strength of the force used.[35] Focusing on a distinction does not take seriously the need to eliminate this type of violence from the lives of children, and it most certainly is a distraction from safeguarding a child's right to be free from physical assaults, no matter the severity.

The 2019 report on child maltreatment examined the disparity between Indigenous and non-Indigenous children's involvement with the child welfare system in Canada. The study found that the most common form of child maltreatment among Indigenous children was neglect (44 percent), whereas among non-Indigenous children it was physical abuse (31 percent). Of investigated Indigenous child maltreatment cases, 14 percent involved physical assaults.[36] The *Ontario Incidence Study of Reported Child Abuse and Neglect* found that physical abuse was the major maltreatment investigation for both Black children (27 percent) and white children (17 percent).[37]

The estimates of child maltreatment are based on cases reported to child welfare, and do not include cases that were never reported, cases that were screened out before the investigation, and those cases investigated by the police. The reporting of physical and sexual abuse of children varies across the country. Some cases are reported to the police rather than child protection agencies, and these cases are not included in the CIS reports.

34 Trocmé et al., *Canadian Incidence Study—2008*, 30.

35 Afifi et al., "Physical Punishment and Mental Disorders," 2.

36 Fallon et al., "Denouncing the Continued Overrepresentation of First Nations Children," 41.

37 Bonnie and Facey, *Ontario Incidence Study*, 31–32.

Statistics Canada has been reporting annually on family violence since 1998. They base their statistics on incidences of family violence reported to police. According to the 2021 Statistics Canada report, there were 127,082 victims of family violence perpetrated by parents, siblings, spouses, and extended family members. Children and youth aged seventeen and younger make up 19 percent of the total, with 24,504 children and youth the victims of police-reported family violence.[38] Six out of ten children and youth victims were girls. Violence against children and youth has increased by 25 percent since 2009. Family violence was 9 percent higher for children and youth in 2021 than it was before the COVID pandemic. The rate of family violence against children and youth increased by 13 percent from 2020 to 2021.[39] Family violence is an issue that has gained international attention and, with it, attempts to protect children in families in Canada and worldwide.

HUMAN RIGHTS AND CHILD WELFARE

As noted earlier, Canada's *Charter of Rights and Freedoms*[40] guarantees all citizens, including children, fundamental rights and freedoms, as well as the right to security of their person (s. 7), the right to be free from cruel and unusual punishment (s. 12), and equality rights (s. 15). The rights granted to children through the United Nations *Convention on the Rights of the Child* (CRC)[41] guarantees similar rights. The rights provided to children in the CRC have been referred to as the three *P*s—namely, provision, protection, and participation.[42] Provision rights, for example, include the right to engage in play and recreational activities (article 31), the right to an education (article 28), an adequate standard of living (article 27), and health-care services (article 24). Protection rights include the right to be free from all forms of abuse (articles 3, 19, 28, and 37) and the right to be protected from

38 Statistics Canada, "Victims of Police-Reported Family and Intimate Partner Violence."

39 Statistics Canada, "Victims of Police-Reported Family and Intimate Partner Violence."

40 *Canadian Charter of Rights and Freedoms*, as enacted by *Canada Act, 1982*, (UK), 1982 c.11.

41 *Convention on the Rights of the Child*, (1989), UN Doc. A/RES/44/25 (1989).

42 Hammarberg, "The UN Convention on the Rights of the Child," 97.

performing work that may be hazardous or will interfere with their education (article 32). Examples of participation rights include the right to be heard and to take part in matters affecting them (article 12) and the right to freedom of association (article 15).

State parties qualify their commitment to the CRC by formally declaring their reservations. These are often based on political, cultural, or religious reasons. For example, one of the Holy See's reservations to the CRC states, "Family planning and education services in article 24.2 [will] mean only those methods of family planning which it considers morally acceptable that is the natural methods of family planning."[43] The most frequently qualified article in the CRC is article 21, regarding a child's right to adoption; second is article 14, regarding a child's right to freedom of thought, conscience, and religion. Tied for third place are the child's right to protection from punishment (article 37); their right to birth registration, name, and nationality (article 7); and protection of children affected by armed conflict (article 38). As noted by Daiute, "Interestingly, 10 of the 12 Articles mentioned most frequently are focused on rights emphasizing children's self-determination."[44] In fact, those articles aimed at self-determination rights are disproportionately cited for reservations (or limitations). The articles protecting children from physical punishment, including article 37, can be seen both as protection and as an assertion of self-determination in that the articles qualify the children to speak out against practices they find unjust.

The CRC has been interpreted such that child physical punishment is viewed as a violation of a child's human right to dignity and physical integrity.[45] The countries that have ratified the CRC are thus obliged, under international law, to ensure that their laws, policies, and practices conform to the rights outlined in the CRC. Articles 3, 19, 28, and 37 of the CRC each address the issue of child physical punishment.

The Government of Canada has ratified the CRC, and Canadian provincial and territorial governments have endorsed the treaty. In doing so, they have made an official commitment to ensure that Canadian laws, policies, and practices conform to it; however, international human rights

---

43 Daiute, "The Rights of Children, the Rights of Nations," 713.

44 Daiute, "The Rights of Children, the Rights of Nations," 714.

45 UNCRC, *General Comment No. 8*.

documents are not enforceable by the United Nations, and they are rarely enforced through domestic law. They are monitored through required reporting to the United Nations Committee on the Rights of the Child, which reviews each State party's implementation of the CRC and issues recommendations. The Committee comprises eighteen experts elected by States parties, with consideration given to equitable geographic distribution and expertise. The Committee's reports are made public and are used as a benchmark for each State's compliance. The reporting process is a means of "holding the politicians' feet to the fire," a process often referred to as the "politics of shame," and a means of ensuring governments abide by their commitments. Its enforcement is carried out "on the basis of public opinion and national and international peer pressure."[46] The Committee's reports are valuable tools for those advocating for policy changes.

The Committee first began monitoring State parties in 1993, paying particularly close attention to the use of child physical punishment in all its forms in homes, schools, and institutions. Since that time, it has recommended prohibition of all forms of child corporal punishment to more than 140 states while at the same time promoting education campaigns to "encourage positive, nonviolent child-rearing and education."[47]

In 2003, the United Nations requested a global study on violence against children to be led by Professor Paulo Sergio Pinheiro, a Brazilian legal scholar. Professor Pinheiro worked in collaboration with the Office of the High Commissioner for Human Rights, UNICEF, and the World Health Organization. The *World Report on Violence Against Children*, released in 2006, documented serious global problems. Such violence, according to the report, "occurs in every country in the world in a variety of forms and settings and is often deeply rooted in cultural, economic and social practices."[48] Corporal punishment was identified as one of the most extensive forms of violence experienced by children. At the time of the study's publication, only 2.4 percent of children worldwide were provided legal protection from corporal punishment in all settings.[49] A 2014 UNICEF investigation into violence against children led to a report demonstrating

46 Howe and Covell, eds., *A Question of Commitment*, 99.
47 Newell, "The Human Rights Imperative," 11.
48 Pinheiro, *World Report on Violence Against Children*, 6.
49 Pinheiro, *World Report on Violence Against Children*, 12.

that the number of children worldwide who are protected from corporal punishment is now 8 percent.[50]

Pinheiro noted that throughout the world, and "in stark contradiction to States' human rights obligations and children's developmental needs, much violence against children remains legal, State-authorised and socially approved."[51] The aim of the study, he said, is "to mark a definitive global turning point: an end to the justification of violence against children, whether accepted as 'tradition' or disguised as 'discipline.'"[52]

The Committee on the Rights of the Child, as a follow-up to the report, issued its own *General Comment* on child corporal punishment, reaffirming the interpretation of the CRC and other international human rights instruments as recognizing "the right of the child to respect for the child's human dignity and physical integrity and equal protection under the law."[53] The Committee reviewed articles 37 of the *Convention on the Rights of the Child*, which requires States to ensure no child is subjected to cruel and degrading treatment or punishment, and 19, which requires states to protect children from all forms of physical or mental violence, and concluded that "there is no ambiguity.... Corporal punishment and other cruel or degrading forms of punishment are forms of violence and States must take all appropriate legislative, administrative, social and educational measures to eliminate them."[54] In addition, they discussed child physical punishment in schools and other institutions, saying that the practice of corporal punishment therein "conflicts with the equal and inalienable right of children to respect for their human dignity and physical integrity."[55] The United Nations Committee on the Rights of the Child further stated that

> addressing the widespread acceptance or tolerance of corporal punishment of children and eliminating it, in the family, schools and other settings, is not only an obligation of States parties under the Convention.

---

50 UNICEF, *Hidden in Plain Sight*, 110. These numbers are based on thirty-nine countries that had prohibited corporal punishment in all settings by 2014. The current number of countries that prohibit corporal punishment is now sixty-seven.

51 UNICEF, *Hidden in Plain Sight*, 3.

52 UNICEF, *Hidden in Plain Sight*, 3.

53 UNCRC, *General Comment No. 8*, at ¶ 2.

54 UNCRC, *General Comment No. 8*, at ¶ 18.

55 UNCRC, *General Comment No. 8*, at ¶ 21.

It is also a key strategy for reducing and preventing all forms of violence in societies.[56]

Canada has been reviewed five times since ratifying the CRC. In each of its subsequent reports, the United Nations Committee on the Rights of the Child the Committee has called for the repeal of s. 43 of the *Criminal Code.* The 2012 report on Canada's compliance with the CRC said,

> The Committee urges the State party [Canada] to repeal Section 43 of the Criminal Code to remove existing authorization of the use of "reasonable force" in disciplining children and explicitly prohibit all forms of violence against all age groups of children within the family, in schools and in other institutions where children may be placed.[57]

Six years after the United Nations *World Report on Violence,* the International NGO Council on Violence Against Children issued its follow-up report.[58] The NGO Council considered harmful practices directed at children worldwide that were based on tradition, culture, religion, and superstition. They expressed support for the "replacement of the concept of parental 'rights' over children with that of parental responsibilities, with the best interest of the child being the parents' 'basic concern.'"[59] Their report detailed a multitude of types of violence perpetrated against children, some by parents or with parental consent, a litany that included female genital mutilation, male circumcision, child marriages, dowry and bride price, corrective rape,[60] cosmetic mutilation, and corporal punishment, among others. The authors note that "corporal punishment kills

---

56 UNCRC, *General Comment No. 8,* at ¶ 3.

57 Committee on the Rights of the Child, *Consideration of Reports Submitted by States Parties Under Article 44 of the Convention: Concluding Observations: Canada,* CRC/C/Can/Co/5-6, June 23, 2022, at ¶ 25. The Committee made an identical statement in its concluding comments from both October 2012 and October 27, 2003. Committee on the Rights of the Child, *Concluding Observations of the Committee on the Rights of the Child: Canada,* CRC/C15/Add.215, October 27, 2003, at ¶ 33.

58 International NGO Council, *Violating Children's Rights.*

59 International NGO Council, *Violating Children's Rights,* 15.

60 The term *corrective rape* is used for sexual assault perpetrated by men against girls and women they presume to be lesbians. International NGO Council, *Violating Children's Rights,* 34.

thousands of children every year, and seriously injures and maims many more."[61] They called on United Nations organizations and others, including religious organizations, to take the lead and address these issues.

The United Nations Sustainable Development Goals (SDGs)[62] direct our attention to corporal punishment as a form of violence to be addressed. In 2015, the SDGs were adopted by heads of state and governments as internationally agreed-upon goals following the previous Millennium Development Goals, which expired in 2015. There are seventeen goals covering social issues such as poverty, health and well-being, gender equality, and environmental sustainability. Each goal has set targets and indicators used to measure the overall success of nations in meeting them.

Sustainable Development Goal 16 aims to "promote peaceful and inclusive societies for sustainable development, provide access to justice for all and build effective, accountable and inclusive institutions at all levels." This goal for a peaceful and inclusive society has set a target to "end abuse, exploitation, trafficking and all forms of violence against and torture of children." The progress information provided by the United Nations notes that "various forms of violence against children persist, including discipline that relies on physical punishment and psychological aggression."[63] To quantify the information needed to meet the targets, nations are to collect information on the proportion of children who have experienced any physical punishment and/or aggression by caregivers within the past month, thus sending a clear message that physical punishment is violence and counter to building a "peaceful and inclusive society."[64]

CONCLUSION

The first Canadian law designed to protect children was Ontario's *Children's Protection Act*,[65] passed in 1893.[66] Since that time, child protection legislation has been passed in every Canadian province and territory and in

61 International NGO Council, *Violating Children's Rights*, 23.
62 United Nations, "The 17 Goals."
63 United Nations, "Goal 16."
64 United Nations, "The 17 Goals."
65 *Children's Protection Act*, S.O. 1893, c. 45.
66 Bala et al., eds., *Canadian Child Welfare Law*; Rooke and Schnell, *Discarding the Asylum*.

approximately 120 First Nations. It wasn't until the 1960s that the reality of child abuse was taken seriously. Child protection legislation gradually evolved to encourage a child's right to be free from excessive forms of physical punishment. However, with the continued retention of s. 43 of the *Criminal Code*, families are sent conflicting messages. Prior to a Supreme Court decision in 2004,[67] s. 43 gave parents the right to use child physical punishment to correct a child's behaviour. As we will see, s. 43 was challenged using the *Charter of Rights and Freedoms*.[68] The case was eventually heard by the Supreme Court of Canada and some limits were placed on the scope of s. 43, but these limits are not enough. The entire section needs to be repealed, giving children and youth the same right to be free from physical assault as adults.

Child corporal punishment has received a great deal of attention over the past number of years, brought on, in part, by the *Canadian Charter of Rights and Freedoms* and the implementation of the United Nations *Convention on the Rights of the Child*.[69] Since the implementation of the *Charter* and the CRC, extensive research has been undertaken that reports on the harmful effects of child physical punishment, however light, adding more urgency to the calls for the repeal of s. 43.

---

67 *Canadian Foundation for Children, Youth and the Law v. Canada (Attorney General)*, [2004] 1 SCR 76.

68 *Canadian Charter of Rights and Freedoms*, as enacted by *Canada Act, 1982*, (UK), 1982 c. 11.

69 *Convention on the Rights of the Child*, (1989), UN Doc. A/RES/44/25 (1989).

SECTION TWO

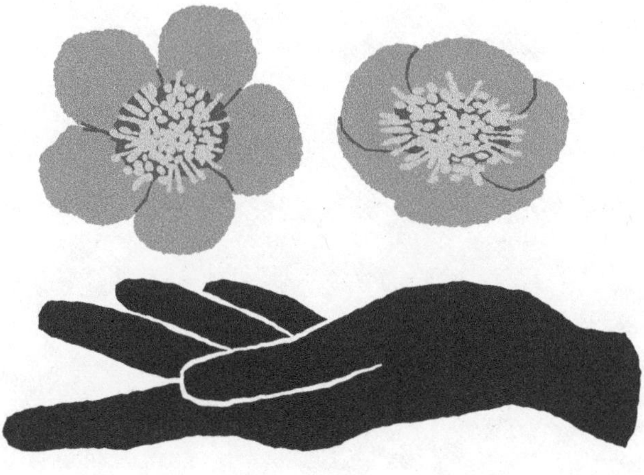

4

LEGAL ARGUMENTS

in the Case of *Canadian Foundation for Children, Youth and the Law v. Canada (Attorney General)*

> *Given that children are highly vulnerable members of our society, and given society's interest in protecting them from harm, fair process in the child protection context must reflect the fact that children's lives and health may need to be given priority where the protection of these interests diverges from the protection of parents' rights to freedom from state intervention.*[1]

INTRODUCTION

THE CASE OF THE *CANADIAN FOUNDATION FOR CHILDREN, Youth and the Law v. Canada (Attorney General)*[2] (herein referred to as *Foundation*) challenged s. 43 of Canada's *Criminal Code*, which provides a defence to those who use physical punishment on children. It

1 *Winnipeg Child and Family Services v. K.L.W.*, [2000] 2 SCR 519 at ¶ 94.

2 *Canadian Foundation for Children, Youth and the Law v. Canada (Attorney General)*, [2004] 1 SCR 76.

began in 1995, when the author applied to the Court Challenges Program for funding to research whether s. 43 violated the rights of children as provided in the *Canadian Charter of Rights and Freedoms.*[3] In order to succeed in obtaining funding from the Court Challenges Program, applicants were required to show that the violation was an equality rights matter, was of national significance and the law or action being challenged fell within federal jurisdiction.[4] The author received $5,000 from the program to conduct research into whether s. 43 might be a violation of the *Charter*.

The Court Challenges Program has had a rocky existence. It began in 1978 as federal funding for minority language rights. When the *Charter* came into effect in 1982, the program's mandate was expanded to include language rights as outlined in the *Charter*. In 1985, when the equality rights section of the *Charter* came into effect, the program was expanded to include funding for equality rights cases. It was closed down in 1992 under the Progressive Conservative government of Brian Mulroney but resurrected in 1994 under the Liberal government of Jean Chrétien. In 2006, its funding, of just over $5 million, was cut by Stephen Harper's Conservative government. The program was partially re-established in 2008 to provide funding for minority language rights. The name was changed to the Language Rights Support Program, and equality rights were left out completely. However, after the election of Justin Trudeau's Liberal government, the Court Challenges Program was reinstated with an expanded mandate in 2017.

It became a politically charged program once it was expanded to include equality rights. This same political tension is reflected in the issue of child physical punishment and others that garner support (or not) based on ideological standpoints—sometimes referred to as culture wars.[5] The phrase *culture wars* comes from the German *Kulturkampf*, a word that described the conflict, erupting in the later part of the nineteenth century, between secular and religious authorities struggling for control of education, marriage, and ecclesiastical appointments in Germany—issues that are as vibrant today as they ever were.

---

3 *Canadian Charter of Rights and Freedoms*, as enacted by *Canada Act, 1982*, (UK), 1982 c.11.

4 For more information on the Court Challenges Program, see https://pcj-ccp.ca/.

5 Davison Hunter, *Culture Wars*.

The Court Challenges Program was defended by those who support substantive equality rights and who recognize the costs of a court challenge—especially for those who historically face discrimination—such as children, persons with disabilities, and those most affected by poverty. Its demise was seen by some as a silencing of the marginalized. Others saw it as an attempt by "left leaning fringe groups" or "social engineers," including "feminists," "language groups," and "homosexuals," to reshape society.[6]

The author's application to the Court Challenges Program was submitted shortly after it had been re-established by the Liberal government in 1994, and while the application was not affected by the political turmoil directed at the program, the court challenge to the constitutional validity of corporal punishment was raised many times to justify closing the Court Challenges Program.[7]

Upon completing the initial research,[8] an application was made for further funding from the Court Challenges Program to take the case forward as a *Charter* challenge. The application was successful, and the adjudicators of the program provided $45,000 to begin the legal process of challenging the constitutionality of s. 43. According to the mandate of the Court Challenges Program, an individual cannot take a case forward on her own. The case was eventually carried forward by the Canadian Foundation for Children, Youth and the Law (CFCYL), an Ontario-based organization, since there was no other Canadian organization that had both a history of working with children and youth as well as experience with equality rights cases. In fact, the CFCYL had tried twice to intervene at the Supreme Court level on cases involving the physical punishment of children so as to challenge the constitutionality of s. 43.[9]

Not surprisingly, the case garnered a great deal of interest. The story of the *Charter* challenge and the funding from the Court Challenges Program hit the *Saskatoon Star Phoenix* on Christmas Eve 1997. A local Reform member of Parliament (later a Conservative Party MP) was particularly

6 See "Court Challenges Program: What Happened," Voices-Voix, May 23, 2017, https://web.archive.org/web/20191223121709/http://voices-voix.ca:80/en/facts/profile/court-challenges-program; "Vellacott Determined to Put End to Court Challenges Program," *Saskatoon Star Phoenix*, March 28, 1998, A6.

7 Gunter, "Kill the Court Challenges Program," A16.

8 Watkinson, "Prohibiting Corporal Punishment."

9 *R. v. Halcrow*, [1993] BCJ No 1227 (BCCA); *R. v. K.(M.)* (1993) 16 Criminal Reports 121.

outraged:[10] Maurice Vellacott held strong fundamentalist religious beliefs and served for fourteen years as a pastor in his riding north of Saskatoon. From the time the story first broke until at least the end of February 1998, there were letters to the editor and opinion pieces on an almost daily basis commenting on the *Charter* challenge. The large majority were angry—accusing the author of ripping off taxpayers, feeding from the "trough," being a liberal-minded social manipulator backed by "left wing" human rights tribunals, and advising the author to "revert to biblical teachings."[11] At one point, MP Vellacott and I were guests on a local radio show. The local newspaper printed an announcement with the heading "Spanking Issue to Be Debated" that began by saying, "Two prominent Saskatonians in the corporal punishment debate will lock horns this morning on local radio. In one corner is..."[12]

The topic of child physical punishment is, as noted earlier, a highly charged political issue. This meant that a number of groups and organizations came forward seeking intervenor status in the case. Intervenors are common in *Charter* litigation as the status allows other interested parties an opportunity to apply to take part and provide input into the case. It is rare for a *Charter* case, and particularly an equality rights case, to be heard before the Supreme Court that does not include a list of organizations representing strong views on the topic in question.

A number of organizations came forward in support of the challenge, including the Ontario Association of Children's Aid Societies, Defence for Children International, the Child Welfare League of Canada, the National Youth in Care Network (now Youth in Care Canada), the Society for Children and Youth of BC, the Canadian Council of Child and Youth Advocates, the Repeal 43 Committee, the Canadian Nurses Association, the United Church of Canada, and the Canadian Association of Social Workers. However, only the Ontario Association of Children's Aid Societies was given intervenor status supporting the *Charter* challenge. The courts

10 Warick, "Tax-Subsidized Fight Irks MP," A1.

11 See also the Letters to the Editor and Opinion sections of the *Saskatoon Star Phoenix* and the *Saskatoon Sun* between December 23, 1997, and March 1, 1998.

12 "Spanking Issue to be Debated," *Saskatoon Star Phoenix*, January 8, 1998, A10; James Parker, "Watkinson Nervously Deals with Limelight," *Saskatoon Star Phoenix: Weekend Extra*, January 17, 1998, C3.

do not provide their reasons for approving or rejecting interveners. Once the case reached the Supreme Court, two other intervenors in support of the challenge were accepted: the Child Welfare League of Canada and the Commission des droits de la personne et des droits de la Jeunesse.

Those supporting the Government of Canada's position (represented by the Attorney General), which argued against the challenge, were the Canadian Teachers' Federation and the Coalition for Family Autonomy. The Canadian Teachers' Federation is an alliance of organizations from across Canada representing around 200,000 school teachers. The Coalition for Family Autonomy, formed specifically to intervene in the case, was made up of the Focus on the Family (Canada) Association, Canada Family Action, the Home School Legal Defence Association of Canada, and REAL Women of Canada (Realistic, Equal, Active, for Life). The coalition described itself as made up of organizations "which have engaged in public policy activities to promote the well-being of families and the primacy of parents to raise and educate their children."[13] A common thread among the individual organizations represented by the Coalition for Family Autonomy are their views on traditional "family values" and "parental rights," which, in this case, are synonymous with the sanctity of the nuclear family, fundamentalist Christian beliefs, and the corresponding view that parents have a right to bring up their children as they see fit.

Focus on the Family's leader at the time was Dr. James Dobson, radio host and author of the bestselling book *Dare to Discipline*.[14] He has published a great deal on the "virtues" of using corporal punishment on children. In his book, Dobson advises parents and teachers to use corporal punishment on children. The following are examples of his advice: "I am recommending a simple principle: when you are defiantly challenged, win decisively";[15] "I recommend [for spanking] a neutral object of some type... a switch or paddle";[16] and "the spanking may be too gentle. If it doesn't hurt it isn't worth avoiding the next time. A slap with the hand on the bottom of a multi-diapered thirty-month old is not a deterrent to anything. While

13 *Canadian Foundation for Children, Youth and the Law v. Canada (Attorney General)*, [2004] 1 SCR 76 (Factum of the Intervener Coalition for Family Autonomy), at ¶ 1.

14 Dobson, *Dare to Discipline*.

15 Dobson, *Dare to Discipline*, 51.

16 Dobson, *Dare to Discipline*, 64.

being careful not to go too far, you should ensure he feels the message."[17] On his website, Dobson responded to questions about using the hand to administer punishment. He again recommended a neutral object, similar to the switch his own mother used on him, since the hand "should be seen as an object of love—to hold, hug, pat and caress."

Canada Family Action, headed by Charles McVety, bills their vision as "promoting the Christian world view in politics, government, society and culture."[18] McDonald reports that McVety proudly displays a front-page story from the *National Post*, following the Supreme Court decision, identifying him "as a self proclaimed 'spanker.'"[19] The Home School Legal Defence Association of Canada represents home-schoolers in courts and legislatures "to promote parent choice in education."[20] REAL Women describe themselves as "a pro-family women's movement"[21] The lawyer representing the Coalition for Family Autonomy was David M. Brown, who was subsequently appointed to the Superior Court of Justice of Ontario in 2006 and then appointed to the Court of Appeal for Ontario in December 2014 by the federal government.

THE CAST OF JUDGES, DECISIONS, AND PLAYERS

The *Foundation* case was heard for the first time in the Ontario Superior Court before Justice David McCombs in December 1999. In a decision dated July 5, 2000, Justice McCombs dismissed the case.[22] The case was appealed to the Ontario Court of Appeal in September 2001. Three judges sat through the appeal.[23] Each day, Judge Doherty, one of those three

17 Dobson, *Dare to Discipline*, 72.

18 Online at https://www.familyaction.ca/about-us/.

19 McDonald, *The Armageddon Factor*, 66.

20 Online at https://www.hslda.ca/membership?&_redirectsecure=true.

21 Online at https://realwomenofcanada.ca.

22 *Canadian Foundation for Children, Youth and the Law v. Canada (Attorney General)*, (2000) 188 DLR (4th) 718 (Ont. Sup. Ct.). I attended each of the three court hearings: the Ontario Superior Court (December 1999), the Ontario Court of Appeal (September 2001), and the Supreme Court of Canada (June 2003).

23 *Canadian Foundation for Children, Youth and the Law v. Canada (Attorney General)*, (2002) 207 DLR (4th) 632 (Ont. CA). Also available at http://www.ontariocourts.on.ca/decisions_index/2002index.htm. The Court was scheduled to hear the case on a number of dates in September, including September 11. But before the day could get started, the Court was shut down.

judges, entered the court room loaded with books and papers. He set them directly in front of him, making it hard to see him. He would at times turn his chair so his back was to the gallery. The Court unanimously dismissed the case and awarded costs to the Government, meaning the plaintiffs were required to pay for the court proceedings.[24]

The CFCYL sought leave of the Supreme Court of Canada to consider an appeal of the Ontario Court of Appeal decision. The Supreme Court agreed, and on the morning of June 6, 2003, in a span of three hours, it heard the arguments of the CFCYL, the Government of Canada (as represented by the Attorney General), and the interveners. The Supreme Court issued its decision six months later. In a 6–3 split, the Court ruled that s. 43 did not violate the rights of children.

The case was argued before the Supreme Court by Cheryl Milne, legal counsel for the CFCYL, and Paul Schabas, who provided his expertise pro bono. Other legal minds aided as well—all pro bono. They argued that s. 43 violated the rights of children under three sections of the *Canadian Charter of Rights and Freedoms*, claiming, first, that s. 43 infringed s. 7 of the *Charter*, which protects all citizens from invasions of their security, and that the infringement could not be justified with reference to the principles of fundamental justice;[25] second, that s. 43 violated a child's rights under s. 12, which prohibits cruel and unusual treatment;[26] and finally, that s. 43 discriminates against children on the basis of their age and is contrary to the equality rights protected under s. 15, which protects all citizens from inequality in law and in the protection afforded by law.[27]

The Attorney General and legal counsel Roslyn Levine led the case in defence of s. 43. They argued that s. 43 served a necessary function by protecting families, which they referred to as the fundamental unit of

---

24 *Canadian Foundation for Children, Youth and the Law v. Canada (Attorney General)*, (2002) 207 DLR (4th) 632 (Ont. CA), at ¶ 69.

25 Section 7 states, "Everyone has the right to life, liberty and security of the person and the right not to be deprived thereof except in accordance with the principles of fundamental justice."

26 Section 12 states, "Everyone has the right not to be subjected to cruel and unusual treatment or punishment."

27 Section 15 (1) states, "Every individual is equal before and under the law and has the right to the equal protection and equal benefit of the law without discrimination and, in particular, without discrimination based on race, national or ethnic origin, colour, religion, sex, age or mental or physical disability."

Canadian society, by allowing parents to raise their children without state interference and the threat of criminal sanctions.

The threat of criminalizing parents dominated the case. On its face, there was a possibility of increased criminalizing of parents since, without the defence of s. 43, parents could be charged with assault and face the consequences meted out to others who commit an assault.

LEGAL ARGUMENT OF THE CFCYL

The CFCYL began their argument before the Supreme Court by quoting from the Government of Canada's own document stating that "it is never okay to spank children; it is a bad idea and it doesn't work."[28] Hitting children, they argued, is a breach of a child's right "to respect for human dignity and physical integrity."[29] They quoted directly from an earlier Supreme Court decision when former Justices Frank Iacobucci and John Mayor said,

> The rights enumerated in the Charter are individual rights to which children are clearly entitled in their relationships with the state and all persons—regardless of their status as strangers, friends, relatives, guardians or parents.[30]

Relying on the evidence of expert witnesses who testified in the case,[31] they noted that "the uncontradicted expert evidence in this case is that the physical punishment of children, including mild spanking, produces no beneficial outcomes for children other than short-term compliance."[32]

---

28 *Canadian Foundation for Children, Youth and the Law v. Canada (Attorney General)*, [2004] 1 SCR 76 (Factum of the Appellant (CFCYL)), at ¶ 1, and quoting from a Health Canada pamphlet.

29 *Canadian Foundation for Children, Youth and the Law v. Canada (Attorney General)*, [2004] 1 SCR 76 (Factum of the Appellant (CFCYL)), at ¶ 1.

30 *Canadian Foundation for Children, Youth and the Law v. Canada (Attorney General)*, [2004] 1 SCR 76 (Factum of the Appellant (CFCYL)), at ¶ 44, citing Supreme Court Justices Iacobucci and Major in *B.(R.) v. Children's Aid*, [1995] 1 SCR 315, at 432.

31 Some of the expert witnesses who submitted affidavits and underwent cross-examination leading up to the Superior Court hearing included Murray Straus, George Holden, James Garbarino, Wayne McKay, Joan Durrant, Peter Newell, Nicholas Bala, Robert Larzelere, and Diana Baumrind.

32 *Canadian Foundation for Children, Youth and the Law v. Canada (Attorney...*

Corporal punishment is harmful to child development, and in support of this position they referred to social science evidence including a meta-analysis conducted by Elizabeth Gershoff that concluded that child physical punishment leads to undesirable behaviours and experiences.[33] Gershoff's study found that child physical punishment leads to an impaired child-parent relationship, poorer child mental health, weaker internalized moral reasoning, higher levels of child aggression, increased anti-social behaviour, and other problems as adults.[34]

The CFCYL pointed out that while "studies cannot prove that corporal punishment is the sole cause of negative child outcomes in each case, most experts are certain that the strength of the association is of such significance as to recommend against its use."[35] They made reference to the expert testimony of University of New Hampshire sociology professor Murray Straus,[36] in which he said, "there was an ever-increasing accumulation of non-definitive evidence which, together, led me to the conclusion that corporal punishment is causally related [to the harmful side effects]."[37] Other expert witnesses, such as University of Texas professor of psychology George Holden and professor of human development and co-director of the Family Life Development Center at Cornell University in New York James Garbarino, agreed.

LEGAL ARGUMENTS OF THE GOVERNMENT OF CANADA

The Government of Canada through the Attorney General introduced their position before the Supreme Court of Canada thus:

... *General)*, [2004] 1 SCR 76 (Factum of the Appellant (CFCYL)), at ¶ 10.

33 Gershoff, "Corporal Punishment by Parents," 531.

34 *Canadian Foundation for Children, Youth and the Law v. Canada (Attorney General)*, [2004] 1 SCR 76 (Factum of the Appellant (CFCYL)), at ¶ 13, citing Gershoff, "Corporal Punishment by Parents," 544.

35 *Canadian Foundation for Children, Youth and the Law v. Canada (Attorney General)*, [2004] 1 SCR 76 (Factum of the Appellant (CFCYL)), at ¶ 12.

36 Murray Straus is also the founder of the Family Violence Research Program, as well as the author of a number of books, including *Beating the Devil Out of Them: Corporal Punishment in American Families*, and many journal articles.

37 *Canadian Foundation for Children, Youth and the Law v. Canada (Attorney General)*, [2004] 1 SCR 76 (Factum of the Appellant (CFCYL)), at ¶ 12, citing Murray A. Straus, cross-examination at 24, Appellant's Record, at 1822.

> Children receive their life education to become productive members of our society within the family—the fundamental unit of Canadian society. Section 43 of the *Criminal Code* addresses the issue of physical discipline in this context and aims to balance the rights of the child with the societal interest in sustaining the family unit.[38]

"Sustaining the family unit" was the cornerstone of their defence: The overall objective of s. 43 was to allow parents and teachers to "train and nurture children without the harm that criminal sanctions would bring to them, their task and their families."[39] To this end, the Government of Canada had developed a two-pronged policy in order to achieve a balance between the rights of the child and society's interest in sustaining the family. The first prong was exempting from criminal law "limited parental and teacher action"; the second prong was promoting and supporting parental education that advocates against the use of physical punishment. The parental education provided by the Government of Canada supports the position that the use of physical force on children is not "desirable" as there are other, more effective ways of dealing with child discipline.[40] As examples of this, the Attorney General (AG) pointed to the government-funded Community Action Program for Children, the parent education program "Nobody's Perfect," and the government's funding of the CFCYL's expert witness Joan Durrant's co-authored booklet *To Spank or Not to Spank?*[41] It is important to note that the Community Action Program for Children provides funding to communities to promote healthy living for children. It is limited to children aged from birth to six years. The booklet *To Spank or Not to Spank* was no longer in circulation at the time of the Supreme Court hearing.

The AG refuted the social science evidence presented by the CFCYL, and maintained that said evidence failed to establish that s. 43 harms

---

38 *Canadian Foundation for Children, Youth and the Law v. Canada (Attorney General)*, [2004] 1 SCR 76 (Factum of the Respondent Attorney General of Canada, at ¶ 1).

39 *Canadian Foundation for Children, Youth and the Law v. Canada (Attorney General)*, [2004] 1 SCR 76 (Factum of the Respondent Attorney General of Canada, at ¶ 4).

40 *Canadian Foundation for Children, Youth and the Law v. Canada (Attorney General)*, [2004] 1 SCR 76 (Factum of the Respondent Attorney General of Canada, at ¶ 5).

41 *Canadian Foundation for Children, Youth and the Law v. Canada (Attorney General)*, [2004] 1 SCR 76 (Factum of the Respondent Attorney General of Canada, at ¶s 8–9).

children.[42] Based on the evidence of expert witness Robert Larzelere, a psychologist and director of behavioural health-care research at Boys Town in Omaha, Nebraska, the AG maintained there were "no negative child outcomes from physical punishment."[43] The AG said the CFCYL based its argument on "a false distinction between the consequences of physical and other corrective measures."[44] Relying further on the evidence of the government's expert witnesses, whom they described as "true academic methodologists and epidemiologists,"[45] the AG challenged the assertion of the CFCYL and their intervenors that physical punishment of children leads to negative outcomes. The AG said, "the majority of 'strong' studies show no negative child outcomes from physical punishment."[46] Mark Roberts, one of the Government's expert witnesses, conducted a study of the efficacy of "time out" sessions backed up with a spanking (defined as "two spanks to the buttocks with an open hand") if necessary. The CFCYL, in their factum, noted, "The children in his studies were hit an average of ten times in sessions lasting on average between 60–90 minutes; one child was hit as many as 50 times in one session."[47]

There are several problems, the AG asserted, with the research on the impact of child physical punishment. First, the studies do not distinguish between abusive punishment and mild punishment; second, the research is further weakened because all variables are not controlled for so as to test a hypothesis; and finally, the studies that have attempted to link negative effects to physical punishment measure only associations, meaning

42 *Canadian Foundation for Children, Youth and the Law v. Canada (Attorney General)*, [2004] 1 SCR 76 (Factum of the Respondent Attorney General of Canada, at ¶ 2).

43 *Canadian Foundation for Children, Youth and the Law v. Canada (Attorney General)*, [2004] 1 SCR 76 (Factum of the Respondent Attorney General of Canada, at ¶ 1), at ¶ 14.

44 *Canadian Foundation for Children, Youth and the Law v. Canada (Attorney General)*, [2004] 1 SCR 76 (Factum of the Respondent Attorney General of Canada, at ¶ 1), at ¶ 4.

45 *Canadian Foundation for Children, Youth and the Law v. Canada (Attorney General)*, [2004] 1 SCR 76 (Factum of the Respondent Attorney General of Canada, at ¶ 1), at ¶ 13.

46 *Canadian Foundation for Children, Youth and the Law v. Canada (Attorney General)*, [2004] 1 SCR 76 (Factum of the Respondent Attorney General of Canada, at ¶ 1), at ¶ 14, citing from Larzelere Affidavit, at ¶s 20 and 50–91.

47 *Canadian Foundation for Children, Youth and the Law v. Canada (Attorney General)*, [2004] 1 SCR 76 (Factum of the Appellant (CFCYL)), footnote 21.

that any causal conclusion drawn from such studies is erroneous.[48] The AG urged the Supreme Court to accept the conclusions of Superior Court Justice McComb, which was in turn accepted by the Ontario Court of Appeal, when he said,

> There is no empirical evidence establishing a definitive, long term causal link between corporal punishment and negative outcomes for children.... In short, it is impossible to determine with scientific precision whether corporal punishment leads to negative outcomes, or whether it is simply a factor among other negative environmental factors that cumulatively impact negatively upon a child's future.[49]

The AG cautioned the Supreme Court against engaging in

> the "truth finding" process of ordinary litigation to cases of "legislative fact" based entirely on social science evidence. The very nature of social science and the process by which its information is obtained and analyzed does not support the acceptance of scientific "conclusions" as factual "truths" in the same way that evidence of personal knowledge and observation or ordinary events does.[50]

The AG was saying that personal knowledge and observations are "the truth" without the rigour and vetting that social science claims are subjected to. But this notion seemed to carry the day. The Supreme Court did not appear to critically review the social science evidence presented to it. It certainly did not comment on it.

---

48 *Canadian Foundation for Children, Youth and the Law v. Canada (Attorney General)*, [2004] 1 SCR 76 (Factum of the Respondent Attorney General of Canada), at ¶ 13, citing from Diane Baumrind Affidavit, at ¶s 27–28 and 115–20.

49 *Canadian Foundation for Children, Youth and the Law v. Canada (Attorney General)*, [2004] 1 SCR 76 (Factum of the Respondent Attorney General of Canada), at ¶ 17, citing Justice McComb, Ontario Superior Court.

50 *Canadian Foundation for Children, Youth and the Law v. Canada (Attorney General)*, [2004] 1 SCR 76 (Factum of the Respondent Attorney General of Canada), at ¶ 91, citing Michael Rustad and Thomas Koenig, "The Supreme Court and Junk Social Science: Selective Distortions in Amicus Briefs," *North Carolina Law Review* 72, no. 1 (1993): 91.

OTHER LEGAL ARGUMENTS

The CFCYL argued that s. 43 interferes with the work of child protection as it makes investigations more difficult and "sends the wrong message to parents."[51] It confounds the distinction between what is considered reasonable force and what is physical abuse. The Ontario Association of Children's Aid Societies, an intervenor in the case, focused on the fact that s. 43 undermines and confuses attempts to protect children, is associated with child abuse, and gives those who advocate the use of corporal punishment the support they need.[52] They asserted that

> child protection and child welfare laws require as their foundation the acceptance by society of children as human beings to be valued, cherished and protected. Section 43 undermines this foundation. It removes children from the criminal law's protection against invasion of physical security or dignity.[53]

The AG agreed that some homes are not safe places for children but disagreed with the position put forward by the CFCYL and their expert witnesses that s. 43 impedes the work of child protection. They argued that children are already protected well through a myriad of systems made up of provincial/territorial legislation, federal criminal law, and public policy initiatives. Referring to the Court of Appeal decision, they said, "there is no impediment to the two levels of protection operating in tandem and they do."[54]

The AG said s. 43 is a narrow defence that can only be used under very specific circumstances—it must be reasonable, for corrective purposes, and implemented by specific individuals such as parents or teachers. S. 43 is "a

---

51 *Canadian Foundation for Children, Youth and the Law v. Canada (Attorney General)*, [2004] 1 SCR 76 (Factum of the Appellant (CFCYL)), at ¶ 16.

52 *Canadian Foundation for Children, Youth and the Law v. Canada (Attorney General)*, [2004] 1 SCR 76 (Factum of the Ontario Association of Children's Aids Societies).

53 *Canadian Foundation for Children, Youth and the Law v. Canada (Attorney General)*, [2004] 1 SCR 76 (Factum of the Ontario Association of Children's Aids Societies), OACAS factum, at ¶ 11.

54 *Canadian Foundation for Children, Youth and the Law v. Canada (Attorney General)*, [2004] 1 SCR 76 (Factum of the Respondent Attorney General of Canada), at ¶ 47.

limited defence to a crime of necessarily broad scope defined by s. 265."[55] The Government said that "outside of the limited application of s. 43, s. 265 protects all children from assault by anyone, in the same manner as any adult."[56] They pointed out that s. 43 is not unique within the *Criminal Code*, as other sections also de-criminalize actions that could otherwise be considered criminal. For example, self-defence after provocation (s. 35), the defence of property, (ss. 38, 40, and 41), actions of a ship's master (s. 44), and surgical operations (s. 45).[57] It is a rational exception that balances the rights of the child and the parent. Without s. 43, "the criminal law is a blunt instrument in the family context."[58]

The CFCYL detailed international laws and the expansion of children's rights making specific reference to the *Convention on the Rights of the Child*, which, among other things, affirms that children are to be protected from "all forms of physical or mental violence" while in the care of parents and other caregivers.[59] The United Nations Committee on the Rights of the Child has consistently interpreted the CRC as requiring State parties, including Canada, to bring an end to child physical punishment. The CFCYL pointed out that at the time of the appeal, in 2003, twelve countries had banned the use of physical force on children.[60]

Throughout the Supreme Court hearing, the CFCYL, the Child Welfare League, and the Ontario Association of Children's Aid Societies all referenced Canada's obligation to uphold international human rights laws and commitments. The AG refuted these claims and cautioned that the members of the Committee on the Rights of the Child who had interpreted

---

55 *Canadian Foundation for Children, Youth and the Law v. Canada (Attorney General)*, [2004] 1 SCR 76 (Factum of the Respondent Attorney General of Canada), at ¶ 61.

56 *Canadian Foundation for Children, Youth and the Law v. Canada (Attorney General)*, [2004] 1 SCR 76 (Factum of the Respondent Attorney General of Canada), at ¶ 56.

57 *Canadian Foundation for Children, Youth and the Law v. Canada (Attorney General)*, [2004] 1 SCR 76 (Factum of the Respondent Attorney General of Canada), at ¶ 58. For more on defences, see chapter 1.

58 *Canadian Foundation for Children, Youth and the Law v. Canada (Attorney General)*, [2004] 1 SCR 76 (Factum of the Respondent Attorney General of Canada), at ¶ 61.

59 *Canadian Foundation for Children, Youth and the Law v. Canada (Attorney General)*, [2004] 1 SCR 76 (Factum of the Appellant (CFCYL)), at ¶ 34, quoting from the *Convention on the Rights of the Child* (see appendix B).

60 As of 2024, sixty-seven countries have done so. See End Corporal Punishment, https://endcorporalpunishment.org/.

Canada's obligations under the *Convention on the Rights of the Child* were there serving in their own personal capacity and thus free to act on their own personal opinions.[61] In addition, the Committee on the Rights of the Child failed to consider s. 43 in the context of Canadian society and its legal system. Thus "the Committee on the Rights of the Child's concluding observations on Canada's response to physical punishment do not fully recognize this Canadian context."[62]

International laws dealing with the rights of the child are consistent, the AG contended, in considering the scope of children's rights from the premise that the family is the fundamental unit of society.[63] The CFCYL's interpretation of the *Convention on the Rights of the Child* was wrong since, according to the AG, the CRC is to be interpreted within the context of the "importance of the family as the natural and fundamental unit of society."[64] The AG pointed out that while article 19 prohibits all physical punishment of children, it must be interpreted in light of article 18, which obliges the State parties to allow parents to raise their children with state support rather than state interference. They maintained that it was "uncontradicted" that those who drafted the CRC did not mean for article 19 to encompass "reasonable corrective measures."[65]

The AG urged the court to abide by its own principles that all *Charter* analysis be done in the total context in which the impugned legislation sits. They argued that this proper context includes the family as the fundamental unit of Canadian society, the realities of child development, the obligations society places on parents and teachers, the legal and social systems in place to protect children, and the role and purpose of the *Criminal Code*.[66]

---

61 *Canadian Foundation for Children, Youth and the Law v. Canada (Attorney General)*, [2004] 1 SCR 76 (Factum of the Respondent Attorney General of Canada), at ¶ 34.

62 *Canadian Foundation for Children, Youth and the Law v. Canada (Attorney General)*, [2004] 1 SCR 76 (Factum of the Respondent Attorney General of Canada), at ¶ 50.

63 *Canadian Foundation for Children, Youth and the Law v. Canada (Attorney General)*, [2004] 1 SCR 76 (Factum of the Respondent Attorney General of Canada), at ¶ 48.

64 *Canadian Foundation for Children, Youth and the Law v. Canada (Attorney General)*, [2004] 1 SCR 76 (Factum of the Respondent Attorney General of Canada), at ¶ 28.

65 *Canadian Foundation for Children, Youth and the Law v. Canada (Attorney General)*, [2004] 1 SCR 76 (Factum of the Respondent Attorney General of Canada), at ¶ 33.

66 *Canadian Foundation for Children, Youth and the Law v. Canada (Attorney General)*, [2004] 1 SCR 76 (Factum of the Respondent Attorney General of Canada), at ¶ 38.

The Attorney General reiterated the point that children lack the capacity and capability of adults. They argued that whatever way a parent chooses to lawfully and reasonably correct a child "is for the benefit of the child's education, in the broadest sense, and is, therefore, a rightful, positive and constructive action."[67]

As noted earlier, the case examined the rights of children under sections 7, 12, and 15 of the *Charter of Rights and Freedoms.* Not surprisingly, views and presentations differed.

SECTION 7

Section 7 states,

> Everyone has the right to life, liberty and security of the person and the right not to be deprived thereof except in accordance with the principles of fundamental justice.

The CFCYL argued that s. 43 violated the security of the person rights under s. 7 (conceded by the Government of Canada) and further that the violation was not in accordance with the "principles of fundamental justice." A s. 7 challenge begins with, first, finding there has been a deprivation of the right to "life, liberty and security of the person" and, second, that the deprivation is contrary to the principles of fundamental justice. Those arguing that a government action or law contravenes the right to "life, liberty and security of the person" were required to clear two hurdles. A claimant was to show that the impugned legislation violates the freedoms protected by s. 7 and also provide evidence that the process for abridging those rights is not in accordance with the principles of fundamental justice. The phrase "principles of fundamental justice" has been interpreted to mean, at a minimum, the right to a fair hearing before an impartial adjudicator, to be properly informed of the case against you, and to be given reasonable notice of the actual hearing.[68] The CFCYL put forth that s. 43 violated the following principles:

---

67 *Canadian Foundation for Children, Youth and the Law v. Canada (Attorney General),* [2004] 1 SCR 76 (Factum of the Respondent Attorney General of Canada), at ¶ 40, referencing *Ogg-Moss v. The Queen,* [1984] 2 SCR 173, at ¶s 185 and 193.

68 Watkinson, *Education, Student Rights and the Charter,* 143.

(1) the principle that the child must be afforded independent procedural rights;
(2) the principle that legislation affecting children must be in their best interests; and
(3) the principle that criminal legislation must not be vague or overbroad.[69]

It is not the child who is protected by s. 43, the CFCYL argued, but rather the parent. Whenever an adult activates s. 43 as a defence, the child is helpless to challenge its use. Once s. 43 is marshalled to the defence of a parent, the onus switches to the prosecution "to rebut the defence beyond a reasonable doubt, again favouring the adult accused over the rights of the child."[70] The CFCYL quoted with approval former Supreme Court judge Madam Justice L'Heureux-Dubé, who said, in a child protection case,

> Given that children are highly vulnerable members of our society, and given society's interest in protecting them from harm, fair process in the child protection context must reflect the fact that children's lives and health may need to be given priority where the protection of these interests diverges from the protection of parents' rights to freedom from state intervention.[71]

---

69 *Canadian Foundation for Children, Youth and the Law v. Canada (Attorney General)*, [2004] 1 SCR 76 (Factum of the Respondent Attorney General of Canada), at ¶ 4.
The Supreme Court has subsequently recognized other principles, including the first and third of three principles put forward by the CFCYL. See *R. v. Malmo-Levine* [2003] 3 SCR 571. The criteria established in this case were set following the arguments in the *Foundation* case, when the Court applied the new criteria. In the *Foundation* case, the Supreme Court noted that "it is a principle of fundamental justice that accused persons must be accorded adequate procedural safeguards in the criminal process." *Winnipeg Child and Family Services v. K.L.W*, [2000] 2 SCR 519, at 572, at ¶ 5. In the case of *R. v. Nova Scotia Pharmaceutical Society*, [1992] 1 SCR 606, the Supreme Court affirmed that the principles of fundamental justice are not met when a law is too vague. The Court said, "a vague provision does not... sufficiently eliminate any area of risk, and thus can provide neither fair notice to the citizen nor a limitation of enforcement discretion" (639).

70 *Canadian Foundation for Children, Youth and the Law v. Canada (Attorney General)*, [2004] 1 SCR 76 (Factum of the Respondent Attorney General of Canada), at ¶ 71.

71 *Canadian Foundation for Children, Youth and the Law v. Canada (Attorney General)*, [2004] 1 SCR 76 (Factum of the Respondent Attorney General of...

Further, s. 43 runs the risk of children being physically punished for something they did not do, as was illustrated in *R. v. Haberstock*.[72] In this case, a teacher slapped a student across the face believing the student had insulted him. The student was innocent. In spite of the student's innocence, the teacher successfully relied on s. 43 as a defence and was acquitted.

BEST INTERESTS OF THE CHILD

The CFCYL attempted to expand the "principles of fundamental justice" to include the principle that a child's best interest must be recognized in the interpretation of legislation affecting them. They made note of earlier cases heard by the Supreme Court in which they "recognized that the 'best interests of the child' forms part of the substantive content of the principles of fundamental justice."[73] They noted that in the case of *Winnipeg Child and Family Services v. K.L.W.*, Justice Arbour stated that the principle of the "best interests of the child" is central when interpreting legislation that affects children,[74] and Madam Justice L'Heureux-Dubé writing for the majority acknowledged that within the s. 7 analysis a child's life and health is an interest of fundamental importance.[75] The CFCYL quoted another previous Supreme Court case, which said,

> this Court has reaffirmed that any decision affecting a child must be made in his or her best interest, which include, but are not limited to, ensuring that the child is protected from harm, whether caused by others or self-inflicted, and, importantly, seeking to foster the healthy development of the child to adulthood.[76]

...Canada), at ¶ 74, citing *Winnipeg Child and Family Services v. K.L.W*, [2000] 2 SCR 519, at 572.

72 *R. v. Haberstock* (1970), 1 CCC (2d) 433 (Sask. CA). For further discussion of *Haberstock*, see Watkinson, *Education, Student Rights and the Charter*.

73 *Canadian Foundation for Children, Youth and the Law v. Canada (Attorney General)*, [2004] 1 SCR 76 (Factum of the Respondent Attorney General of Canada), at ¶ 76.

74 *Winnipeg Child and Family Services v. K.L.W*, [2000] 2 SCR 519, at 572, at ¶ 9.

75 *Winnipeg Child and Family Services v. K.L.W*, [2000] 2 SCR 519, at 572, at ¶s 93 and 107.

76 *Canadian Foundation for Children, Youth and the Law v. Canada (Attorney General)*, [2004] 1 SCR 76 (Factum of the Respondent Attorney General of Canada), at ¶ 76, citing from *R. v. Sharpe*, [2001] 1 SCR 45, at ¶ 174.

Additionally the CFCYL pointed out that when determining the principles of fundamental justice the practice is to consider not just Canadian law but also international law, in particular article 3 of the *Convention on the Rights of the Child*, which states,

> In all actions concerning children, whether undertaken by public or private social welfare institutions, courts of law, administrative authorities or legislative bodies, the best interests of the child shall be a primary consideration. [77]

As noted in the CFCYL's factum, the best interest of children is the "only 'primary consideration' stated in the Convention. Article 18, dealing with the parental responsibilities, provides that 'the best interest of the child will be their basic concern.'"[78]

The Child Welfare League of Canada, an intervenor at the Supreme Court level, argued that s. 7 is to be interpreted within the purview of international law, and that one guiding principle found in international law is "the prohibition against punishment that violates the dignity and integrity of the child."[79] They said the international prohibition amounts to "customary international law...,[which is] reflected in the Principles of Fundamental Justice."[80]

The CFCYL argued the Ontario Court of Appeal's ruling that s. 43 was needed to allow parents to "carry out their important responsibilities to train and nurture children without the harm that [criminal] sanctions would bring to them, to their tasks and to the families concerned"[81] was an "adult-centered approach" that ignores the rights of children. Equality rights are to inform the balancing rights of s. 7, and "by drawing the boundary of the parent's liberty rights under s. 7 to permit the continued use of

---

77 United Nations *Convention on the Rights of the Child*, Can. T.S. 1992 no. 3, art. 3(1).

78 *Canadian Foundation for Children, Youth and the Law v. Canada (Attorney General)*, [2004] 1 SCR 76 (Factum of the Appellant (CFCYL)), at ¶ 33.

79 *Canadian Foundation for Children, Youth and the Law v. Canada (Attorney General)*, [2004] 1 SCR 76 (Factum of the Intervener Child Welfare League of Canada), at ¶ 3.

80 *Canadian Foundation for Children, Youth and the Law v. Canada (Attorney General)*, [2004] 1 SCR 76 (Factum of the Intervener Child Welfare League of Canada), at ¶ 3.

81 *Canadian Foundation for Children, Youth and the Law v. Canada (Attorney General)*, [2004] 1 SCR 76 (Factum of the Appellant (CFCYL)), at ¶ 77.

corporal punishment on children... [we fail] to consider the equality right of children and their particular vulnerabilities."[82]

In support of the CFCYL's position that the principles of fundamental justice included the best interests of the child, the CFCYL reminded the Supreme Court of its earlier decisions in which it had ruled that parental rights could not outweigh the security rights of children,[83] nor could a parent override a child's right to equal treatment.[84]

VAGUE AND BROAD

The CFCYL referred to case law that demonstrated that the law fails to set any adequate legal standard. They noted that s. 43 is applied differently within provinces[85] and across the country.[86] They concluded that s. 43 "results in an arbitrary and discriminatory application of the law.... [and] may 'trap the innocent by not providing fair warning'[87] while permitting and condoning unlawful and violent conduct towards children."[88] As examples of the arbitrariness of the interpretations given to s. 43 and the apparent tolerance of child injury, humiliation, and the use of weapons, the CFCYL provided examples of recent acquittals. For example, the following were acquitted through an s. 43 defence: a grandfather who struck his granddaughter with

82 *Canadian Foundation for Children, Youth and the Law v. Canada (Attorney General)*, [2004] 1 SCR 76 (Factum of the Appellant (CFCYL)), at ¶ 77.

83 *Canadian Foundation for Children, Youth and the Law v. Canada (Attorney General)*, [2004] 1 SCR 76 (Factum of the Appellant (CFCYL)), at ¶ 78, referring to *B.(R.) v. Children's Aid*, [1995] 1 SCR 315, at 387.

84 *Canadian Foundation for Children, Youth and the Law v. Canada (Attorney General)*, [2004] 1 SCR 76 (Factum of the Appellant (CFCYL)), at ¶ 79, citing Eaton, at 278–79.

85 *Canadian Foundation for Children, Youth and the Law v. Canada (Attorney General)*, [2004] 1 SCR 76 (Factum of the Appellant (CFCYL)), ¶ 8. See Landau, "Policing the Punishment."

86 *Canadian Foundation for Children, Youth and the Law v. Canada (Attorney General)*, [2004] 1 SCR 76 (Factum of the Appellant (CFCYL)), at ¶ 82.

87 *Canadian Foundation for Children, Youth and the Law v. Canada (Attorney General)*, [2004] 1 SCR 76 (Factum of the Appellant (CFCYL)), at ¶ 83, citing *Grayned v. City of Rockford*, 408 U.S. 104 (1972), 108–09 (USSC).

88 *Canadian Foundation for Children, Youth and the Law v. Canada (Attorney General)*, [2004] 1 SCR 76 (Factum of the Appellant (CFCYL)), at ¶ 83.

a belt;[89] a father who struck his fourteen-year-old daughter with a belt, leaving welts and bruises on her legs;[90] and a father who struck his eleven-year-old son with a belt, leaving a buckle-shaped mark on his thigh.[91]

The AG conceded that s. 43 violates a child's s. 7 security rights, but, they said, it is done so in accordance with the "principles of fundamental justice."[92] The AG maintained that s. 43 is not parent-centred, as the CFCYL argued, but supports societal interests of which children are the central focus by "maintaining the family unit and parent–child relations.... [and] excusing some actions from criminal culpability for good reason."[93] In exercising their parental roles, the AG said, parents require a "protected sphere" to carry out their role in making important decisions concerning their children, something "that the state is ill-equipped to do."[94] When the state interferes with a parent, it may violate a parent's "liberty interest" under s. 7.[95] Parental autonomy "is a competing and compelling societal interest and principle."[96]

Section 43, the AG argued, is not inconsistent with the "best interests of the child" but acknowledges the fact that children are part of a family unit and that context has to be part of considering the child's best interests.[97] It is neither vague nor overbroad as was put forward by the CFCYL. The law, the AG noted, is not an exact art: "A degree of generality in the law is essential and is not to be confused with vagueness."[98] The interpretation of s. 43

---

89 [tk]

90 *R. v. C.(G.C.)* [2001], N.J. No. 290 (Nfld. T.D.).

91 *R. v. Bell*, [2001] OJ No. 1820 (Sup. Ct.).

92 *Canadian Foundation for Children, Youth and the Law v. Canada (Attorney General)*, [2004] 1 SCR 76 (Factum of the Respondent Attorney General of Canada), at ¶ 62.

93 *Canadian Foundation for Children, Youth and the Law v. Canada (Attorney General)*, [2004] 1 SCR 76 (Factum of the Respondent Attorney General of Canada), at ¶ 67.

94 *Canadian Foundation for Children, Youth and the Law v. Canada (Attorney General)*, [2004] 1 SCR 76 (Factum of the Respondent Attorney General of Canada), at ¶ 68.

95 *Canadian Foundation for Children, Youth and the Law v. Canada (Attorney General)*, [2004] 1 SCR 76 (Factum of the Respondent Attorney General of Canada), at ¶ 70, citing *B.(R.) v. Children's Aid Society*, at 370 and 373. See chapter 4 for further discussion.

96 *Canadian Foundation for Children, Youth and the Law v. Canada (Attorney General)*, [2004] 1 SCR 76 (Factum of the Respondent Attorney General of Canada), at ¶ 70.

97 *Canadian Foundation for Children, Youth and the Law v. Canada (Attorney General)*, [2004] 1 SCR 76 (Factum of the Respondent Attorney General of Canada), at ¶ 72.

98 *Canadian Foundation for Children, Youth and the Law v. Canada (Attorney General)*, [2004] 1 SCR 76 (Factum of the Respondent Attorney General of Canada), at ¶ 75.

relies on judicial discretion, and such discretion is not synonymous with vagueness or overbreadth.[99]

The AG maintained that the CFCYL was exaggerating and misleading the Court in their submission of cases relied upon to show how s. 43 has been interpreted, and warned "they must be read with caution."[100] Many of the cases the CFCYL cited were twenty years old and did not reflect what the AG said are "evolving community social values."[101]

SECTION 12

Section 12 states that "every person has the right not to be subjected to any cruel and unusual treatment or punishment." In a 1987 decision, the Supreme Court of Canada directed that a central consideration in determining whether a form of punishment is cruel and unusual "is the principle of human dignity which lies at the heart of s. 12. It is the dignity and importance of the individual which is the essence and the cornerstone of democratic government."[102] The CFCYL, in reference to this case, said that corporal punishment not only degrades a child's dignity but is also unnecessary and harmful. The punishment imposed under s. 43 "is arbitrary, inconsistent and irrational, as s. 43 fails to provide ascertained or ascertainable standards."[103]

Section 12 applies to the actions of governments and thus those of parents and teachers since it is the government that permits the use of child physical punishment through its own legislation. The CFCYL said, "by exempting children from protection from assault, and saying it is right

---

99 *Canadian Foundation for Children, Youth and the Law v. Canada (Attorney General)*, [2004] 1 SCR 76 (Factum of the Respondent Attorney General of Canada), at ¶ 77.

100 *Canadian Foundation for Children, Youth and the Law v. Canada (Attorney General)*, [2004] 1 SCR 76 (Factum of the Respondent Attorney General of Canada), at ¶ 80.

101 *Canadian Foundation for Children, Youth and the Law v. Canada (Attorney General)*, [2004] 1 SCR 76 (Factum of the Respondent Attorney General of Canada), at ¶ 79.

102 *R. v. Smith*, [1987] 1 SCR, 1074. The accused challenged the constitutional validity of the seven-year minimum sentence for importing narcotics as being cruel and unusual punishment contrary to the *Charter* because of the potential disproportionality of the sentence. The majority of the Supreme Court ruled that the minimum sentence violated s. 12 and could not be justified using s. 1.

103 *Canadian Foundation for Children, Youth and the Law v. Canada (Attorney General)*, [2004] 1 SCR 76 (Factum of the Appellant (CFCYL)), at ¶ 86.

to hit children the state is responsible for its infliction contrary to s. 12 of the *Charter*."[104] It pointed out that the United Nations Rapporteur on the Commission on Human Rights likened corporal punishment to torture and other cruel and degrading treatments contrary to the *Universal Declaration of Human Rights*.[105]

Section 12 is not breached, the AG submitted, as it is not cruel and unusual and is not meted out by a state actor. Section 12 has been interpreted strictly to apply only to state-imposed punishment or treatment as a result of criminal or quasi-criminal offences. This does not apply in the case of child physical punishment. Nor does the term *treatment* apply in this case as, again, it is not state imposed.[106]

SECTION 15

Section 15 of the *Charter* provides that every individual has the right to equal protection and equal benefit of the law without discrimination because of age. However, s. 43 of the *Criminal Code* uses age as a marker in permitting physical force to be exerted upon a person. It approves the use of force as a means of correction to be used on children but not on adults.[107]

In 1984, the Supreme Court heard the case of *Ogg-Moss v. The Queen*,[108] in which a counsellor for mentally disabled people unsuccessfully attempted to use s. 43 as a defence for charges of common assault. Mr. Ogg-Moss had hit a twenty-one-year-old developmentally handicapped resident five times on the forehead with a large metal spoon to punish him for spilling his milk. The CFCYL made reference to this case, quoting from the then–chief justice, who said, "I cannot believe that it is the intention of the *Criminal Code* to create such a category of permanent second-class

---

104 *Canadian Foundation for Children, Youth and the Law v. Canada (Attorney General)*, [2004] 1 SCR 76 (Factum of the Appellant (CFCYL)), at ¶ 85.

105 *Canadian Foundation for Children, Youth and the Law v. Canada (Attorney General)*, [2004] 1 SCR 76 (Factum of the Appellant (CFCYL)), at ¶ 87, referencing United Nations, *Report of the Special Rapporteur*, at ¶s 46–53.

106 *Canadian Foundation for Children, Youth and the Law v. Canada (Attorney General)*, [2004] 1 SCR 76 (Factum of the Respondent Attorney General of Canada), at ¶ 93.

107 Watkinson, *Education, Student Rights and the Charter*, 143.

108 *Ogg-Moss v. The Queen*, [1984] 2 SCR 173. This case, though not a *Charter* case, considered the use of s. 43 as a defence for a counsellor who struck a mentally disabled adult who had spilled his dinner.

citizens on the basis of a mental or physical handicap."[109] The classification of children as "second-class citizens," the CFCYL argued, clearly violates a child's right to dignity, which is a core value of s. 15(1) of the *Charter*.[110] Dignity is at the heart of any s. 15 analysis as the Supreme Court made clear in a 1999 decision. In that case the Court concluded "that the purpose of s. 15(1) is to prevent the violation of essential human dignity and freedom through the imposition of disadvantage, stereotyping, or political or social prejudice."[111]

Subsequently, the Supreme Court set down a test to be met in order to establish a violation of s. 15. The first part of the test, known as the *Law* test,[112] is that proof is needed to show that the law treats people differently; second, that the treatment is based on one of the enumerated or analogous grounds under s. 15 (such as age); and third, that the law has a discriminatory effect in that it denies human dignity or treats people as less worthy on the basis of an enumerated ground (such as age).[113]

The CFCYL argued that s. 43 clearly treats people differently based on their age. It does not protect children in the way it protects adults from assault. Section 43, the CFCYL pointed out, "only applies to children, i.e., all individuals under the age of 18."[114] Section 43 draws a clear distinction between

109 *Canadian Foundation for Children, Youth and the Law v. Canada (Attorney General)*, [2004] 1 SCR 76 (Factum of the Appellant (CFCYL)), at ¶ 55.

110 *Canadian Foundation for Children, Youth and the Law v. Canada (Attorney General)*, [2004] 1 SCR 76 (Factum of the Appellant (CFCYL)), at ¶ 55.

111 *Canadian Foundation for Children, Youth and the Law v. Canada (Attorney General)*, [2004] 1 SCR 76 (Factum of the Appellant (CFCYL)), at ¶ 55, citing *Law v. Canada*, [1999] 1 SCR 497, at 529.

112 In the case of *Law v. Canada (Minister of Employment and Immigration)*, Nancy Law, a thirty-year-old widow, was denied survivor benefits under the Canada Pension Plan on the basis of her age. She challenged the decision, saying it infringed on her right to equality under s. 15(1) of the *Charter*. The Supreme Court disagreed and dismissed her appeal.

113 *Canadian Foundation for Children, Youth and the Law v. Canada (Attorney General)*, [2004] 1 SCR 76 (Factum of the Appellant (CFCYL)), at ¶ 58, citing *Gosselin v. Quebec (Attorney General)*, [2002] 4 SCR 84, at ¶ 17. The case of *Gosselin* challenged a 1984 Quebec social assistance scheme that provided funding on a different scale based on a person's age. Louise Gosselin argued that the age differentiation violated ss. 7 and 15 of the *Charter*. The majority of the Supreme Court found the differentiation did not violate the *Charter*.

114 *Canadian Foundation for Children, Youth and the Law v. Canada (Attorney General)*, [2004] 1 SCR 76 (Factum of the Appellant (CFCYL)), at ¶ 63.

children and adults. Of all the defences available to charges of assault in the *Criminal Code*, no other defence singles out an identifiable group.

The CFCYL relied on the further interpretation of *Law* as discussed in *Gosselin*, in which the Supreme Court said any distinction on the basis of age must be shown to be in the best interest of the group or individual. In the case of *Gosselin*, the Court determined that the imposition of certain criteria placed on unemployed Quebec citizens on the basis of their age did not violate s. 15 of the *Charter*. They made the distinction based on the fact that the age criterion was in the best interest of the unemployed person. The CFCYL noted that the chief justice in the case of *Gosselin* had stated that "a key marker of discrimination and denial of human dignity under s. 15(1) is whether the affected individual or group has suffered from 'pre-existing disadvantages, vulnerability, stereotyping, or prejudice.'"[115] All of these criteria, the CFCYL submitted, are met in this case. The distinction on the basis of age is not in a child's best interest, and any "assertion that s. 43 does not increase the vulnerability of children is contradicted by the evidence and common-sense."[116] Section 43, the CFCYL stated, "permits and perpetuates the notion that hitting a child is not only acceptable but beneficial" with the result that "their right to be free of physical harm is devalued," thus offending "the dignity and security of children."[117] The CFCYL reminded the Court of the overwhelming evidence given not only by their expert witnesses but by those of the Government that demonstrated that hitting children does not work as a disciplinary measure and has no beneficial effects. They said that s. 43 "perpetuates the notion that children... need to be taught a lesson 'for the benefit of their education.'"[118]

The AG argued that the distinction found in s. 43 does not amount to discrimination, but rather "the distinction is based on the natural features of

---

115 *Canadian Foundation for Children, Youth and the Law v. Canada (Attorney General)*, [2004] 1 SCR 76 (Factum of the Appellant (CFCYL)), at ¶ 64, citing CJ McLauchlin, *Gosselin v. Quebec (Attorney General)*, [2002] 4 SCR 84, at ¶ 30.

116 *Canadian Foundation for Children, Youth and the Law v. Canada (Attorney General)*, [2004] 1 SCR 76 (Factum of the Appellant (CFCYL)), at ¶ 64.

117 *Canadian Foundation for Children, Youth and the Law v. Canada (Attorney General)*, [2004] 1 SCR 76 (Factum of the Appellant (CFCYL)), at ¶ 66.

118 *Canadian Foundation for Children, Youth and the Law v. Canada (Attorney General)*, [2004] 1 SCR 76 (Factum of the Appellant (CFCYL)), at ¶ 66, referencing *Ogg-Moss v. The Queen*, [1984] 2 SCR, at 187.

childhood—a child's needs and capacities—and not on stereotypes."[119] The AG reminded the Court that equality claims are to be examined contextually. In the case at hand, the contextual factors were reiterated again: "the family as the fundamental unit of society, parental roles and legal responsibilities, the social science evidence related to child capacities and development; and the framework and purpose of the criminal law and *Criminal Code*."[120]

Discrimination on the basis of age, the AG maintained, is unlike other enumerated grounds as it is dependent on need, capacity, or circumstance.[121] A child's development capacities, they argued, are central to this case. Children need correction and are, due to their age, dependent on their parents. Section 43 is based on these "informed general assumptions that are neither demeaning nor based in stereotype."[122] Relying on scientific evidence to support the notion of "human development," the AG referred to other "age" discrimination cases to show that the Court "has recognized that age' is not strongly associated with discrimination."[123]

The AG argued that children are not a "traditionally disadvantaged group" but a "special group" that requires special treatment to accommodate their vulnerabilities,[124] and asserted that section 43 recognizes "the inherent capacities and circumstances of childhood"[125] and is neither

---

119 *Canadian Foundation for Children, Youth and the Law v. Canada (Attorney General)*, [2004] 1 SCR 76 (Factum of the Respondent Attorney General of Canada), at ¶s 94, 107, and 108.

120 *Canadian Foundation for Children, Youth and the Law v. Canada (Attorney General)*, [2004] 1 SCR 76 (Factum of the Respondent Attorney General of Canada), at ¶ 96. Within their factum they listed these contextual factors numerous times. See for example ¶s 38 and 66.

121 *Canadian Foundation for Children, Youth and the Law v. Canada (Attorney General)*, [2004] 1 SCR 76 (Factum of the Respondent Attorney General of Canada), at ¶ 100, citing *Law v. Canada (M.E.I.)*, [1999] 1 SCR 497, at ¶ 69.

122 *Canadian Foundation for Children, Youth and the Law v. Canada (Attorney General)*, [2004] 1 SCR 76 (Factum of the Respondent Attorney General of Canada), at ¶ 101.

123 *Canadian Foundation for Children, Youth and the Law v. Canada (Attorney General)*, [2004] 1 SCR 76 (Factum of the Respondent Attorney General of Canada), at ¶ 100. See for example *Gosselin v. Quebec (A.G.)*; *Law v. Canada (M.E.I.)*; *Granovsky v. Canada (M.E.I.)*, [2001] 1 SCR 703.

124 *Canadian Foundation for Children, Youth and the Law v. Canada (Attorney General)*, [2004] 1 SCR 76 (Factum of the Respondent Attorney General of Canada), at ¶ 102.

125 *Canadian Foundation for Children, Youth and the Law v. Canada (Attorney General)*, [2004] 1 SCR 76 (Factum of the Respondent Attorney General of Canada), at ¶ 107.

"demeaning nor based in stereotype."[126] Parliament has enacted s. 43 so as not to criminalize parents, the effect of which would be to exacerbate a child's vulnerability,[127] they insisted, noting that "the context of human developmental capacity forms the basis for innumerable distinctions in law and society based on age, including the designation of an age of majority, rules governing substitute decision-making for the elderly, or laws for obtaining a driver's license."[128] It is the developmental capacities of children that underpins their "need for education including correction and which distinguish childhood from adulthood."[129]

The AG concluded that "s. 43 represents the very antithesis of stereotype or prejudice and does not violate the essential human dignity of children."[130] Rather, s. 43 corresponds to the "unique circumstances of children's psychological development and limitations, in light of their needs, capabilities and the circumstances of the parent-child relationship in this society."[131] The intervener group, the Coalition for Family Autonomy, accused the CFCYL of seeking "to drive the enforcement mechanisms of the criminal law deep into the day-to-day activities of millions of Canadian families. If successful, Canada will be the only country to criminalize such conduct."[132]

The coalition adopted the facts as set out in the factum of the Attorney General, setting their arguments within what they called the "social and political context of this application."[133] They put forward a number of con-

---

126 *Canadian Foundation for Children, Youth and the Law v. Canada (Attorney General)*, [2004] 1 SCR 76 (Factum of the Respondent Attorney General of Canada), at ¶ 101.

127 *Canadian Foundation for Children, Youth and the Law v. Canada (Attorney General)*, [2004] 1 SCR 76 (Factum of the Respondent Attorney General of Canada), at ¶ 104.

128 *Canadian Foundation for Children, Youth and the Law v. Canada (Attorney General)*, [2004] 1 SCR 76 (Factum of the Respondent Attorney General of Canada), at ¶ 101.

129 *Canadian Foundation for Children, Youth and the Law v. Canada (Attorney General)*, [2004] 1 SCR 76 (Factum of the Respondent Attorney General of Canada), at ¶ 101.

130 *Canadian Foundation for Children, Youth and the Law v. Canada (Attorney General)*, [2004] 1 SCR 76 (Factum of the Respondent Attorney General of Canada), at ¶ 110.

131 *Canadian Foundation for Children, Youth and the Law v. Canada (Attorney General)*, [2004] 1 SCR 76 (Factum of the Respondent Attorney General of Canada), at ¶ 108, citing from Baumrind Affidavit.

132 *Canadian Foundation for Children, Youth and the Law v. Canada (Attorney General)*, [2004] 1 SCR 76 (Factum of the Coalition for Family Autonomy), at ¶ 3. The Coalition for Family Autonomy's submission was misleading, as by 2003 a dozen countries had already banned corporal punishment.

133 *Canadian Foundation for Children, Youth and the Law v. Canada (Attorney...*

textual principles that they believed should be considered by the Court, including that the family has a natural, not legal, origin and that "families are the primary unit of Canadian society";[134] that Canadian law is reluctant to intrude into the sphere of family decisions relating to the upbringing of children[135] and extensive state involvement in raising children is an idea "repugnant to democrats";[136] that a child's decision-making capabilities are not the same as an adult's;[137] and that applying the concept of "rights talk" to the family structure possesses an artificial air and stands at odds with the pre-existing obligations of parents to their children. The Rights talk, they said, turns the relationship into a legal relationship, which it is not. While the coalition was made up of many conservative Christian organizations,[138] they did not raise any religious points.

The Canadian Teachers' Federation, while opposing the use of corporal punishment in schools, worried that if s. 43 were removed they would not be able to restrain students. In their factum, they expressed concern that this would mean teachers would not be able to separate a bully from the classmate he is taunting, guide a child by the shoulder to line up in rows, or remove a disruptive student from the classroom or school bus.[139]

SECTION 1

Another section of the *Charter* that played an important role in this discussion, but which in the end was ignored, is s. 1, the government's "ace in the hole." It gives governments or their agents the means to limit rights if

---

...*General)*, [2004] 1 SCR 76 (Factum of the Coalition for Family Autonomy), at ¶ 7.

134 *Canadian Foundation for Children, Youth and the Law v. Canada (Attorney General)*, [2004] 1 SCR 76 (Factum of the Coalition for Family Autonomy), at ¶ 8.

135 *Canadian Foundation for Children, Youth and the Law v. Canada (Attorney General)*, [2004] 1 SCR 76 (Factum of the Coalition for Family Autonomy), at ¶ 13.

136 *Canadian Foundation for Children, Youth and the Law v. Canada (Attorney General)*, [2004] 1 SCR 76 (Factum of the Coalition for Family Autonomy), at ¶ 20.

137 *Canadian Foundation for Children, Youth and the Law v. Canada (Attorney General)*, [2004] 1 SCR (Factum of the Coalition for Family Autonomy), at ¶ 16, citing John Stuart Mill, *On Liberty* (Oxford University Press, 1991), 14.

138 See footnotes 13 through 24 above, as well as the accompanying text.

139 *Canadian Foundation for Children, Youth and the Law v. Canada (Attorney General)*, [2004] 1 SCR 76 (Factum of the Intervener Canadian Teachers' Federation Factum, at ¶ 18).

doing so is reasonable and justifiable in a free and democratic society. The Supreme Court of Canada has established a test that the government must meet whenever it attempts to justify limiting rights.[140]

The test calls upon governments to outline two central criteria: First, limiting a right or freedom is acceptable if the objective (or end) to be gained by the limit is found to be of sufficient importance. The standards to be used in measuring the worth of the objective must be high to ensure that "objectives which are trivial or discordant with the principles integral to a free and democratic society do not gain s. 1 protection."[141] The second criterion requires governments to show that the method chosen (the means) to limit a right or freedom is reasonable and demonstrably justified.[142] The task of the courts at this stage is to identify the underlying functional values of the government's objectives so as to expose "legislation aimed at effecting a less than worthy goal [that] may be cloaked in the rhetoric of justice and reason."[143] The government or its agent must provide cogent and persuasive evidence that clearly shows the method is designed to achieve the objective and is rationally connected to it. The Court said, "where a distinction or limit is irrelevant to the achievement of the objective the limit cannot be saved."[144] The government must also show that the method impairs as little as possible the right or freedom in question because there are no alternative methods available that are less restricting and will achieve the same objective. Finally, the government or its agent must show that there is proportionality between the effect of the method and the objective to be met.[145]

140 *R. v. Oakes*, [1986] 65 N.R. 87. See also *Dagenais v. Canadian Broadcasting Corp*, [1994] 3 SCR 835, which amended, in part, the third part of the *Oakes* test.

141 *R. v. Oakes*, [1986] 65 N.R. 87, at 129.

142 *R. v. Oakes*, [1986] 65 N.R. 87, at 128.

143 *Miron v. Trudel*, [1995] 2 SCR 418, at 503.

144 *Egan v. Canada*, [1995] 2 SCR 513, at 559.

145 *R. v. Oakes*, [1986] 65 N.R. 87, at 129. Since the test was first articulated, it has suffered a great deal of criticism. The criticism is focused not so much on the stringency of the test but on the Court's diluting of its impact. In addition, the Supreme Court has produced tests and limits on rights and freedoms within the *Charter*, which has meant the justification under s. 1 is avoided and formal equality remains. See McIntyre, "Answering the Siren Call of Abstract." See also Chapman, "The Politics of Judging." The author argues that the Supreme Court has avoided using the *Oakes* test, using instead threshold tests (*R.W.D.S.U. v. Dolphin Delivery Ltd*, [1986] 2 SCR 573), bowing to legislative deference (*R. v. Edwards Books and Art Ltd*, [1986] 2 SCR 713), and ignoring it altogether (*Jones v. The Queen*, [1986] 2 SCR 284).

Both parties in the *Foundation* case—the CFCYL and the Government of Canada (Attorney General)—considered s. 1 based on the possibility of the Supreme Court finding that s. 43 of the *Criminal Code* violated the *Charter* rights of children. The CFCYL argued that s. 43 cannot be justified under s. 1 of the *Charter* while the Attorney General argued otherwise.

The CFCYL asserted that s. 43 fails the first criteria as the objective behind s. 43 is not pressing and substantial. The objective the CFCYL focused on was the original purpose behind s. 43 as stated by the judge and legal scholar Blackstone in the eighteenth century.[146] At the time of the drafting of the original version of s. 43, Blackstone wrote that the legislation allowing parents to use force on their children was "to keep the child in order and obedience... for the benefit of his education."[147] However, the Ontario Court of Appeal produced a new objective for s. 43 in their decision. The Court of Appeal said the purpose of s. 43 was to allow parental and teacher latitude to "train and nurture children without the harm" of criminalization.[148] The CFCYL took issue with the shift away from the original objective of s. 43 as outlined by Blackstone, reminding the Court that, according to a previous Supreme Court decision, "it is not open to the government to assert *post facto* a purpose which did not animate the legislation in the first place."[149] When considering the purpose of legislation, they argued, the focus should be the "intent of those who drafted and enacted the legislation at the time, and not of any shifting variables."[150] The CFCYL said that s. 43 is not rationally connected to its original objective, which was to permit the physical punishment of children for their benefit and education. Current research shows the punishment "does not benefit a child's

146 Blackstone, *Commentaries on the Laws of England*, chapter 1.

147 *Canadian Foundation for Children, Youth and the Law v. Canada (Attorney General)*, [2004] 1 SCR 76 (Factum of the Appellant (CFCYL)), at ¶ 92, citing Blackstone, *Commentaries on the Laws of England.*

148 *Canadian Foundation for Children, Youth and the Law v. Canada (Attorney General)*, [2004] 1 SCR 76 (Factum of the Appellant (CFCYL)), at ¶ 93, quoting from the Ontario Court of Appeal decision.

149 *Canadian Foundation for Children, Youth and the Law v. Canada (Attorney General)*, [2004] 1 SCR 76 (Factum of the Appellant (CFCYL)), at ¶ 94, quoting from *Irwin Toy Ltd. v. Quebec*, [1989] 1 SCR 927, at 983.

150 *Canadian Foundation for Children, Youth and the Law v. Canada (Attorney General)*, [2004] 1 SCR 76 (Factum of the Appellant (CFCYL)), at ¶ 94, citing *R. v. Big M Drug Mart*, [1985] 1 SCR 295, at 331.

education but causes harm."[151] The CFCYL made a distinction between child physical punishment and restraint, saying, "parents and teachers must be permitted to use restraint,"[152] but that retaining s. 43 to allow for the use of restraint does not justify the existence of s. 43.[153] The *Criminal Code* provides other defences to deal with situations of restraint or prevention of harm. The CFCYL argued that there are more effective alternative means to discipline and educate children that do not impede their rights. In addition, there is a lack of proportionality between the objective of s. 43 and its negative effects. Apart from the harm it causes, s. 43 "conflicts with child protection legislation and impedes child protection efforts."[154]

The Attorney General's position was that the legislative objective of s. 43 "is to ensure that criminal sanctions are not brought in respect of conduct that the evidence demonstrates is not harmful."[155] It asserted that the Court of Appeal was correct in assessing "the historical objective of s. 43 as assisting parents (and teachers) in educating their children and providing reasonable leeway for them to carry out their responsibility, which is of fundamental importance to society."[156] This is not a shift as stated by the CFCYL but rather "a permissible 'shift in emphasis' with the modern patterns of benefiting a child's education and socialization."[157] The AG said s. 43

151 *Canadian Foundation for Children, Youth and the Law v. Canada (Attorney General)*, [2004] 1 SCR 76 (Factum of the Appellant (CFCYL)), at ¶ 96.

152 *Canadian Foundation for Children, Youth and the Law v. Canada (Attorney General)*, [2004] 1 SCR 76 (Factum of the Appellant (CFCYL)), at ¶ 99.

153 *Canadian Foundation for Children, Youth and the Law v. Canada (Attorney General)*, [2004] 1 SCR 76 (Factum of the Appellant (CFCYL)), at ¶ 104. The CFCYL quoted the Supreme Court in the case of *Ogg-Moss v. The Queen*, [1984] 2 SCR, at 183, when they said, "Section 43 is not necessary for the protection of persons using physical force in response to violent or dangerous behaviour or in the course of approved treatment. The former situations are already covered by, *inter alia*, ss. 34, 35, 37, 38, 39, 41 of the criminal code.... Section 43 only applies to 'correctional' force unrelated to treatment or to the protection of self or others."

154 *Canadian Foundation for Children, Youth and the Law v. Canada (Attorney General)*, [2004] 1 SCR 76 (Factum of the Appellant (CFCYL)), at ¶ 108.

155 *Canadian Foundation for Children, Youth and the Law v. Canada (Attorney General)*, [2004] 1 SCR 76 (Factum of the Respondent Attorney General of Canada), at ¶ 118.

156 *Canadian Foundation for Children, Youth and the Law v. Canada (Attorney General)*, [2004] 1 SCR 76 (Factum of the Respondent Attorney General of Canada), at ¶ 119.

157 *Canadian Foundation for Children, Youth and the Law v. Canada (Attorney General)*, [2004] 1 SCR 76 (Factum of the Respondent Attorney General of Canada), at ¶ 120.

is rationally connected to the objective of providing parents with the scope to "fulfill their responsibilities to their children and society."[158] Section 43 also meets the criteria of minimally impairing a child's right "because it is limited in its application and can respect *Charter* rights when properly applied."[159] Section 43 minimally impairs a child's right since all provinces and territories have child protection legislation that already allows for state intervention.[160] The salutary effects of s. 43, the AG asserted, outweigh any negative effects by allowing parents the liberty to make decisions without the interference of the state regarding their own children and most importantly without the possibility of criminalization. Any possible negative effects associated with maintaining s. 43 are minimal considering that the social science evidence has not established that "normative physical punishment is harmful."[161] The AG made reference to an earlier case, saying, "This Court has elevated the liberty interest of parents—to be free of state intervention in parent–child relations—to a constitutional principle, excepting only in situations of harm."[162] This, they argued, was an important consideration in balancing the interests of parents and an important factor to consider in determining the salutary effects of s. 43.[163]

CONCLUSION

The differing opinions and arguments in the case of the *Canadian Foundation of Children Youth and the Law v. Canada (Attorney General)*

---

158 *Canadian Foundation for Children, Youth and the Law v. Canada (Attorney General)*, [2004] 1 SCR 76 (Factum of the Respondent Attorney General of Canada), at ¶ 121.

159 *Canadian Foundation for Children, Youth and the Law v. Canada (Attorney General)*, [2004] 1 SCR 76 (Factum of the Respondent Attorney General of Canada), at ¶ 123.

160 *Canadian Foundation for Children, Youth and the Law v. Canada (Attorney General)*, [2004] 1 SCR 76 (Factum of the Respondent Attorney General of Canada), at ¶ 125.

161 *Canadian Foundation for Children, Youth and the Law v. Canada (Attorney General)*, [2004] 1 SCR 76 (Factum of the Respondent Attorney General of Canada), at ¶s 128–29.

162 *Canadian Foundation for Children, Youth and the Law v. Canada (Attorney General)*, [2004] 1 SCR 76 (Factum of the Respondent Attorney General of Canada), at ¶ 130, referring to the case of *New Brunswick (Minister of Health and Community Services) v. G.(J.)*, [1999] 3 SCR 46. This case involved a mother's right to legal representation in a case of child apprehension.

163 *Canadian Foundation for Children, Youth and the Law v. Canada (Attorney General)*, [2004] 1 SCR 76 (Factum of the Respondent Attorney General of Canada), at ¶ 130.

highlight the diversity of opinions centred on this topic. In this case, the differing opinions were for the Supreme Court to decide—which it did. On January 30, 2004, the Supreme Court of Canada, in a 6–3 decision, ruled that s. 43 of the *Criminal Code of Canada* does not violate the constitutional rights of children. Legally, their decisions are the "end of the line." But they are not the end of the discussion, research, education, and plans for other means to bring about change.

5

THE SUPREME COURT'S DECISION

No other criminal law provisions compares to section 43's sanctioning of the use of violence by private individuals against innocent and uniquely vulnerable third parties—children—based upon the unfortunate accident of the children's relationships to their attackers.[1]

INTRODUCTION

ON JANUARY 30, 2004, THE SUPREME COURT OF CANADA issued its ruling in the case of the *Canadian Foundation for Children, Youth and the Law v. Canada (Attorney General)*[2] (herein referred to as *Foundation*). In a 6–3 split decision, the Supreme Court of Canada ruled that s. 43 of the *Criminal Code of Canada*[3] does not violate the constitutional rights of children as enshrined in the *Canadian Charter of Rights and Freedoms.*[4] It was an extremely disappointing ruling

1 Carter, "Constitutional Validity of the Corporal Punishment Defence," 201.

2 *Canadian Foundation for Children, Youth and the Law v. Canada (Attorney General)*, [2004] 1 SCR 76.

3 *Criminal Code of Canada*, RSC 1985, c. C-46.

4 *Canadian Charter of Rights and Freedoms*, as enacted by *Canada Act, 1982*, (UK), 1982 c.11.

for those advocating for children's rights and a decision that has been roundly denounced.[5]

The Supreme Court of Canada, in upholding the constitutionality of s. 43, ruled that the purpose of s. 43 was to "carve out a sphere within which children's parents and teachers may use minor corrective force in some circumstances without facing criminal sanction,"[6] and that "this section provides a workable, constitutional standard that protects both children and parents."[7] Mark Carter, a legal scholar, observes that "no other criminal law provisions compares to section 43's sanctioning of the use of violence by private individuals against innocent and uniquely vulnerable third parties—children—based upon the unfortunate accident of the children's relationships to their attackers."[8]

The decision of the Court's majority considered, first and foremost, the rights of parents and adults. It missed the rights of children. The outcome in this significant *Charter* challenge was derailed by the Court's focus on parental rights, referred to by Sykes as "an important third force at work" in this decision.[9] While the intent in challenging s. 43 using the *Charter of Rights and Freedoms* was to focus on the rights of children and "the broader values and interests of society,"[10] parental rights trumped. The Court did this while rejecting any consideration of scientific evidence regarding the harm of child physical punishment, Canada's obligations under the *Convention on the Rights of the Child*, subsequent international directives, and possible alternatives to child physical punishment. The decision fits squarely within the traditional conservative model associated with the notion that children are the property of their parents. This view, as explained by legal scholar

---

5 Carter, "Fundamentally Flawed," 1; McGillivray, "Nowhere to Stand," 57; Durrant et al., "Protection of Children from Physical Maltreatment in Canada," 64; Watkinson, "Corporal Punishment and Education"; McGillivray and Durrant, "Child Corporal Punishment," 177; Sykes, "Bambi Meets Godzilla," 131; Carter, "Constitutional Validity of the Corporal Punishment Defence," 189; Mosoff and Grant, "Upholding Corporal Punishment," 177.

6 *Canadian Foundation for Children, Youth and the Law v. Canada (Attorney General)*, [2004] 1 SCR 76, at ¶ 1.

7 *Canadian Foundation for Children, Youth and the Law v. Canada (Attorney General)*, [2004] 1 SCR 76, at ¶ 2.

8 Carter, "Constitutional Validity of the Corporal Punishment Defence," 201.

9 Sykes, "Bambi Meets Godzilla," 132.

10 Sykes, "Bambi Meets Godzilla," 133.

Jeffery Wilson, rests "in the common law principle of the parent's rights to discipline and the child's duty to submit."[11] The traditional conservative model stands in opposition to a social democratic model that respects and takes seriously the rights of children.

The majority decision was written by Chief Justice Beverley McLachlin and concurred with by Justice Charles Gonthier,[12] Justice Frank Iacobucci, Justice John Major, Justice Michel Bastarache, and Justice Louis LeBel. The dissenting judges were Justice Louise Arbour,[13] Justice Ian Binnie, and Justice Marie Deschamps. The dissenting judges each wrote their own decisions.

THE DECISION

The majority of the Supreme Court judges sided with the Government of Canada, the Canadian Teachers' Federation, and the Coalition for Family Autonomy and found that while the defence available to parents and teachers under s. 43 violates a child's "security of the person" rights under s. 7, it is not done in contravention of the principles of fundamental justice. They found that s. 12 of the *Charter* was not offended by s. 43 since s. 12 applies to the actions of governments and their agents, not to parents. Finally, the Court found that s. 43 did not constitute discrimination against children.[14] They acknowledged that s. 43 "permits conduct toward children that would be criminal in the case of adult victims,"[15] but the distinction on the basis of age is, they said, designed to protect children by not criminalizing their parents and teachers. Chief Justice McLachlin, writing for the majority, said,

> The decision not to criminalize such conduct is not grounded in devaluation of the child, but in a concern that to do so risks ruining lives

11 Wilson, *Children and the Law*, 241.

12 Justice Charles Gonthier retired from the Supreme Court in August 2003 but took part in the hearing and provided his support to the majority decision issued in January 2004.

13 Justice Louise Arbour resigned from the Supreme Court in June 2004 to take up her new position as the United Nations high commissioner for human rights.

14 The three dissenting judges came to different conclusions, but one—Justice Binnie—agreed that s. 43 discriminates against children on the basis of their age. However, he found that the discrimination could be justified under s. 1.

15 *Canadian Foundation for Children, Youth and the Law v. Canada (Attorney General)*, [2004] 1 SCR 76, at ¶ 50.

> and breaking up families—a burden that in large part would be borne by children and outweigh any benefit derived from applying the criminal process.[16]

In the majority's opinion, the benefit to be gained by the existence of s. 43 outweighed the deleterious effects of the use of physical force on children and corresponded to their need for the assurance that their parents and teachers would not be criminalized. One by one they rejected all of the *Charter* arguments presented to them by the Canadian Foundation for Children, Youth and the Law.

SECTION 7

As discussed in chapter 4, the CFCYL argued that s. 43 violated the security of the person rights under s. 7 and, further, that it was done in a manner that was not in accordance with the "principles of fundamental justice." Section 7 involves two steps that are the responsibility of the person or group claiming a violation of their rights: first, their right has been violated, and second, it was not done in accordance with the principles of fundamental justice. The Government, represented by the Attorney General (AG), conceded that s. 43 violates a child's right to security of the person, but argued that it was done in accordance with the principles of fundamental justice. The onus was on the CFCYL to show that the principles had not been upheld. The CFCYL argued that s. 43 violated the following principles: that the child must be afforded independent procedural rights; that legislation affecting children must be in their best interests; and that criminal legislation must not be vague or overbroad.[17]

In response to the first principle, the Court said children do not need separate representation of their interests in cases where they are the victim as they are well represented by the Crown.[18] I always found this to be

---

16 *Canadian Foundation for Children, Youth and the Law v. Canada (Attorney General)*, [2004] 1 SCR 76, at ¶ 62.

17 *Canadian Foundation for Children, Youth and the Law v. Canada (Attorney General)*, [2004] 1 SCR 76, at ¶ 4.

18 *Canadian Foundation for Children, Youth and the Law v. Canada (Attorney General)*, [2004] 1 SCR 76, at ¶ 6.

a disingenuous argument considering it was the Crown who was leading the challenge to retain s. 43. Second, the Court said that the best interest of the child is not a principle of fundamental justice since it "is not vital or fundamental to our societal notion of justice."[19] Finally, the Court found that the principle of vagueness and overbreadth was not abridged since, as part of the discussion on this point, the Court set out to limit the scope of s. 43, saying,

> It follows that s. 43 of the *Criminal Code* will satisfy the constitutional requirement for precision if it delineates a risk zone for criminal sanctions. This achieves the essential task of providing general guidance for citizens and law enforcement officers.[20]

In subsequent paragraphs, within the decision, the Court set out limits to s. 43, which they referred to as the "zone of risk."[21]

Justice Louise Arbour, in her dissenting opinion, argued that the Court's attempt to limit the scope of s. 43 by setting out specific criteria—the "zone of risk"—was an error. Limiting a defence can only be done if it is determined that, in this case, the defence of s. 43 offends the *Charter*. Justice Arbour said to reduce a defence by picking away at it is not the role of courts. The impact of the Court's decision could result in enlarging "criminal responsibility by limiting defences enacted by Parliament." Justice Arbour said that, "in fact, the role of the courts is precisely the opposite."[22]

In her dissenting opinion, Justice Arbour relied upon the breach of a child's security of the person under s. 7 of the *Charter* to conclude that s. 43

19 *Canadian Foundation for Children, Youth and the Law v. Canada (Attorney General)*, [2004] 1 SCR 76, at ¶ 10.

20 *Canadian Foundation for Children, Youth and the Law v. Canada (Attorney General)*, [2004] 1 SCR 76, at ¶ 18. See also Carter, "Constitutional Validity of the Corporal Punishment Defence," 195–204, for a more in-depth analysis of the Supreme Court's s. 7 reasoning.

21 *Canadian Foundation for Children, Youth and the Law v. Canada (Attorney General)*, [2004] 1 SCR 76, at ¶s 19–40.

22 *Canadian Foundation for Children, Youth and the Law v. Canada (Attorney General)*, [2004] 1 SCR 76, at ¶ 135. Carter, "Fundamentally Flawed," cites the work of Peter Hogg, *Constitutional Law of Canada*, vol. 2, 5th ed. (Carswell, 2007), 47-64.8, 47-64.9 (this is how it is referred to in Carter's paper), who uses the *Foundation* case to illustrate the question "Where does interpretation end and redrafting begin?"

does violate the *Charter* rights of children. She said that the phrase "reasonable under the circumstances" in s. 43 violated the rights of children and the deprivation did not meet the requirements of the principles of fundamental justice because it is "unconstitutionally vague."[23] She went on to note that

> vagueness in defining the terms of a defence which affects the physical integrity of children may be even more invidious than is vagueness in defining an offence or a defence in another context and may therefore call for a stricter standard.[24]

Justice Arbour referred to Canada's international obligations regarding the rights of the child and relied on the fact that the United Nations Committee on the Rights of the Child had made similar observations regarding comparable legislation in the United Kingdom. The Committee said, "the imprecise nature of the expression of reasonable chastisement as contained in these [United Kingdom] legal provisions may pave the way for it to be interpreted in a subjective and arbitrary manner."[25]

SECTION 12

The majority of the Court ruled that the prohibition against cruel and unusual punishment under s. 12 applies only to governments and their agents, and that "corrective force in the family setting is not treatment by the state."[26] The Court dismissed any connection with parents to government despite the fact that it is an act of government that provides parents with the right to use physical force on children. The bigger challenge, however, was trying to separate teachers from the net of "government."

---

23 *Canadian Foundation for Children, Youth and the Law v. Canada (Attorney General)*, [2004] 1 SCR 76, at 191.

24 *Canadian Foundation for Children, Youth and the Law v. Canada (Attorney General)*, [2004] 1 SCR 76, at 185.

25 *Canadian Foundation for Children, Youth and the Law v. Canada (Attorney General)*, [2004] 1 SCR 76, at 196, referring to the Committee on the Rights of the Child, *Report Adopted by the Committee*, at ¶ 218.

26 *Canadian Foundation for Children, Youth and the Law v. Canada (Attorney General)*, [2004] 1 SCR 76, at ¶ 48.

Teachers are employed by the state, and their connection to government is clear. Nevertheless the majority found that the conduct permitted by s. 43 did not rise to the level of "cruel and unusual treatment," nor did it outrage standards of decency, and thus s. 12 did not apply to teachers either.[27] It must be noted, again, the majority had only just clarified a few paragraphs earlier[28] what conduct would not be permitted by teachers under s. 43, thus setting their own stage for their own conclusion.

Justice Binnie, in his dissenting opinion, found that the inclusion of teachers under s. 43 could no longer be justified. He argued that a teacher does not share the same commitment as a parent to a particular child. According to Justice Binnie, "The pupil-teacher relationship is closer to the master-apprentice relationship for which s. 43 protection was abolished by Parliament in 1955."[29]

SECTION 15

The majority on the Supreme Court found that s. 43 did not discriminate against children on the basis of their age. This was an especially confounding and distressing conclusion. While the distinction was based on a child's age, the Court reasoned that the distinction was designed to protect children by not penalizing their parents or teachers. The justification comes from the Court's rigid interpretation of the 1999 Supreme Court decision *Law v. Canada*,[30] which set out the perspective, specific steps, and factors to be considered when determining whether discrimination has occurred.

It was the CFCYL's position that children do not receive equal protection or equal benefit from the *Criminal Code*. The *Criminal Code of Canada* prohibits assaults and applies punitive measures to those who assault

---

27 *Canadian Foundation for Children, Youth and the Law v. Canada (Attorney General)*, [2004] 1 SCR 76, at ¶ 49.

28 *Canadian Foundation for Children, Youth and the Law v. Canada (Attorney General)*, [2004] 1 SCR 76, at ¶ 38.

29 *Canadian Foundation for Children, Youth and the Law v. Canada (Attorney General)*, [2004] 1 SCR 76, at ¶ 125. Prisoners were removed from s. 43 in 1972 and sailors in 2001 by Parliament.

30 *Law v. Canada (Minister of Employment and Immigration)*, [1999], 1 SCR 497. Recall that the case involved the denial of CPP survivor benefits to widow Nancy Law on the basis of her age (thirty years old). Her challenge under s. 15 of the *Charter* alleging age discrimination was unsuccessful.

adults, but it does not protect children in the same way.[31] As distressing as this decision was for those who attempted to show that s. 43 is a violation of the rights of children, it was even more so considering the strange and perhaps harmful analysis given to the equality rights section of the *Charter*. Throughout the series of court decisions in this case, the s. 15 argument was given alarmingly short shrift. The Superior Court of Ontario found, in two short paragraphs, that s. 15 was not abridged by s. 43—end of story.[32] The Ontario Court of Appeal found that s. 43 appeared to discriminate on the basis of age, but acknowledged they were only prepared to admit to such since s. 43 could be saved by s. 1, which "guarantees the rights and freedoms set out in it subject to such reasonable limits prescribed by law as can be demonstrably justified in a free and democratic society."[33] They said this but without showing how. Once the matter reached the Supreme Court, Chief Justice McLachlin gave it slightly more attention but with disturbing twists that are discussed below.

Equality

The CFCYL argued that equality for children can only be assured "if the criminal law treats simple assaults on children in the disciplinary context the same as it treats simple assaults on adults."[34] The Supreme Court said this was equating equal treatment with identical treatment, an interpretation the Court has consistently rejected. This was an astonishing interpretation as it implies that the failure to provide children with the same protection from assault as that afforded to adults does not amount to inequality/discrimination. This appears to fly in the face of earlier court

31 The *Criminal Code* does not define the term *child*. However, according to the *Convention on the Rights of the Child*, "a child means every human being below the age of eighteen years unless, under the law applicable to the child, majority is attained earlier." The age of eighteen is used as the age of majority in Canada for purposes of voting. In addition, Saskatchewan legislation establishing the Children's Advocate defines children as being under the age of eighteen.

32 *Canadian Foundation for Children, Youth and the Law v. Canada (Attorney General)*, (2000) 188 DLR (4th) 718, at ¶s 130 and 131.

33 *Canadian Foundation for Children, Youth and the Law v. Canada (Attorney General)*, (2002) 207 DLR (4th) 632, at ¶ 57. Also at http://www.ontariocourts.on.ca/decisions_index/2002index.htm.

34 *Canadian Foundation for Children, Youth and the Law v. Canada (Attorney General)*, [2004] 1 SCR 76, ¶ 50.

rulings on the evolution of equality.[35] Ryder, Faria, and Lawrence, in their analysis of s. 15 jurisprudence over the past fifteen years, point out that it is "sometimes remarked that *Charter* equality jurisprudence has rejected formal equality in favour of a substantive understanding of equality."[36] But both formal equality (referred to by the Court as equal treatment) and substantive equality inform equality jurisprudence.[37]

Ryder and colleagues describe formal equality as focusing on the individual and the relevance of their characteristics to the challenged law or policy. It is a process of determining whether discrimination has occurred based on the fact that not all people are given the same treatment. Concomitantly, substantive equality focuses on the group and the impact of laws and policies on those already suffering from social, political, and economic disadvantages. It is concerned with ensuring that laws and policies applied to everyone do not result in more burdensome consequences to an identifiable group. The authors use as an example the issue of same sex marriage, which considered whether the opposite-sex requirement in marriage violates s. 15. The Court found that the proposed legislation put forward by the federal government legalizing same sex marriage to be within the jurisdiction of the government and that it did not violate the *Charter* but rather "flows from it."[38]

Ryder and colleagues argue that both formal equality and substantive equality play an important role in equality jurisprudence and describe the distinction between formal equality and substantive equality this way:

> Formal equality focuses on whether sexual orientation is relevant to the objectives of the legal definition of marriage; substantive equality focuses on whether the exclusion from marriage has the effect of further subordinating gays and lesbians in Canadian society.[39]

---

35 Ryder et al., "What's *Law* Good For?"

36 Ryder et al., "What's *Law* Good For?," 106.

37 Ryder et al., "What's *Law* Good For?," 106.

38 This issue was heard by the Supreme Court of Canada in the case of *Reference re Same-Sex Marriage*, [2004] 3 SCR, in which the Court was asked to rule on the constitutionality of proposed legislation legalizing same sex marriage (at ¶ 43).

39 *Reference re Same-Sex Marriage*, [2004] 3 SCR, at 106.

The authors note that formal and substantive understandings of equality often work together and come to the same conclusion, but they can also cause tensions in legal interpretations.

The Chief Justice's analysis in the *Foundation* case failed to acknowledge that our evolving notions of equality, directed in large part by the Court itself, take into account the impact of direct discrimination and discrimination arising from neutral practices. Though substantive equality acknowledges that not all differentiations among groups violate equality rights, the Chief Justice's implication that cases of differential treatment (or direct discrimination) aimed at members of a vulnerable group does not amount to a violation of equality rights is troubling and underscores the need to justify such interpretations, where it belongs—within a s. 1 discussion.

As Justice Binnie notes in his dissenting opinion, in the view of Chief Justice McLachlin, "the objective of substantive equality (as distinguished from formal equality) justifies the differential treatment of children."[40] It appears the Chief Justice's interpretation has taken the phrase "equality with a vengeance"[41] to include "substantive equality with a vengeance." Carter describes the reasoning of the majority in this regard as "bizarre."[42]

"Reasonable Person"

The perspective to be taken when determining whether discrimination has occurred is that of the "reasonable person," and the discussion and analysis of the facts are to be framed within the perspective of the "reasonable person." The Court in *Law* said the issue is "whether a reasonable person in circumstances similar to those of the claimant would find that the legislation which imposes differential treatment has the effect of demeaning his or her dignity."[43] In the *Foundation* case, Chief Justice McLachlin opined that since the idea of the reasonable child confronts us with "the fiction of a reasonable, fully apprised preschool-aged child,"[44] what is needed is some-

---

40 *Canadian Foundation for Children, Youth and the Law v. Canada (Attorney General)*, [2004] 1 SCR 76, at ¶ 91.

41 *Schachter v. Canada et al.*, [1992] 2 SCR 679.

42 Carter, "Constitutional Validity of the Corporal Punishment Defence," 205.

43 *Law v. Canada (Minister of Employment and Immigration)*, [1999] 1 SCR 497, ¶ 60.

44 *Canadian Foundation for Children, Youth and the Law v. Canada (Attorney General)*, [2004] 1 SCR 76, at ¶ 53.

one to speak on his or her behalf. The best way to consider the perspective of the child, the majority said, is through the "perspective of the reasonable person acting on behalf of a child, who seriously considers and values the child's views and development needs."[45] In other words, the determination as to whether a child's dignity has been demeaned is made by the parent or teacher, "the very person from whom the child may need protection."[46] That is to say, the very person with the most to gain by leaving the law as it is. Justice Binnie in his dissenting opinion warned against using the notion of "dignity" such that it becomes an "unpredictable side-wind powerful enough to single-handedly blow away the protection that the *Criminal Code* would otherwise provide."[47]

Ignoring the views of children in regard to child physical punishment is an obvious lacuna in this matter. Save the Children conducted the first major report into children's views of child physical punishment in the United Kingdom. The survey compiled the views of more than 1,300 young people between the ages of six and seventeen from across Scotland and found that three-quarters of respondents "believe it is wrong for an adult to hit a child under any circumstances."[48] A 2010 study examined African American and Anglo-American children's evaluation of discipline methods. The study considered whether the age of the children, their race, socioeconomic status, and exposure to spanking influenced their evaluations. A total of 108 children, aged six to ten years old, and one of their parents participated in the study. The children were presented with scenarios of a child misbehaving and had to evaluate which form of discipline was the best. The forms of discipline were time-out, withdrawal of privileges, reasoning, or spanking. The youth chose reasoning as the best method (37 percent), second was withdrawal of privileges (27 percent), then spanking (23 percent), and, finally, time-out (12 percent). As one nine-year-old participant noted, "Spanking doesn't show him how to do something better, it just shows you have more power over him."[49]

---

45 *Canadian Foundation for Children, Youth and the Law v. Canada (Attorney General)*, [2004] 1 SCR 76, at ¶ 53.

46 Mosoff and Grant, "Upholding Corporal Punishment," 193.

47 *Canadian Foundation for Children, Youth and the Law v. Canada (Attorney General)*, [2004] 1 SCR 76, at ¶ 72.

48 Collins, "Children Reject Smacking."

49 Vittrup and Holden, "Children's Evaluation of Discipline," 215.

Justice Louise Arbour, in her dissenting opinion, canvassed over twenty cases decided within the previous ten to fifteen years that were deemed reasonable by, one might assume, the "reasonable person" acting on behalf of the child. They included a teacher who used karate chops to the face and shoulders of students; a father who struck his fourteen-year-old daughter with a belt, leaving welts and bruises; a foster mother who hit two two-year-olds on their diapered bottoms with a belt, leaving red marks; an aunt and uncle who ordered their two teenaged nieces to strip to their underwear, and beat them with a belt on their buttocks and thighs; and a father who struck his four-year-old son across the face, leaving an imprint—the child was suffering from an ear infection at the time that eventually required medical attention.[50]

Mosoff and Grant point out that displacing the perspective of the child with that of an adult illustrates poignantly the ambiguity around the idea of the rights of the child. It discounts the child's perspective and trivializes their disempowerment and vulnerability which is the "very sense of disempowerment and vulnerability, that is exacerbated by excluding children from the usual assault provisions of the *Criminal Code*."[51] The silencing of children's voices assumes all children from birth to age eighteen are incapable of expressing reasonable views. Anand cautions that the Court's reasoning may also be used to discount other groups as well, including those with mental disabilities or claimants of colour.[52] Removing the voices of vulnerable rights claimants "perpetuates legal inequality by silencing the voices of the marginalized."[53] If children cannot be given a voice in an issue as fundamental to a child's dignity and security of the person, Mosoff and Grant comment that they "cannot imagine in what circumstances their perspective would be considered."[54]

---

50 *Canadian Foundation for Children, Youth and the Law v. Canada (Attorney General)*, [2004] 1 SCR 76, at ¶s 153–70.

51 Mosoff and Grant, "Upholding Corporal Punishment," 193.

52 Anand, "Reasonable Chastisement," 877.

53 Sykes, "Bambi Meets Godzilla," 161.

54 Mosoff and Grant, "Upholding Corporal Punishment," 193. A 2006 special report from the United Nations recommended that children be allowed to express their concerns in accordance with article 12 of the UN *Convention on the Rights of the Child*: "1. States Parties shall assure to the child who is capable of forming his or her own views the right to express those views freely in all matters affecting the child, the views of the child being given due weight in accordance with the age and...

Law *Test and Correspondence Factor*

In addition, *Law* outlined three steps necessary to prove a violation of s. 15. First, does the law create a distinction; second, is the distinction based on an enumerated or analogous ground; and third, is the distinction discriminatory. The answer to the first step in the *Foundation* case is yes, the law makes a distinction between children and adults in that s. 43 of the *Criminal Code* permits the use of force upon children and not adults. Similarly, the answer to the second step is that the distinction is made on the enumerated ground of age. The third requires the courts to look at the contextual factors to determine if the distinction is discriminatory. Within the third step are four important contextual factors: first, whether the group experiences pre-existing disadvantages, stereotypes, prejudice, or vulnerability; second, whether there is correspondence between the ground on which the claim is based and the needs, capacity, or circumstances of the claimant; third, whether the law is designed for an ameliorative purpose; and fourth, what the nature of the interest is that is affected by the law.[55]

The Court found that the first factor regarding vulnerability and pre-existing disadvantage was met since children were indeed a "highly

---

...maturity of the child. 2. For this purpose, the child shall in particular be provided the opportunity to be heard in any judicial and administrative proceedings affecting the child, either directly, or through a representative or an appropriate body, in a manner consistent with the procedural rules of national law." See Pinheiro, *World Report on Violence Against Children*, and recommendation 7, which calls for the full participation of children in "all aspects of prevention, response and monitoring of violence against them, taking into account article 12 of the *Convention on the Rights of the Child.* Recommendation 28 which calls on state governments to 'Develop and strengthen national policies and action plans on child protection that include mechanisms to ensure children's participation in the implementation, monitoring and evaluation of programs and services (for example, the establishment of a National Commission on Child Protection or Ombudsman for Children).'"

55 *Canadian Foundation for Children, Youth and the Law v. Canada (Attorney General)*, [2004] 1 SCR 76, at ¶ 51. For further discussion on the impact of the "*Law* test" on s. 15 litigation, see Faraday et al., *Making Equality Rights Real.* Supreme Court decisions *R. v. Kapp*, [2008] 2 SCR 483, and *Withler v. Canada (Attorney General)*, [2011] 1 SCR 396, are reminders to ease the restrictions associated with the second factor in the *Law* test. The Supreme Court ruled that the primary indicators of discrimination are "the perpetuation of disadvantage and stereotyping" and identified that the second factor in *Law* (correspondence) "deals with stereotyping" (*R. v. Kapp*, at ¶ 23; *Withler v. Canada*, at ¶ 38).

vulnerable group,"[56] and the fourth factor was likewise met since "the nature of the interest affected—psychological integrity—is profound."[57] The third factor did not apply in this case.[58] And while two of the three relevant factors met the test of discrimination, the Court found that the correspondence factor nullified any further considerations. This factor looks at the correspondence between the legislation under review and the needs, capacities, and circumstances of those affected by it. Section 43, the Court reasoned, is necessary to meet the needs of children to have secure family and school settings. It is "Parliament's attempt to accommodate both of these needs."[59] These needs would not be met, the Court reasoned, if parents and teachers were criminalized for using "minimal force of transient or trivial impact."[60]

In other words, the Supreme Court's decision to dismiss the equality rights claim rested exclusively on the second factor and the majority's determination that a "correspondence" existed between the needs of the child in circumstances such as these.[61] Ryder and colleagues comment that Chief Justice McLachlin's conclusion

> turned entirely on the correspondence factor: age, she held, corresponds to the need to use corrective and reasonable force in some circumstances.

The result of permitting the correspondence factor to trump the other three factors is that even differential treatment on a prohibited ground that further subordinates a disadvantaged group will not be found to violate section 15 if the claimant fails to demonstrate that the law or policy at issue lacks a rational basis.[62]

---

56 *Canadian Foundation for Children, Youth and the Law v. Canada (Attorney General)*, [2004] 1 SCR 76, at ¶ 56.

57 *Canadian Foundation for Children, Youth and the Law v. Canada (Attorney General)*, [2004] 1 SCR 76, at ¶ 56.

58 *Canadian Foundation for Children, Youth and the Law v. Canada (Attorney General)*, [2004] 1 SCR 76, at ¶ 56.

59 *Canadian Foundation for Children, Youth and the Law v. Canada (Attorney General)*, [2004] 1 SCR 76, at ¶ 59.

60 *Canadian Foundation for Children, Youth and the Law v. Canada (Attorney General)*, [2004] 1 SCR 76, at ¶ 59.

61 Ryder et al., "What's *Law* Good For?," 124.

62 Ryder et al., "What's *Law* Good For?," 124.

The majority's interpretation of the *Law* test in this case has been described as "unprecedented"[63] due to its rigidity in the application of the test. Indeed, in a subsequent decision, the Supreme Court of Canada cautioned that the *Law* test concerning the substance of a s. 15 equality rights claim was not to be applied in a rigid manner, saying a s. 15 "analysis is contextual, not formalistic, grounded in the actual situation of the group and the potential of the impugned law to worsen their situation."[64]

Justice Binnie, in his dissenting opinion, disagreed strongly with the majority's interpretation of s. 15, saying,

> There can be few things that more effectively designate children as second-class citizens than stripping them of the ordinary protection of the assault provisions of the *Criminal Code*. Such stripping of protection is destructive of dignity from any perspective including that of a child.[65]

The Supreme Court constructed an insurmountable legal wall to keep at bay the equality rights of children. They confounded their own prior understandings of substantive equality, dismissed the perspective of the children and youth as being antithetical to that of a "reasonable person," and even though all parts of the *Law* test applied to the circumstances of child corporal punishment and two out of the three relevant contextual factors were met, it relied solely on its own interpretation of the "correspondence" factor to justify the continued legality of child physical assault.

In Terrorem

The majority ruled that while children need to be protected from abuse, they also need their parents and teachers: a "stable and secure family and school setting is essential to this growth process."[66] The Chief Justice then began what legal scholars Mosoff and Grant refer to as the majority's *in*

63 Sykes, "Bambi Meets Godzilla," 164.

64 *Withler v. Canada (Attorney General)*, [2011] 1 SCR 396, at ¶ 37.

65 *Canadian Foundation for Children, Youth and the Law v. Canada (Attorney General)*, [2004] 1 SCR 76, at ¶ 72.

66 *Canadian Foundation for Children, Youth and the Law v. Canada (Attorney General)*, [2004] 1 SCR 76, at ¶ 58.

terrorem[67] arguments, using a Latin phrase that translates as "by way of threat" or "to produce fear or frighten."

The Chief Justice said it made little sense to "bring the blunt hand of the criminal law down on minor disciplinary contacts"[68] and risk having the state incur "considerable expense."[69] It must be remembered the Court had only just circumscribed what was to be considered "minor" a few paragraphs earlier.[70] The Chief Justice portrayed a devastating picture of criminalized parents "being dragged into Court for a 'pat on the bum'"[71] and families torn asunder. The majority saw the need for parental and teacher protection from assault charges so as to avoid ruining lives, breaking up families,[72] and "rupturing the family setting."[73] It was, the Court said, a means that "protects both children and parents."[74] The rationale for s. 43 is based, the Chief Justice said, "on the interest of the child and on family and school relationships."[75] The benefit to be gained for children was the assurance that their family setting would not be broken nor their teacher "detained pending bail, with the inevitable harm to the child's crucial educative setting."[76] But as Mosoff and Grant point out, "It is not clear why a teacher would be denied bail in such a circumstance and this example further demonstrates the approach of the majority in creating unlikely counter-factual scenarios

67 Mosoff and Grant, "Upholding Corporal Punishment," 177.

68 *Canadian Foundation for Children, Youth and the Law v. Canada (Attorney General)*, [2004] 1 SCR 76, at ¶ 51.

69 *Canadian Foundation for Children, Youth and the Law v. Canada (Attorney General)*, [2004] 1 SCR 76, at ¶ 60, quoting, with approval from the Canadian Committee on Corrections, Ouimet, *Toward Unity* (the Ouimet Report), 12–13.

70 *Canadian Foundation for Children, Youth and the Law v. Canada (Attorney General)*, [2004] 1 SCR 76, at ¶ 51.

71 *Canadian Foundation for Children, Youth and the Law v. Canada (Attorney General)*, [2004] 1 SCR 76, at ¶ 207.

72 *Canadian Foundation for Children, Youth and the Law v. Canada (Attorney General)*, [2004] 1 SCR 76, at ¶ 60, quoting with approval from the Ouimet Report.

73 *Canadian Foundation for Children, Youth and the Law v. Canada (Attorney General)*, [2004] 1 SCR 76, at ¶ 68.

74 *Canadian Foundation for Children, Youth and the Law v. Canada (Attorney General)*, [2004] 1 SCR 76, at ¶ 2.

75 *Canadian Foundation for Children, Youth and the Law v. Canada (Attorney General)*, [2004] 1 SCR 76, at ¶ 51.

76 *Canadian Foundation for Children, Youth and the Law v. Canada (Attorney General)*, [2004] 1 SCR 76, at ¶ 68.

to support its argument."[77] However, it is worth restating that s. 43 does not protect any other professional groups who work with children. It does not provide childcare workers, daycare workers, religious leaders, coaches, and nurses with a s. 43 defence, yet they continue to perform their work relying, if necessary, on other defences available to us all (ss. 37, 38, 45).

As others have pointed out, there are legal principles and guidelines that limit the criminalizing of individuals who have technically "broken the law."[78] Justice Arbour in her dissenting opinion pointed out that the legal defence of *de minimis*, which encapsulates the notion that the law will not concern itself with trivial matters, is available for those circumstances in which assaults should not fall under criminal sanctions. She said that if s. 43 was struck down "parents would be no more at risk of being dragged into court for a 'pat on the bum' than they currently are for 'tasting' a single grape in the supermarket."[79]

In addition, the prospect of the increased criminalization of parents seems unlikely. The police and prosecutors have a great deal of discretion in deciding whether charging a parent, or anyone for that matter, is in the "public's interest." It is easy to see that charging a parent, who is to provide for their children, would not make sense at times; however, the Supreme Court still fixated on hypothetical scenarios of parents languishing in prisons while providing no supporting evidence to show that such outcomes are likely, nor that parents in countries that have done away with their equivalent of s. 43 are more likely to be criminalized.

Perhaps this reasoning illustrates more than anything how the gaze of the majority turned full face onto the rights of parents, thus eclipsing any need to justify the use of force on children or acknowledge the risks children encounter from physical punishment overwhelmingly evident in social science research available and presented to the Court at the time.[80]

In the first s. 15 case heard by the Supreme Court of Canada in 1987, the Court said,

---

77 Mosoff and Grant, "Upholding Corporal Punishment," 181n17.

78 McGillivray, "Child Physical Assault," 133; Durrant, "Corporal Punishment: A Violation," 99; Stuart, *Canadian Criminal Law: A Treatise*.

79 *Canadian Foundation for Children, Youth and the Law v. Canada (Attorney General)*, [2004] 1 SCR 76sd, at ¶ 207.

80 Durrant, "Evaluating the Success of Sweden's Corporal Punishment Ban," 435; Gershoff, "Corporal Punishment by Parents," 539; along with the affidavits of expert witnesses such as Murray Straus, James Gargarino, George Holden, and others.

> s. 15 is designed to protect those groups who suffer social, political and legal disadvantage in our society, the burden resting on government to justify the type of discrimination against such groups is appropriately an onerous one.[81]

Clearly children meet the requirement of a group who suffers social, political, and legal disadvantages. However, the disadvantage facing children was constructed by the Chief Justice as a benefit consistent with the oldest reasoning known to humankind, the cliché that it is "for your own good." And as if to reassure every child, she remarked, "Parliament's choice not to criminalize this conduct does not devalue or discriminate against children, but responds to the reality of their lives by addressing their need for safety and security in an age-appropriate manner."[82]

Legal scholar Mark Carter summarized the majority's development of sections 7, 12, and 15 of the *Charter* as a "disturbing development in our understanding of how law directly and indirectly allows children to be the victim of violence."[83] He states,

> There is cruel irony in the extent to which the majority decision in the *Foundation* case is characterized by the identification of teachers and parents as the most deserving recipients of our concern about victimization in the debate over the retention of the corporal punishment defence.... Equally troubling is the Court's willingness to compromise the constitutional standard of children's equality in the interests of vague concepts of family integrity. The majority does so by usurping the language of substantive equality.[84]

---

81 *Andrews v. Law Society of British Columbia*, [1989] 1 SCR 143, at 151. This initial interpretation of the purpose of s. 15, first formalized in 1989, is now well established and referred to consistently. See, for example, *Law v. Canada (Minister of Employment and Immigration)*, [1999], 1 SCR 497, at ¶ 43; *Withler v. Canada (Attorney General)*, [2011] 1 SCR 396, at ¶ 35.

82 *Canadian Foundation for Children, Youth and the Law v. Canada (Attorney General)*, [2004] 1 SCR 76, at ¶ 51.

83 Carter, "Constitutional Validity of the Corporal Punishment Defence," 191.

84 Carter, "Constitutional Validity of the Corporal Punishment Defence," 191.

THE ABSENCE OF SECTION 1

One of the questions asked in a study undertaken by the former Law Commission of Canada was "What does criminal law provide that is not available through other means or alternatives?"[85] A section 1 analysis as provided for in the *Charter* directs us to the same question by requiring the government or its agent to justify the need to limit a right or freedom such as the right to equal treatment, security of the person, or to be protected from cruel and unusual treatment and to then consider alternatives that are less limiting. Had the Supreme Court, in the *Foundation* case, undertaken this procedure, it would have come face to face with what is paramount in the challenge to the use of physical force on children—a consideration of alternative responses to ensure children are granted their inherent right to dignity and equality while avoiding what the majority of the Supreme Court decided would be the criminalizing of parents and teachers.

Whenever a court considers a *Charter* challenge, a determination is made as to whether the law or practice that is being challenged limits a guaranteed right. The onus of proof at this stage is placed upon the individual or group who is challenging the law or government action. If the court finds that the challenged law limits a guaranteed right, this does not automatically mean the law is unconstitutional. The court then moves to consider, under s. 1 of the *Charter*, whether the limit is a reasonable one and can be "demonstrably justified in a free and democratic society."[86] The onus of proof switches at this point to the government to justify the need to limit the right. The government must show that limiting a right meets a sufficiently important objective and that the limit is reasonable and demonstrably justified.

The objective, or "aim," of s. 43 was described by the majority of the Supreme Court as a means

> to permit parents and teachers to apply strictly limited corrective force to children without criminal sanctions so that they can carry out their important responsibilities to train and nurture children without the

85 Law Commission of Canada, *What Is a Crime?*

86 [tk]

> harm that such sanctions would bring to them, to their tasks and to the families concerned.[87]

As discussed in chapter 4, identifying the objective behind s. 43 was a contested issue.[88] The *Foundation* argued that the objective of s. 43, flowing from the original nineteenth-century works of Blackstone, was to correct children for the good of their education.[89] The Attorney General convinced the Supreme Court that the purpose of s. 43 was to protect children from the possibility that their parents would be criminalized. The reframing of s. 43's objective was significant in terms of the justification process under s. 1, a process that in the end was not considered by the Supreme Court because they found there had been no breach of children's *Charter* rights. It had, however, been given passing consideration by the Ontario Court of Appeal.

Once a sufficiently important objective has been established, the government is compelled to show that the limit is reasonable and can be justified. This is known as the *Oakes* test,[90] a part of which asks government to address three components that are designed to "balance the interest of society with those of individuals and groups."[91] First, the government must provide cogent and persuasive evidence that clearly shows that the method used to limit a right or freedom is designed to achieve the objective and is rationally connected to it. Second, the government must show that the method impairs as little as possible the right or freedom in question because there are no less-restricting methods available that will achieve the same objective. Finally, the government must show that there is proportionality between the negative and positive effects of limiting the rights under consideration.[92]

However, since the majority of the Supreme Court in the *Foundation* case found that no sections in the *Charter* had been violated, there was no

87 *Canadian Foundation for Children, Youth and the Law v. Canada (Attorney General)*, [2004] 1 SCR 76, at ¶ 59.

88 McGillivray, "Nowhere to Stand," 57; Watkinson, *Education, Student Rights and the Charter*; Watkinson, "Prohibiting Corporal Punishment."

89 Blackstone, *Commentaries on the Laws of England.*

90 *R. v. Oakes*, [1986] 65 N.R. 87. See also *Dagenais v. Canadian Broadcasting Corp*, [1994] 3 SCR 835, which amended, in part, the third part of the *Oakes* test.

91 *Miron v. Trudel*, [1995] 2 SCR 418, at 503.

92 *R. v. Oakes*, [1986] 65 N.R. 87, at 139.

limit to be justified. In so ruling, they managed to sidestep the s. 1 inquiry. Justice Binnie in his dissenting opinion criticized the majority of the Supreme Court for their interpretation of s. 15. His disagreement centred in part on the narrowing of the equality rights protection under s. 15 and "the technique by which this narrowing is accomplished, namely by moving into s. 15(1) a range of consideration that, in my view, ought properly to be left to government justification under s. 1."[93]

The limiting of rights at the front end—that is, within the parameters of s. 15 and s. 7 rather than under s. 1—is a contentious issue and one that is constantly debated.[94] The majority of the Supreme Court limited the right of children to equal protection and benefit of the law under s. 15 rather than justifying limiting their rights under s. 1 and having the onus fall to the government to prove it was reasonable and justifiable. They did this by shaving away at the meaning of *discrimination* such that its essence was diminished, leaving nothing of substance. Equally significant was the fact that by narrowing the scope of the right to equal treatment and benefit of the law under s. 15 it "unfairly shifts the burden of proof from the government to the rights-claimant."[95] The rights claimant must continue arguing for an expansive interpretation of s. 15 while the government ducks the onus to prove otherwise. That is, limiting rights within the sections of the *Charter* has the potential to constrict rights unnecessarily and lets governments off the hook too easily.

While the majority of the Supreme Court did not consider s. 1, the Ontario Court of Appeal did give it passing consideration. The Ontario Court of Appeal unanimously decided to examine the argument that s. 43 violated s. 15, but only because in their opinion "s. 43 is clearly defended by s. 1 of the *Charter*."[96] To support their position the Court of Appeal quoted the s. 1 test as described in 1995's *Egan*.[97] Of interest is the Court of Appeals's description of the three criteria to be followed:

93 *Canadian Foundation for Children, Youth and the Law v. Canada (Attorney General)*, [2004] 1 SCR 76, at ¶ 74.
94 Sykes, "Bambi Meets Godzilla," 131.
95 Sykes, "Bambi Meets Godzilla," 147.
96 *Canadian Foundation for Children, Youth and the Law v. Canada (Attorney General)*, (2002), 207 DLR (4th) 632 (Ont. CA), at ¶ 57.
97 *Egan v. Canada*, [1995] 2 SCR 513.

(1) the rights violation must be rationally connected to the aim of the legislation;
(2) the impugned provision must minimally impair the *Charter* guarantee; and
(3) there must be a proportionality between the effect of the measure and its objective.[98]

What is missing from their description of the s. 1 test, as originally detailed in the *Oakes* test,[99] is the requirement, under step two, that the government or agent must show "that the method impairs as little as possible the right or freedom in question *because there are no workable or less restricting alternatives*."[100]

If the lower courts and the majority on the Supreme Court had seriously contemplated workable and less-restrictive alternatives, they may have collectively taken up the challenge of the Law Reform Commission and considered "What does criminal law provide that is not available through other means or alternatives?"[101] Or, put another way, "What alternatives are available that do not involve criminal law?" This will be discussed further in chapter 8.

"ZONE OF RISK"

As noted earlier, the majority of the Court set out their "zone of risk," as a means to assuage the historically devastating impact of s. 43. Chief Justice McLachlin, writing for the majority, offered this compromise:

> The purpose of s. 43 is to delineate a sphere of non-criminal conduct within the larger realm of common assault. It must, as we have seen, do this in a way that permits people to know when they are entering a

---

98 *R. v. Oakes*, [1986] 65 N.R. 87, at 139.
99 *Miron v. Trudel*, [1995] 2 SCR 418, at 139.
100 *Miron v. Trudel*, [1995] 2 SCR 418, emphasis mine. In a more recent Supreme Court decision that contemplated the minimal impairment part of the *Oakes* test, Justice McLachlin said, "Another way of putting this question is to ask whether there are less harmful means of achieving the legislative goal." See *Alberta v. Hutterian Brethren of Wilson Colony*, [2009] 2 SCR 567, at ¶ 53.
101 Law Commission of Canada, *What Is a Crime?*

> zone of risk of criminal sanction and that avoids ad hoc discretionary decision-making by law enforcement officials.[102]

The Chief Justice then, as Justice Arbour noted, undertook "a laudable effort to take the law where it ought to be."[103] This was, in Justice Arbour's opinion, beyond the proper role of the Court since the process has enlarged "criminal responsibility by limiting defences enacted by Parliament."[104] The limitations are those set down by the Court in their determination of the kind of conduct that will not be protected under s. 43.

Section 43, the Chief Justice said, is less precise in "what conduct falls within its sphere."[105] Even so, s. 43 provides some guidance by defining the conduct of physical punishment in two ways: the force is to be "by way of correction" and it is to be "reasonable under the circumstances."[106]

By Way of Correction

Chief Justice McLachlin noted that the requirement that the force be "by way of correction" sets two limitations on the type of conduct protected by s. 43. First, the force used must be for "educative or corrective purposes" and cannot be justified by outbursts of anger or frustration.[107] Second, the child upon whom the force is applied must be capable of understanding why they are being hit and be able to benefit from the correction. This eliminates children under the age of two and children who, due to a disability, are "incapable of learning from the application of force."[108]

---

102 *Canadian Foundation for Children, Youth and the Law v. Canada (Attorney General)*, [2004] 1 SCR 76, at ¶ 19.

103 *Canadian Foundation for Children, Youth and the Law v. Canada (Attorney General)*, [2004] 1 SCR 76, at ¶ 35.

104 *Canadian Foundation for Children, Youth and the Law v. Canada (Attorney General)*, [2004] 1 SCR 76, at ¶ 35.

105 *Canadian Foundation for Children, Youth and the Law v. Canada (Attorney General)*, [2004] 1 SCR 76, at ¶ 22.

106 *Canadian Foundation for Children, Youth and the Law v. Canada (Attorney General)*, [2004] 1 SCR 76, at ¶ 22.

107 *Canadian Foundation for Children, Youth and the Law v. Canada (Attorney General)*, [2004] 1 SCR 76, at ¶ 24.

108 *Canadian Foundation for Children, Youth and the Law v. Canada (Attorney General)*, [2004] 1 SCR 76, at ¶ 25.

Reasonable Under the Circumstances

The second requirement of conduct is that the force be "reasonable under the circumstances." This phrase has been roundly criticized for its vagueness and the fact that its interpretation by police, judges, and prosecutors is often based on what they went through as children. Chief Justice McLachlin acknowledged that the words are broad and determined to provide their own precision. She turned for assistance to selected international human rights documents and to what she referred to as social consensus and expert evidence to determine what constitutes reasonable corrective discipline. However, she did not provide any references to support their reliance on "social consensus and expert evidence." The first limitation is that the behaviour for which s. 43 provides an exemption is the "non-consensual application of force that results neither in harm nor in the prospect of bodily harm. This limits its operation to the mildest forms of assault."[109] She said that "s. 43 exempts from criminal sanction only minor corrective force of a transitory and trifling nature."[110]

Canada's international obligations direct that physical correction must not be harmful or degrading to children. Chief Justice McLachlin quoted from articles 5, 19, and 37 of the United Nations *Convention on the Rights of the Child* and also made reference to the *Convention on Civil and Political Rights*.[111] She noted that the Human Rights Committee of the United Nations "has expressed the view that corporal punishment of children in schools engages Art. 7's prohibition of degrading treatment or punishment... [but] the committee has not expressed a similar opinion regarding parental use of mild corporal punishment."[112] Despite the Human Rights

---

109 *Canadian Foundation for Children, Youth and the Law v. Canada (Attorney General)*, [2004] 1 SCR 76, at ¶ 30.

110 *Canadian Foundation for Children, Youth and the Law v. Canada (Attorney General)*, [2004] 1 SCR 76, at ¶ 40. Section 2 of Canada's *Criminal Code* refers to the words *transient* and *trifling* in the definition of "bodily harm." It states that "'bodily harm' means any hurt or injury to a person that interferes with the health or comfort of the person and that is more than merely transient or trifling in nature."

111 The full text of these United Nations conventions can be found at https://www.ohchr.org/en/core-international-human-rights-instruments-and-their-monitoring-bodies.

112 *Canadian Foundation for Children, Youth and the Law v. Canada (Attorney General)*, [2004] 1 SCR 76, at ¶ 33.

Committee's conclusions, the Chief Justice did not remove teachers from the scope of s. 43, but said that when a teacher uses corporal punishment it is "unreasonable." Thus, if it is "unreasonable," it is obvious that it can never be considered "reasonable under the circumstances."

As noted earlier, the Chief Justice turned to international human rights documents to assist her, but for reasons that seem unfathomable, concluded they did not require states to outright ban corporal punishment. In her dissenting opinion, Justice Arbour points out that this is an erroneous conclusion and quotes directly from the Committee on the Rights of the Child's 1995 report: "Physical punishment of children in families [should] be prohibited."[113]

The Chief Justice also failed to refer to the most recent report from the Committee regarding Canada's compliance with the *Convention on the Rights of the Child*, in which it also clearly states that corporal punishment should be banned for both parents and teachers:

> The Committee recommends that the State party [Canada] adopt legislation to remove the existing authorization of the use of "reasonable force" in disciplining children and explicitly prohibit all forms of violence against children, however light, within the family, in schools and in other institutions where children may be placed.
>
> The Committee recommends that the State party further improve the quality of education throughout the State party in order to achieve the goals of article 29, paragraph 1, of the Convention and the Committee's general comment No. 1 on the aims of education by, inter alia:
>
> - Adopting appropriate legislative measures to forbid the use of any form of corporal punishment in schools and encouraging child participation in discussions about disciplinary measures.[114]

This directive was not lost on Justice Arbour, who quoted directly from the Committee's report in her dissenting opinion.

---

113 *Canadian Foundation for Children, Youth and the Law v. Canada (Attorney General),* [2004] 1 SCR 76, at ¶ 187, citing the Committee on the Rights of the Child, *Report Adopted by the Committee*, at ¶ 93.

114 Committee on the Rights of the Child, CRC/C/15/Add.215, October 27, 2003, at ¶s 4, 5, 32, 33, and 45(d).

The majority of the Court expanded on the limitations to s. 43, specifically listing actions that will not be considered "reasonable." These actions enter what the Court called a "zone of risk," meaning that the s. 43 defence will not be available in certain circumstances. The Court said it is never reasonable to use corporal punishment on children under two years of age because they do not have the capacity to understand "why they are hit."[115] Similarly, a child with a "disability or some other contextual factor" will not understand the reasons for the use of force.[116] The Court said, "in these cases, force will not be 'corrective' and will not fall within the sphere of immunity provided by s. 43"[117] since children must be capable of learning and have the capacity to successfully correct their behaviour.[118] Corporal punishment is not to be used on teenagers as it can induce aggressive or anti-social behaviour in them.[119] Corporal punishment cannot be justified under s. 43 when an object or weapon is used, such as a ruler or belt,[120] nor in cases involving slaps or blows to the head.[121] or when the force is "degrading, inhuman or harmful conduct."[122] Section 43 cannot be used as a defence to charges of assault when corporal punishment is applied in anger stemming from "frustration, loss of temper or abusive personality."[123]

These limitations are themselves worthy of further comment. Age is arbitrary and does not consider any objective data. As Carter notes, the Supreme Court did not reference a single study on the impact of corporal

---

115 *Canadian Foundation for Children, Youth and the Law v. Canada (Attorney General)*, [2004] 1 SCR 76, at ¶s 25 and 40.

116 *Canadian Foundation for Children, Youth and the Law v. Canada (Attorney General)*, [2004] 1 SCR 76, at ¶ 25.

117 *Canadian Foundation for Children, Youth and the Law v. Canada (Attorney General)*, [2004] 1 SCR 76, at ¶ 25.

118 *Canadian Foundation for Children, Youth and the Law v. Canada (Attorney General)*, [2004] 1 SCR 76, at ¶ 25.

119 *Canadian Foundation for Children, Youth and the Law v. Canada (Attorney General)*, [2004] 1 SCR 76, at ¶s 37 and 40.

120 *Canadian Foundation for Children, Youth and the Law v. Canada (Attorney General)*, [2004] 1 SCR 76, at ¶s 37 and 40.

121 *Canadian Foundation for Children, Youth and the Law v. Canada (Attorney General)*, [2004] 1 SCR 76, at ¶s 37 and 40.

122 *Canadian Foundation for Children, Youth and the Law v. Canada (Attorney General)*, [2004] 1 SCR 76, at ¶ 40.

123 *Canadian Foundation for Children, Youth and the Law v. Canada (Attorney General)*, [2004] 1 SCR 76, at ¶ 40.

punishment of three- to twelve-year-olds: "This is not surprising in that no such study would support the conclusion that children in this age range benefit from being subjected to corporal punishment."[124]

The majority of the Court found that teachers remain within the parameter of s. 43. However, the Court said that s. 43 is not available as a defence for teachers who use corporal punishment on students. It noted that "Substantial societal consensus, supported by expert evidence and Canada's treaty obligations, indicate that corporal punishment by teachers is unreasonable."[125] Section 43 will protect teachers from charges of assault only when "a teacher uses reasonable, corrective force to restrain or remove a child in appropriate circumstances."[126] In other words, teachers are in the "zone of risk" whenever they use corporal punishment on their students. Section 43 can only be used to defend teachers from charges of assault when they restrain a child. However, teachers were always adequately protected in fulfilling the need to restrain children under s. 37 and other sections of the *Criminal Code*. The majority of the Court did not remove teachers from s. 43 as was called for by Justice Binnie, and it is obvious that the only reason teachers were not removed was the Court's concern that if this happened teachers would not be able to use restraint to control disruptive students.[127]

But even restraints can be tricky. Restraint is considered a security measure designed to protect the student, others, and property. A review of the use of restraints on patients in one U.S. government report "found conclusively that children are especially targeted by facility staff for this unsafe practice (restraints), and are at greater risk of injury and death."[128] Ironically, they noted that most injuries occur to staff and the subject of

124 Carter, "Constitutional Validity of the Corporal Punishment Defence," 200.

125 *Canadian Foundation for Children, Youth and the Law v. Canada (Attorney General)*, [2004] 1 SCR 76, at ¶ 38.

126 *Canadian Foundation for Children, Youth and the Law v. Canada (Attorney General)*, [2004] 1 SCR 7, at ¶ 38.

127 This is another curious example of judicial reasoning. Sections 34 through 42 provide not just teachers but all citizens with a defence to charges of assault when force or restraint are considered necessary to protect oneself, others, or property. This point was also made by Justice Louise Arbour in her dissent (see ¶ 143).

128 Mohr et al., "Adverse Effects Associated with Physical Restraint," 331, citing the US General Accounting Office, *Mental Health*.

the restraint during the process of restraint or seclusion.[129] The authors of the report recommend that alternative interventions be used, such as "promoting self-management for some children... with poor self-control,"[130] and appropriate protection be provided to others from acutely aggressive individuals. If restraint is to be used it is to be carried out by judicious and well-trained staff. While this review was focused on patients, it provides useful advice and warnings for teachers as well.

In summary, those who use corporal punishment on children in Canada risk criminal sanctions when

- it exceeds minor corrective force of a transitory and trifling nature;
- it is used on children under the age of two;
- it is used on teenagers;
- it is used on children with disabilities;
- a child is hit on the head;
- the force is degrading or inhuman;
- it is applied in anger;
- an object is used; and
- it is used by teachers.

CONCLUSION

The outcome in the case of the *Canadian Foundation for Children Youth and the Law v. Canada (Attorney General)* was a missed opportunity to expand upon and protect in a substantive way the rights of children. A substantive understanding of children's rights would mean considering the unique needs and developing nature of children and our understanding of childhood. Instead, the Court turned their full attention to the rights of parents. This was not a decision about children's rights—to security, protection from physical punishment, and equality—as those rights were abandoned on the steps of the Supreme Court of Canada.

129 Mohr et al., "Adverse Effects Associated with Physical Restraint," 335.

130 Mohr et al., "Adverse Effects Associated with Physical Restraint," 335.

6

THE AFTERMATH OF THE SUPREME COURT'S DECISION

The current confusion in the law regarding the legality of various forms of discipline would, of course, disappear if the parental right to use physical punishment was abolished altogether.[1]

INTRODUCTION

THE INTENT IN CHALLENGING S. 43 OF THE *CRIMINAL CODE*[2] using the *Charter of Rights and Freedoms*[3] was to focus on the rights of children to be free from physical assault in a manner similar to the protections to which adults are entitled.[4] However, the Court's majority considered first and foremost the rights of parents and adults, raising alarms over the possibility of parents and teachers ending up in jails.[5] The

---

1 Fortin, *Children's Rights and the Developing Law*, 329.

2 *Criminal Code of Canada*, RSC 1985, c. C-46.

3 *Canadian Charter of Rights and Freedoms*, as enacted by *Canada Act, 1982*, (UK), 1982 c.11.

4 *Canadian Foundation for Children, Youth and the Law v. Canada (Attorney General)*, [2004] 1 SCR 76.

5 Mosoff and Grant, "Upholding Corporal Punishment."

anticipated outcome was derailed by the Court's focus on parental rights, eclipsing the rights of children. The Court made their decision without adequately considering the scientific evidence regarding the harms associated with child physical punishment, Canada's obligations under the *Convention on the Rights of the Child*,[6] and possible alternatives to child physical punishment.

The Court's decision placed some restrictions on the application of s. 43,[7] but regrettably the outcome of the Supreme Court's majority decision left in its wake utter confusion. Practices considered reasonable one day were criminal the next. There was no educational undertaking by the government to describe the changes or even impose a delay to allow for a full understanding of the changes to the interpretation of s. 43. The government argued during the case that their educational policy was a major part of their strategy to inform parents that child physical punishment is not a good idea,[8] but they had yet to develop one.

Fortin, a British legal scholar, argues that "the current confusion in the law regarding the legality of various forms of discipline would, of course, disappear if the parental right to use physical punishment was abolished altogether."[9] It would focus our attention instead on a child's right to protection and a recognition of their inherent dignity and the obligation of parents and society to uphold those rights. A separate analysis of 420 online postings to a national newspaper in the days following the Supreme Court decision demonstrated the confusion surrounding the decision. Of those writing, 60 percent interpreted the decision as giving parents permission to physically punish children. Only 11 percent referred to the limitations the decision placed on the use of child physical punishment.[10]

6 *Convention on the Rights of the Child*, (1989), UN Doc. A/RES/44/25 (1989).

7 *Canadian Foundation for Children, Youth and the Law v. Canada (Attorney General)*, [2004] 1 SCR 76, at ¶s 37–40.

8 *Canadian Foundation for Children, Youth and the Law v. Canada (Attorney General)*, [2004] 1 SCR 76 (Factum of the Respondent Attorney General of Canada, at ¶ 4).

9 Fortin, *Children's Rights and the Developing Law*, 329.

10 Durrant et al., "What Did the Canadian Public Learn," 229.

A CONFUSED PUBLIC

Eighteen months after the Supreme Court issued its decision, a colleague and I conducted research into the public's knowledge of the case.[11] The purpose of the study was to determine the degree to which parents knew and understood the limits placed on them by the Supreme Court's decision; whether the limits interfered with their cultural, religious, or other traditional values or beliefs; and what parents need in order to abide by the limits placed on their use of corporal punishment.

Thirty-four participants took part in focus groups. Two were male. Of the thirty-four, 47 percent were members of cultural minority groups and 74 percent described themselves as being associated with some religious or spiritual group. Only twelve participants said they were aware of the Supreme Court decision limiting the authority of parents to use physical punishment on children. Of these twelve who answered yes to the question "Are you aware of the Supreme Court's decision on the use of physical punishment?" only five had any correct information on the changes. This means that, while 35 percent of all participants said they knew of the decision, only 15 percent (five participants) could demonstrate what the decision said, and even then, only in a very limited and peripheral way. For example, one of the five knew that physical punishment could not be used in anger and that only an open hand could be used to apply physical force on a child, but she did not indicate that force could not be applied to the head. Another of the five knew you could not hit a child on the head and that physical force on a toddler was prohibited, but nothing more. One participant who said she knew about the limitations arising from the Supreme Court decision said that only mild force could be used (which is correct) but also thought it could be used only on children under five years of age (it is limited to children between two and twelve). Four of the remaining seven participants who said they knew of the Supreme Court decision gave incorrect information, such as saying the Court ruled it was permissible to hit a child on the face. Two participants thought the Court had said there was to be no hitting of children at all. Another participant, a recent immigrant to Canada who was not aware of the Supreme Court's decision and therefore could not provide any

11 Watkinson, "Physical Punishment in Childhood."

examples of how the law had changed, reported that she had been told by immigration authorities that children cannot be spanked in Canada.

Participants were asked whether the limits on the use of physical punishment (spanking) interfere in any way with their cultural, religious, or other traditional values or beliefs. This question was asked in response to those who were concerned that any changes to the law concerning the physical punishment of children could be seen as violating the religious, cultural, or traditional practices of parents. None of the participants found that the limitations interfered with any religious, cultural, or other traditional values or beliefs. Nor were there any concerns raised about how the law has changed. In fact, three of the participants believed the law had always prohibited the use of physical punishment on children.

The participants discussed what they considered to be their needs or the needs of other parents to abide by the changes to the law. The most common theme was parental support. Many identified a need for respite for parents "just to sit for a moment." Some suggested a drop-off centre for kids to allow time for the parent to "de-stress." The establishment of such a facility would acknowledge that others share the frustrations and intensities of child rearing and "you wouldn't feel so alone." However, others worried that if they took part in such a service it might "red flag" them: a fear that by asking for help you draw attention to a weakness. Another common theme was the need for parenting classes and that the health system, the one common denominator in the lives of children and their parents, take the lead in the dissemination of information on healthy child-rearing practices. Each focus group raised the need for more public education on physical punishment, its impact, and the related Supreme Court decision.

Toronto Public Health conducted a similar study between January and March 2006, exploring the knowledge of respondents regarding the Supreme Court's decision on the use of physical punishment of children.[12] The study was conducted through telephone interviews and included 2,451 English- and French-speaking respondents over the age of eighteen. The survey found that two-thirds of the respondents were not aware of the Supreme Court's decision and, of those who were aware of the decision, "less than one in five knew the legal limitations placed on its use by the

12 Toronto Public Health, *National Survey*.

Supreme Court."[13] One of the most startling findings in the Toronto Public Health study was the fact that those who were aware of the Supreme Court decision, compared to those who were not, were "more likely to believe that parents are allowed to physically punish their children and less likely to feel unsure that this is allowed."[14] The study concludes that "the law is ineffective in protecting children in the way the Court had intended, and it also places caregivers at risk of prosecution for acts that they do not know are criminal offences."[15]

"ZONE OF RISK": UNRELIABLE

The majority of the Supreme Court reasoned that the limits to a s. 43 defence would lessen the chance of criminalizing parents and teachers. The ruling assumes, though it is not explicitly stated by the majority, that child physical punishment meted out within "reasonable" limits would not lead to harm or the maltreatment of children. Researchers tested this hypothesis by comparing the criteria on reasonable force set by the Supreme Court in the *Foundation* case with substantiated child physical abuse cases.[16]

As discussed in chapter 5, the Supreme Court limited the defence of "reasonable" force by setting what is referred to as the "zone of risk," outlining the circumstances under which a person using physical punishment on a child could not use s. 43 as a defence. A person steps outside the s. 43 defence when he or she is not the child's parent, when the child is younger than two or older than twelve, when the child is not capable of learning from the correction, when the force used exceeds what is considered trifling and transitory, when an object is used, when the force is not for corrective purposes but rather is the result of anger, and when the punishment is degrading, inhuman, and harmful. Or as Durrant and colleagues explained,

> the court suggests that children between the ages of 2 and 12 who are struck by a parent's hand with the intent to correct are not at risk of maltreatment; that there is a "safe zone" of physical punishment in which

---

13 Toronto Public Health, *National Survey*, 1.

14 Toronto Public Health, *National Survey*, 9.

15 Toronto Public Health, *National Survey*, 11.

16 Durrant et al., "Protection of Children from Physical Maltreatment in Canada."

children are not harmed. The court also believes that the criteria it identified to define reasonable force are adequate to protect children from maltreatment in their homes.[17]

The researchers used the Supreme Court's criteria and compared them to child maltreatment cases identified in the 2003 *Canadian Incidence Study of Reported Child Abuse and Neglect* (CIS).[18] They found that the Court's criteria of what is reasonable corporal punishment actually characterized findings of child physical maltreatment. In other words, the criteria used to define reasonable use of force on children made up the majority of substantiated child physical maltreatment cases. The researchers reasoned that "if the court's criteria can distinguish between harmless and harmful use of force, there should be consistency between those criteria and the characteristics of substantiated cases of child physical maltreatment."[19] They found otherwise. For example, most maltreated children harmed by their parents were between the ages of two and twelve and were capable of learning. The maltreated children in the CIS were not harmed with an object and three-quarters of the child maltreatment cases were for corrective purposes. The authors reported that "one in five cases of substantiated physical maltreatment cases in Canada are not characterized by *any* of the court's criteria for defining unreasonable force."[20] In other words, 80 percent of substantiated child physical maltreatment cases involved criteria that the Court deemed "reasonable." The "zone of risk" criteria are unworkable. Based on their findings, the researchers concluded that "ending all physical punishment is more likely to reduce physical maltreatment than placing arbitrary limits on its use."[21]

SUBSEQUENT CASES AND MORE CONFUSION

Professor Anne McGillivray reviewed forty-seven post-*Foundation* cases recorded online at Repeal 43. The website, since deleted, compiled all reported and unreported cases of child physical punishment. McGillivray

17 Durrant et al., "Protection of Children from Physical Maltreatment in Canada," 67.
18 Trocmé et al., *Canadian Incidence Study—2003*.
19 Durrant et al., "Protection of Children from Physical Maltreatment in Canada," 69.
20 Durrant et al., "Protection of Children from Physical Maltreatment in Canada," 86.
21 Durrant et al., "Protection of Children from Physical Maltreatment in Canada," 86.

found what she referred to as "the futility of redefining the indefinable."[22] Despite the limits placed on its use, McGillivray provides case examples that suggest parents and teachers accused of assault still have successfully used s. 43 as a defence. Such examples include acquitting an angry father who shoved his son, causing him to stumble and bruise his head;[23] finding not guilty a bus driver who taped a special needs boy to his seat, put the boy's sock in his mouth, and taped it in place;[24] acquitting a teacher charged with fourteen counts of assault and four of assault with a weapon against learning-disabled students in her grade 1 and 2 classes;[25] acquitting a father who burned his seven-year-old son with a lighter to teach him not to play with fire. The Court in this last case found "the assault to be both unintentional and educational in intent."[26]

A review of another twenty-six subsequent cases reported on the Repeal 43 website,[27] but not included in McGillivray's study, found that of the twenty-six cases, eighteen were found guilty (two pled guilty). The remaining eight cases either acquitted the perpetrator, dismissed the case, or found him or her not guilty. The cases included a father acquitted of assault after pushing his ten-year-old son and causing him to fall. The appeal judge found the trial judge had erred in concluding the accused was frustrated (the Supreme Court said physical punishment can never be used in anger) even though the alleged assault resulted after the boy refused to help push his father's car after it was stuck in the snow.[28] The case of assault against the father of a one-and-a-half-year-old who was having a temper tantrum on the floor was dismissed. The father lifted the child by one arm and set him on the stairs. The child continued crying. When the mother attempted to intervene, the father blocked her way and prevented her from going to the phone. The

22 McGillivray, "Nowhere to Stand," 68.

23 *R. v. Demelo*, [2009] OJ No. 2387 (CtJ).

24 *R. v. Morro*, [2009] ABPC 114.

25 *R.v. Persaud*, [2007] OJ No. 1752 (Sup Crt).

26 McGillivray, "Nowhere to Stand," 69, referencing *R. v. T.E.*, [2006] NSJ No. 61 (SC).

27 These cases are from a compilation of reported and unreported cases recorded on the website of the Repeal 43 Committee. See https://www.repeal43.org/. Regrettably this website is no longer updated. This was the same source originally used by McGillivray, "Nowhere to Stand." The other twenty-six cases were reviewed by the author following McGillivray's review.

28 *R. v. Gervin*, [2012] MBQB 44.

judge ruled the force used was "reasonable."[29] A 2012 case arising from allegations of assault upon a small child resulted in eight separate charges. The accused, the common-law spouse of the child's mother, was acquitted of all charges based in part on the judge's perception of animosity among the female witnesses to the alleged abuser, raising doubts as to their intent, and the fact that none of them had reported the incidents to child welfare.[30]

Other cases reported in CanLii between 2012 and 2022 provide a broad range of conclusions to assault charges and the use of s. 43 as a defence. Forty-one cases were reviewed: twenty-three of those charged with assault were found guilty, six pled guilty, and the others were either dismissed or given conditional discharges.[31] One of the dismissed cases involved a school principal who was charged with four counts of assault and one of uttering threats against students, who were all described as having "exceptionalities."[32] The principal was alleged to have raised and banged the chairs the student were sitting in several times, causing them to cry. He allegedly held students' faces, shouted at them, and tipped a student out of his chair, dragged him into the shower, and sprayed him with cold water. The judge ruled that the touching that happened in the cases did not exceed what was justified under s. 43. He noted that in criminal cases, including child physical punishment, the threshold in proving the guilt of the accused is to be beyond a "reasonable doubt," which the Crown had not met. In addition, the judge doubted the credibility of the witnesses who had not reported the incidents at the time they happened.

The case of *R. v. A.(M.)* provides a compelling case study of the confusion and arbitrariness that abounds in adjudicating child physical punishment within the current context of s. 43 of the *Criminal Code of Canada*. The father, referred to as A.M., of a six-year-old girl, A.A., was acquitted of three charges of assault on his daughter because the judge was not satisfied "beyond a reasonable doubt"[33] that the incidents either occurred or that they exceeded what was considered "reasonable." The father was charged with three counts of assault, the first related to the alleged spanking, the

---

29 *R. v. Catellier*, [2011] MBQB 77.

30 *R. v. Fitzpatrick*, [2012] N.J. No. 19 (Prov. Ct.) per Porter J.

31 The cases reviewed were limited to English-language and non-historical cases.

32 *R. v. McGrath*, [2021] CanLii 7914 (NL), at ¶ 2.

33 *R. v. A.(M.)*, [2011] ONCJ 91, at ¶ 52.

second resulting from allegedly knocking his daughter off the bed, and the third charge referring to the father shaking his fist at his daughter.

The parents were separated and A.A. had been staying with her father for the weekend when the incident happened. The mother of the child called police after noticing bruises on A.A.'s buttocks that she said looked like handprints.[34] According to the decision, the daughter was in bed and started screaming, waking her younger brother. The father told her to stop or he would spank her. She continued screaming, and he spanked her. She also fell to the floor while the father was removing her urine-soaked pajama bottoms. The child said her father spanked her ten times. She was cross-examined and again said he spanked her ten times. During re-examination she said he spanked her two times.[35] The father said he spanked her two or three times.[36] Later during cross-examination he said he slapped her once.[37]A forensic pathologist provided expert evidence. He had examined the pictures of A.A.'s bruised bottom and said the bruises were typical of those made by a strike of an adult hand. He said, "we characterize this as forceful spanking, these types of injuries."[38]

However, the judge in this case, after making reference to the *Foundation* case, described the boundaries set by the Supreme Court in the case as including "the fact that the force applied to the child must have been intended to be for educative or corrective purposes, relating to restraining, controlling or expressing disapproval of the actual behaviour of a child capable of benefiting from the correction."[39] The judge stated that the s. 43 defence is available to the father only if he "subjectively believed" that he was using reasonable force and the force was "objectively" reasonable under the circumstances.[40]

Even though the judge found that the father "spanked her hard enough,"[41] and "with sufficient force to leave... bruises... that took one to two weeks to go away,"[42] he was not convinced it exceeded what is deemed "trifling

---

34 *R. v. A.(M.)*, [2011] ONCJ 91, at ¶ 20.
35 *R. v. A.(M.)*, [2011] ONCJ 91, at ¶ 29.
36 *R. v. A.(M.)*, [2011] ONCJ 91, at ¶ 44
37 *R. v. A.(M.)*, [2011] ONCJ 91, at ¶ 49.
38 *R. v. A.(M.)*, [2011] ONCJ 91, at ¶ 37.
39 *R. v. A.(M.)*, [2011] ONCJ 91, at ¶ 14.
40 *R. v. A.(M.)*, [2011] ONCJ 91, at ¶ 17.
41 *R. v. A.(M.)*, [2011] ONCJ 91, at ¶ 50.
42 *R. v. A.(M.)*, [2011] ONCJ 91, at ¶ 57.

or transitory." He reviewed several cases presented to him by the father's counsel to determine the limits of "trifling or transitory." He accepted as a legitimate guideline a 2001 decision in which the parent of a child had used a belt to administer "a spanking of two or three blows, one of which left a bruise in the shape of the belt buckle."[43] The judge quoted from the 2001 decision, which said, "When appropriate deference is shown to the parent's value system and to their decision that they see the transgression as serious, the infliction of some pain and a bruise that is merely transient or trifling in nature... cannot... constitute unreasonable force,"[44] and since the "spanking" was considered "transient or trifling," it was not unreasonable force.[45] Other cases taken into consideration by the judge in determining what was considered "transitory and trifling" included striking an eleven-year-old on the face hard enough to leave finger marks,[46] and another case of spanking a child "hard enough to produce two small bruises and hand marks which lasted for at least several hours."[47] All of the cases referred to by the judge in order to determine what is considered "transitory or trifling" were heard prior to the 2004 *Foundation* case.

The judge quoted the Supreme Court saying that "the gravity of the precipitating event is not relevant,"[48] yet when the mother was being cross-examined, she "conceded... that A.A. is a handful at times and does not always do what she was told to do." This comment from the mother, which one might interpret as evidence of the child's behaviour leading to the "precipitating event," was considered by the judge.[49]

CONCLUSION

Parents, members of the public, and even the lower courts were confused following the Supreme Court's decision about the newly delineated "zone of risk," and the government did little to educate the public on the new

---

43 *R. v. A.(M.)*, [2011] ONCJ 91, at ¶ 69.

44 *R. v. A.(M.)*, [2011] ONCJ 91, at ¶ 70, referring to the case of *R. v. Bell*, [2001] OJ No. 1820 (Ont. S.CJ) per Langdon J.

45 *R. v. A.(M.)*, [2011] ONCJ 91.

46 *R. v. James*, [1998] OJ No. 1438 (Ont. CJ) per Weagant J.

47 *R. v. A.(M.)*, [2011] ONCJ 91, at ¶ 73.

48 *R. v. A.(M.)*, [2011] ONCJ 91, at ¶ 16.

49 *R. v. A.(M.)*, [2011] ONCJ 91, at ¶ 25.

limits placed on the scope of s. 43 and what it might mean for them.[50] The government failed to provide guidance to parents whose actions were deemed legal one day but criminalized the next. What's more, research found these new limits were ineffective in reducing child maltreatment, calling into question whether children were really being protected.

As long as s. 43 exists within the *Criminal Code*, children and their advocates will be burdened with proving the assault took place "beyond a reasonable doubt."[51] This is a significant wall to climb when relying on the evidence of children who find themselves confronting the social normalcy of child physical punishment. The criminal law system was not made with children in mind. To leave things as they are is unconscionable. Children are being harmed, and Canada is disregarding its international obligations to protect children from all forms of physical violence and ignoring the overwhelming evidence concerning the harms associated with child physical punishment.

As we know, all persons charged with a criminal offence are innocent until proven guilty—that is, when they are deemed guilty "beyond a reasonable doubt."[52] This is the standard of proof in a criminal case. Thus, every case of child physical punishment must meet this standard. Clearly, this is worrisome for several reasons as evidenced in this case of A.A.[53] One wonders what chance any child has if they carry the burden of proof, have been a "handful at times," and suffer the bruises. It is clear from this case and the other disheartening array of cases that, in the words of McGillivray and Milne, "the Supreme Court's compromise—keep the defense, narrow the scope—is not a success."[54]

---

50 See the following government document: "Criminal Law and Managing Children's Behaviour" (2015), https://www.canada.ca/en/public-health/services/publications/healthy-living/pamphlet-what-s-wrong-with-spanking.html.

51 While the burden of proof lies with the Crown, children frequently provide information regarding assaults, which can be difficult to assess as "beyond a reasonable doubt."

52 *R. v. Lifchus*, [1997] 3 SCR 320; *R. v. Fitzpatrick*, [2012] N.J. No. 19 per H. Porter Prov. Ct.J; Jonathan Pyzer, "What Is 'Beyond a Reasonable Doubt' in Canadian Law," *Pyzer Criminal Lawyers* blog, March 26, 2025, https://www.torontodefencelawyers.com/beyond-reasonable-doubt-canadian-criminal-law.

53 *R. v. A.(M.)*, [2011] ONCJ 91.

54 McGillivray and Milne, "Canada: The Rocky Road of Repeal," 105.

SECTION THREE

7

CURRENT RESEARCH AND CHILD WELL-BEING

The UN General Assembly has included the protection of children from all forms of violence as Sustainable Development Goal 16.2. Such human rights arguments, along with an aligned body of research indicating that physical punishment is harmful to children, have led to a growing consensus among health professionals that physical punishment to children is detrimental and ineffective.[1]

INTRODUCTION

Social science evidence demonstrates that child physical punishment has long-term negative outcomes "whether measured in terms of social, emotional, intellectual, or physical development and shows a degree of consistency that is unusual in the social sciences."[2]

In 2002, Elizabeth Gershoff undertook a seminal meta-analysis of all studies, conducted over fifty years, into the effects of corporal punishment

1 Heilmann et al., "Physical Punishment and Child Outcomes," 355.
2 Smith and Durrant, "Introduction to the Global Movement," 5.

on children.[3] She selected eighty-eight studies on the basis that they focused only on mild to moderate corporal punishment, excluding all studies that looked at the outcomes of serious physical abuse. Her findings concluded that mild to moderate corporal punishment had a harmful effect on child development and health, effects that followed them through to adulthood. Specifically, she found that in twelve studies on the relationship between child physical punishment and mental health and another eight studies on the relationship between child physical punishment and later adult mental health, all studies revealed an association with an increased probability of mental health problems such as anxiety and depression. Other findings included decreased child moral internalization, increased child aggression, increased child delinquent and anti-social behaviours, decreased child-parent attachment thus decreasing the quality of their relationship, increased risk of being a victim of physical abuse, increased adult aggression, increased adult criminal and anti-social behaviour, and increased risk of abusing one's own child or spouse. Similar studies, controlling for a range of variables such as parental age, family structure, poverty, emotional support, racialized status, and interactives among such variables, have replicated Gershoff's findings.[4]

In the view of the United Nations Committee on the Rights of the Child, corporal punishment is invariably degrading. In addition, there are other non-physical forms of punishment that are also cruel and degrading and thus incompatible with the *Convention on the Rights of the Child*. These include, for example, punishment that belittles, humiliates, denigrates, scapegoats, threatens, scares, or ridicules the child.[5]

This chapter explores the physical and mental health hazards associated with child physical punishment. The Committee includes "mild" corporal punishment such as "spanking" and "smacking" alongside more

3 Gershoff, "Corporal Punishment by Parents," 231.

4 Cuartas et al., "Corporal Punishment"; Gershoff, "More Harm Than Good," 31; Durrant and Ensom, "Physical Punishment of Children"; Berlin et al., "Correlates and Consequences," 1403; Durrant, "The Empirical Rationale," 42; Ma et al., "Corporal Punishment and Youth," 481; Afifi et al., "Physical Punishment and Mental Disorders"; Gershoff and Grogan-Kaylor, "Spanking and Child Outcomes," 453; Durrant and Ensom, "Twenty-Five Years of Physical Punishment Research," 20; Afifi et al., "Associations Between Spanking Beliefs."

5 UNCRC, *General Comment No. 8*, at ¶ 11.

extreme or injurious types of punishment such as whipping, burning, and throwing children. There is a continuum of physical punishment meted out to children, and all those on the continuum are included in the terms *corporal punishment* and/or *physical punishment*. The Committee considers all forms of corporal punishment a breach of children's rights.[6] This broad definition of child physical punishment has been criticized for confounding even the mildest forms, such as spanking, with forms of maltreatment or physical abuse.[7] The argument is that these acts do not cause serious harm.

In 2016, Gershoff (along with Grogan-Kaylor) responded again to these criticisms by conducting another meta-analysis of studies that examined the impact of physical punishment on children. They started with 1,574 articles, eliminating all those that were not peer reviewed and retaining only those that met the following definition of spanking: "hitting a child on their buttocks or extremities using an open hand."[8] In total, their meta-analysis examined seventy-five articles.

Gershoff and Grogan-Kaylor found that even spanking (often considered to be a "mild" form of physical punishment) is associated with an increased risk of thirteen detrimental outcomes, including "more aggression, more anti-social behavior, more externalizing problems, more internalizing problems, more mental health problems, and more negative relationships with parents. Spanking was also significantly associated with lower moral internalization, lower cognitive ability, and lower self-esteem."[9] They also found the more children are spanked, the greater the risk that spanking will lead to physical abuse. The researchers found no evidence that spanking improves a child's behaviour in any way.[10]

In summary, the severity of the punishment does not eliminate the possibility of negative outcomes associated with its use. The following discussion highlights some of the evidence illuminating the impact of childhood experiences and outcomes with corporal punishment.

---

6 UNCRC, *General Comment No. 8*, at ¶ 11.

7 Larzelere and Baumrind, "Are Spanking Injunctions Scientifically Supported?," 57.

8 Gershoff, "Corporal Punishment by Parents," 231; Gershoff and Grogan-Kaylor, "Spanking and Child Outcomes," 453.

9 Gershoff and Grogan-Kaylor, "Spanking and Child Outcomes," 463.

10 Brown et al., "Spank, Slap or Hit?," 1.

ADVERSE CHILDHOOD EXPERIENCES

Some of the most important research to emerge over the past few decades has investigated the effects of adverse childhood experiences (ACEs) on brain development/hindrance, mental health, physical health, and longevity. ACEs are events that cause trauma to children: be it abuse, neglect, dysfunctional households, or violence.

The Adverse Childhood Experiences (ACE) Study was originally conducted between 1995 and 1997. It was a collaborative study undertaken by the Centers for Disease Control and Prevention and the Kaiser Permanente Health Appraisal Clinic in San Diego. Adult patients receiving physical exams agreed to take part in a confidential survey about their childhood experiences of abuse, neglect, and family dysfunction. In all, seventeen thousand adults took part in two waves of data collection. The ACE Study questionnaire consists of ten questions built around seven categories inquiring as to whether the adults had experienced psychological, physical, or sexual abuse, whether violence occurred in the home against the mother, and whether they lived with a household member who used substances, was mentally ill, or ever imprisoned. The findings have contributed to scores of peer-reviewed articles covering the topics of health outcomes for children and adults.

The questionnaire begins by asking participants if any of ten specific incidences happened during their first eighteen years of life. The first question asks, "Did a parent or other adult in the household often swear at you, insult you, put you down, or humiliate you? or act in a way that made you afraid that you might be physically hurt?" The second question asks, "Did a parent or other adult in the household often push, grab, slap, or throw something at you? or ever hit you so hard that you had marks or were injured?"[11]

One of the first published articles arising from the study of the first wave of 8,056 participants found a strong relationship between the number of adverse categories experienced in childhood and the participant's poor physical and mental health. Of respondents, 52 percent had experienced one or more adverse childhood events. Persons who had four or more adverse experiences, as compared to those who had none, had increased health risks for alcoholism, drug abuse, depression, suicide attempts,

---

11 Felitti et al., "Relationship of Childhood Abuse," 245.

dangerous sexual activity, and obesity. Persons who had multiple ACES were likely to have multiple health complications later in life such as heart disease, cancer, lung disease, and liver disease. The authors concluded that "the findings suggest that the impact of these Adverse Childhood Experiences on adult health status is strong and cumulative."[12]

Other research has substantiated these early findings and provides compelling evidence as to the harm caused to a child's brain development by disrupting normal neuronal development and function.[13] The disruptions are caused by stress, more specifically toxic stress that "gets under the skin."[14] There are three kinds of stress. First, positive stress is a physiological state that is mild to moderate in strength and brings forth tolerable and necessary chemical responses. Second is tolerable stress, brought on by exposure to a greater magnitude of stress such as the death of a family member or a natural disaster. The third is toxic stress. It is the most dangerous and can result from "prolonged activation of the body's stress response systems."[15] The plasticity of a young developing brain makes it more sensitive to chemical influences, "and there is growing evidence from both animal and human studies that persistently elevated levels of stress hormones can disrupt its developing architecture."[16] Toxic stress impacts development in the architecture of a child's brain and "confers lasting changes at the most basic level of the nervous, endocrine, and immune systems, and such exposure can alter the physical structure of DNA."[17] Shonkoff and Garner explain that "alterations in a child's ecology can have a measurable effect on his or her developmental trajectory, with lifelong consequences for educational achievement, economic productivity, health status, and longevity."[18]

The stress hormones of note include corticotropin-releasing hormone, cortisol, norepinephrine, and adrenaline, which, in combination with other bodily responses, can be harmful.[19] The essential characteristics of this type

12 Felitti et al., "Relationship of Childhood Abuse," 251.

13 McEwen, "Understanding the Potency"; Shonkoff and Garner, "The Lifelong Effects," 232; Cuartas et al., "Corporal Punishment," 821.

14 Shonkoff and Garner, "The Lifelong Effects," 235.

15 Shonkoff and Garner, "The Lifelong Effects," 236.

16 Shonkoff and Garner, "The Lifelong Effects," 236.

17 Massetti et al., "Global Perspective on ACES," 209.

18 Shonkoff and Garner, "The Lifelong Effects," 234.

19 Shonkoff and Garner, "The Lifelong Effects," 235.

of toxic stress result from the "postulated disruption of brain circuitry and other organ and metabolic systems during sensitive developmental periods."[20] It has been shown to alter the size and neuronal architecture of the hippocampus and prefrontal cortex—areas of the brain that affect memory, learning, and "executive functioning." "Thus, the developing architecture of the brain can be impaired in numerous ways that create a weak foundation for later learning, behavior, and health."[21]

Further studies have shown "a strong graded relationship between the ACE score and the risk of premature death of a family member."[22] Households characterized as "chaotic" impact the lives of children living there, as well as the lives of current adult family members. There is evidence "that violence and serious household dysfunction tends to be intergenerational."[23] As the study reports, the impact of ACEs may be transmitted intergenerationally through social and biological risk occurring at different life stages, "such as neurological development during childhood, and health behaviors inculcated during adolescence and adulthood."[24]

The association between adverse childhood experiences, including physical punishment, has shown links to mental health issues, anti-social behaviour, impaired cognitive development, and societal violence. These effects follow individuals into adulthood, suggesting "that the impact of these adverse childhood experiences on adult health status is strong and cumulative."[25]

CHILD PHYSICAL PUNISHMENT AND MENTAL HEALTH

As noted earlier, research has turned to the association between child physical punishment and mental health. A review of research over the last twenty years shows an association with a plethora of mental health problems from

---

20 Shonkoff and Garner, "The Lifelong Effects," 236.
21 Shonkoff and Garner, "The Lifelong Effects," 236.
22 Anda et al., "The Relationship of Adverse Childhood Experiences," 106.
23 Anda et al., "The Relationship of Adverse Childhood Experiences," 107.
24 Anda et al., "The Relationship of Adverse Childhood Experiences," 110.
25 Felitti et al., "Relationship of Childhood Abuse," 251; Anda et al., "The Relationship of Adverse Childhood Experiences," 106; Asmundson and Afifi, eds., *Adverse Childhood Experiences*; Jaffee and Christian, "The Biological Embedding of Child Abuse and Neglect," 1.

childhood into adulthood.[26] Corporal punishment, which includes child abuse and child physical punishment, have been linked to anxiety, depression, substance dependency, diminished coping strategies, and anti-social personality.[27] Afifi and colleagues studied the effects of "harsh physical punishment," which they described as pushing, slapping, and shoving, with a population of over 36,000 adults aged twenty and older.[28] The respondents were asked, "As a child how often were you ever pushed, grabbed, shoved, slapped or hit by your parents or any adult living in your house?"[29] The research, adjusted for socio-demographic variables and family histories of dysfunction, found relationships between harsh physical punishment and lifetime mental disorders such as major depression, anxiety, alcohol and drug abuse, as well as some personality disorders.[30]

CHILD PHYSICAL PUNISHMENT, AGGRESSION, AND ANTI-SOCIAL BEHAVIOUR

Research has been specific in finding that the use of child physical punishment is a risk factor for child aggression and anti-social behaviour.[31] Heilmann and colleagues reviewed sixty-nine prospective longitudinal studies on the outcomes associated with child physical punishment and, among other findings, concluded that physical punishment worsens a child's behaviour over time compared to children who were not physically punished.[32] The adverse effects are manifested in externalizing behaviours that violate social norms and are harmful to others, such as aggression toward others, including siblings and parents. The authors made note of

26 Fortier et al., "Associations Between Lifetime Spanking/Slapping"; Bomysoad and Francis, "Adverse Childhood Experiences"; Afifi et al., "Spanking and Adult Mental Health Impairment"; Mersky et al., "Impacts of Adverse Childhood Experiences on Health," 37; Gershoff, "Corporal Punishment by Parents"; Gershoff and Grogan-Kaylor, "Spanking and Child Outcomes."

27 Sheffler et al., "ACEs and Mental Health Outcomes," 47.

28 Afifi et al., "Physical Punishment and Mental Disorders," 184.

29 Afifi et al., "Physical Punishment and Mental Disorders," 186.

30 Afifi et al., "Physical Punishment and Mental Disorders," 192; Felitti et al., "Relationship of Childhood Abuse," 245.

31 Gershoff, "Corporal Punishment by Parents," 23; Taylor et al., "Mothers' Spanking of 3-Year-Old Children," 1058.

32 Heilmann et al., "Physical Punishment and Child Outcomes," 355–64.

several studies whose methodological design helped rule out other variables and thus increased "confidence that the findings are consistent with a causal conclusion."[33] The authors found that children who were physically punished increased their externalizing behaviour (aggression toward others, bullying) more than the children who were not physically punished.

Researchers in another study sought to answer the question, "Is a mother's use of CP [corporal punishment] on a 3 year old child linked to risk for that child being more aggressive at 5 years of age, even after controlling for the child's initial level of aggression at age 3 and other important maternal parenting risk factors and demographic features?"[34] The research included 2,461 respondents who were mothers of three-year-old children. The mothers were assessed on their use of corporal punishment when the child was three. Each child was assessed for aggressive behaviours at age three and again at age five. The study considered and controlled for the children's initial level of aggression at age three as well as eight known family characteristics associated with child aggression: psychological maltreatment, physical maltreatment (not including spanking), child neglect, intimate partner violence, maternal stress, depression, use of drugs or alcohol, and consideration of aborting the child. The research found that "even when all of those maternal parenting risks were controlled for—a mother's more frequent use of CP with their 3 year old children increased the odds of those children being more aggressive at age 5."[35] The researchers summarized their findings as supporting "a social learning approach to understanding the cycle of violence, whereby the child learns to be aggressive by being treated directly with aggression."[36]

A later study found that harsh physical punishment (absent abuse and injury) and child maltreatment (including physical, sexual, emotional abuse and neglect) were also associated with anti-social behaviour.[37] When looking at the outcomes associated with harsh physical punishment and/or child maltreatment in childhood, the authors estimated that if all experiences of harsh physical punishment and child maltreatment were

33 Heilmann et al., "Physical Punishment and Child Outcomes," 355–64.
34 Taylor et al., "Mothers' Spanking of 3-Year-Old Children."
35 Taylor et al., "Mothers' Spanking of 3-Year-Old Children," 1063.
36 Taylor et al., "Mothers' Spanking of 3-Year-Old Children," 1063.
37 Afifi et al., "Associations of Harsh Physical Punishment," 8.

eliminated, there would be a reduction of anti-social behaviours among 47.3 percent of women and 45.5 percent of men.[38]

In response to the question raised by other researchers as to whether the anti-social behaviour exhibited by children who are physically punished is due to a child's genetics rather than environmental factors,[39] Burt and colleagues designed and conducted a twin study to determine whether genetics or environment (being hit by their parents) played a role in the anti-social behaviour of children who were physically punished.[40] The study was conducted in two parts and involved identical and fraternal twins in which one twin received harsher physical punishment than the other. The research concluded that the twin who received harsh physical punishment showed more anti-social behaviour than the twin who did not. The findings were the same, regardless of the status of the twins (identical or fraternal). The researchers concluded that the "results convincingly show that these associations are, to a significant degree, environmental in origin; harsh parenting, including hitting in anger, is associated with increases in children's anti-social behaviour for nongenetic reasons."[41]

CHILD PHYSICAL PUNISHMENT AND SOCIETAL VIOLENCE

Researchers are also documenting the connection between child physical punishment and a violent society demonstrated in levels of societal bullying, dating violence, family violence, physical aggression, homicide rates, anti-social behaviour, and warfare.[42]

Adverse environments such as inequality, poverty, and war have a corresponding negative impact on children's experiences, resulting in increased risk for child abuse and intimate partner violence as the violence

38 Afifi et al., "Associations of Harsh Physical Punishment," 8.

39 Larzelere et al., "Improving Causal Inferences in Meta-Analyses," 2038.

40 Burt et al., "Twin Differences in Harsh Parenting," 395–409.

41 Burt et al., "Twin Differences in Harsh Parenting," 407.

42 Smith and Durrant, "Introduction to the Global Movement," 5; Douglas and Straus, "Assault and Injury of Dating Partners"; Ember and Ember, "Explaining Corporal Punishment of Children," 609; Lansford and Dodge, "Cultural Norms for Adult Corporal Punishment of Children," 257; Dussich and Maekoya, "Physical Child Harm and Bullying-Related Behaviors," 495.

then transfers into the home.[43] Afifi promotes the expansion of the definition of ACES to include community violence such as war, poverty, and exposure to physical and emotional violence in the home and community.[44] Lansford and Dodge found that the frequent use of corporal punishment on children in varying cultures was related to a higher prevalence and endorsement of violence in society at large.[45] The authors cautioned that "frequent corporal punishment may contribute to increasing societal rates of violence, but high rates of societal violence may also contribute to a social climate in which corporal punishment is acceptable and, therefore, more frequent."[46]

Andero and Stewart, in their discussion of corporal punishment, note that there are some isolated societies in which children are never hit. And while such societies are the exception, they are locations "where relationships between adults tend to be non-violent."[47]

CHILD PHYSICAL PUNISHMENT AND COGNITIVE DEVELOPMENT

Straus and Paschall found that the use of corporal punishment by mothers, even moderate corporal punishment such as slapping a child's hand, is associated with lower cognitive development or IQ.[48] It is measured by rating a child's motor and social development, memory, and recognition. Corporal punishment was measured by asking the mothers at the start of their study and four years later, "Did you find it necessary to spank your child in the past week?"[49] The researchers found that the two- to four-year-old children who did not receive corporal punishment in the week prior to the sample weeks gained a mean of 5.5 cognitive ability points (IQ) in comparison to children who received corporal punishment. The five- to nine-year-olds whose mothers did not use corporal punishment in either

43 Massetti et al., "Global Perspective on ACES," 221.
44 Afifi, "Considerations for Expanding the Definition of ACES," 35.
45 Lansford and Dodge, "Cultural Norms for Adult Corporal Punishment of Children," 257–70.
46 Lansford and Dodge, "Cultural Norms for Adult Corporal Punishment of Children," 266.
47 Andero and Stewart, "Issue of Corporal Punishment: Re-Examined," 90.
48 Straus and Paschall, "Corporal Punishment by Mothers," 459–83.
49 Straus and Paschall, "Corporal Punishment by Mothers," 465.

week gained a mean of about two points in comparison to children who received corporal punishment. Their analysis controlled for ten parenting and demographic variables such as the mother's supportiveness, cognitive stimulation, education, and race/ethnicity. They found there to be a lack of significant interaction with these contextual variables, indicating "that the relation of CP to slower development of cognitive ability may apply even when done by loving and attentive parents, and even when it occurs among a sector of the population with cultural norms that approve CP."[50]

Cuartas explored the effect of spanking on the social/emotional skills of Bhutanese children.[51] He used a national longitudinal sample of 1,377 children whose median age was 50.5 months (a little over four years of age). He found that the developmental consequences of spanking showed evidence of slower cognitive growth and increased aggression and that the developmental consequences did not differ based on normative social practices or socio-economic status. Another study undertaken with 1,167 Colombian families also found that children who were physically punished gained fewer cognitive skills than children who were not physically punished.[52] Gershoff and Grogen-Kaylor's meta-analysis supported the findings of a reduction in cognitive growth of children who were spanked leading to poorer school performance.[53]

A similar study found that spanking at ages one, two, and three predicted lower mental development scores at age three. The study was based on the Bayley Scales of Infant and Toddler Development, a measurement of a child's motor, language, and cognitive development.[54]

CONCLUSION

The plethora of evidence as to the harms of child physical punishment is overwhelming. Researchers have found that there are no long-term benefits to child physical punishment, it negatively impacts children's cognitive development, and its use does not improve a child's behaviour in any

50 Straus and Paschall, "Corporal Punishment by Mothers," 477.
51 Cuartas, "The Effect of Spanking on Early Social/Emotional Skills," 180.
52 Cuartas et al., "Physical Punishment as a Predictor."
53 Gershoff and Grogan-Kaylor, "Spanking and Child Outcomes," 453.
54 Berlin et al., "Correlates and Consequences," 1403.

way.[55] These harms follow children into adulthood, negatively impacting their mental and physical health. The effects of childhood physical punishment shortens one's life due to physical complications from heart disease, cancer, lung and liver disease, and more.[56]

As noted earlier, there are those who argue that "customary" or "normative" child discipline is harmless.[57] Regardless, one fact remains—children, like adults, have the right not to be hit. This inalienable right overrides the questionable and perhaps unethical attempts by some researchers to justify the use of physical punishment on children.

Entitlements to human rights have evolved over the past century, and children's rights are just now gaining momentum. We have seen the expansion of child protection throughout Canada to include child protection legislation in every province and territory.[58] The *Canadian Charter of Rights and Freedoms*, as part of Canada's Constitution, came into force in 1982. This meant that for the first time, equality rights and fundamental freedoms were protected in Canada's supreme law.[59] The *Charter* protects every person's right to security, as well as the right not to be subjected to cruel punishment and to be treated as equals under the law—sections that apply to the rights of children to be protected from threats to their physical security and to enjoy the same protection rights as adults. Seven years later, the United Nations *Convention on the Rights of the Child* joined the ranks of international human rights documents providing human rights protections and entitlements to children.[60] Since the CRC's inception, Canada has

55 Gershoff and Grogan-Kaylor, "Spanking and Child Outcomes," 453.

56 Anda et al., "The Relationship of Adverse Childhood Experiences," 106; Felitti et al., "Relationship of Childhood Abuse," 245; McEwen, "Understanding the Potency"; Shonkoff and Garner, "The Lifelong Effects," 232; Cuartas et al., "Corporal Punishment," 821.

57 Baumrind et al., "Ordinary Physical Punishment," 580; Fuller, "The Science and Statistics," 243; Larzelere and Baumrind, "Are Spanking Injunctions Scientifically Supported?," 57; Larzelere et al., "Do Nonphysical Punishments Reduce," 10.

58 Clément and Chamberland, "Physical Violence and Psychological Aggression," 1001. The *Civil Code of Quebec* removed the parental right to "moderately discipline their children" in 1994.

59 *Slaight Communications Inc. v. Davidson*, [1989] 1 SCR 1038.

60 Durrant et al., "Recognizing the Child's Right to Protection from Physical Violence," 104297; Durrant and Ensom, *Joint Statement on Physical Punishment of Children and Youth.*

been called on numerous times by the United Nations Committee on the Rights of the Child to explicitly prohibit corporal punishment and protect children from corporal punishment in all settings, including the home.[61]

And while these two human rights documents form an impressive combination, enhancing the rights of children to be free from child physical punishment—a right that is protected in sixty-seven countries—such punishment is not prohibited in Canada.[62] In 2004, the Supreme Court of Canada was asked to consider the constitutionality of child physical punishment as allowed for in Canada's *Criminal Code*.[63] It found that the law permitting physical or corporal punishment on children did not violate children's rights. This meant that the only way Canada can join the list of countries who have banned the use of corporal punishment on children in all settings is for the Government of Canada to repeal s. 43 of the *Criminal Code*.

---

61 Committee on the Rights of the Child, "Concluding Observations on the Combined Third and Fourth Periodic Report of Canada," CRC/C/CAN/CP/3-4, 2012, para. 44.

62 See note 58 in chapter 1 for a full list of the states that have prohibited the use of child physical punishment in all settings.

63 *Canadian Foundation for Children, Youth and the Law v. Canada (Attorney General)*, [2004] 1 SCR 76. Please see the previous chapter for a full discussion of the case and its impact.

8

WHERE TO FROM HERE?

Children have the right to care, security and a good upbringing. Children are to be treated with respect for their person and individuality and may not be subjected to physical punishment or other injurious or humiliating treatment.[1]

FULL REPEAL—BUT WHEN?

A SIGNIFICANT STEP IN ENSURING THAT CHILDREN ARE NO longer subject to physical punishment is to get rid of the defence in the *Criminal Code of Canada* that exempts parents and others from charges of assault when they use force on children. This requires the federal government to repeal section 43 of the *Criminal Code*.[2] Attempts at repealing s. 43 have spanned decades and involved at least nineteen

1 This is Sweden's positive statement about the treatment of children as written in their *Parental Code*, Janson, Langberg, and Svensson, "Sweden: A 30-Year Ban," 247. See other examples, such as Denmark's *Parental Custody and Care Act* (1997), which states: "A child has the right to care and security. [The child] shall be treated with respect as an individual and may not be subjected to corporal punishment or other degrading treatment." CYC, "Prohibition of Corporal Punishment."

2 *Criminal Code of Canada*, RSC 1985, c. C-46. Section 43 states, "Every school teacher, parent or person standing in the place of the parent is justified in using force by way of correction toward the pupil or child, as the case may be, who is under his care, if the force does not exceed what is reasonable under the circumstances."

Private Member's Bills (PMBs) and numerous legislative reports.[3] More recently, the Truth and Reconciliation Commission's (TRC) *Final Report* documented the history and impact of residential schools on the lives of Indigenous and Métis children and called on the government to repeal s. 43 of the *Criminal Code of Canada*.[4] The *Final Report* contains ninety-four Calls to Action designed to address the intergenerational impact of residential school on Indigenous people and to address systemic racism.

Call to Action 6 focuses on the issue of child physical punishment, which was a traumatic part of residential schooling. The TRC detailed the physical abuse meted out on Indigenous students in order "to 'civilize' and Christianize" them. The TRC said it "believes that corporal punishment is a relic of a discredited past and has no place in Canadian schools or homes."[5]

When Prime Minister Justin Trudeau won the federal election in 2015, he promised to enact all ninety-four Calls to Action, saying, "We will, in partnership with Indigenous communities, the provinces, territories, and other vital partners, fully implement the Calls to Action of the Truth and Reconciliation Commission."[6] In 2015 the Liberals had a majority government; this was reduced to a minority government in the following election. However, between 2022 and 2024, the federal Liberals were supported by the New Democratic Party, which might have allowed them to repeal s. 43, but they did not do so.[7]

In 2023, two PMBs were introduced into Parliament within a few weeks of each other. The first was tabled in the House of Commons on May 19, 2022, by MP Peter Julian (Bill C-273), and the second was tabled in the Senate by Senator Stan Kutcher on June 16, 2022.[8] Both bills sought full

---

3 See, for example, CHEO, "Joint Statement"; the Honourable Raynell Andreychuk and the Honourable Joan Fraser, *Children: The Silenced Citizens*, April 2007, https://sencanada.ca/content/sen/committee/391/huma/rep/rep10apr07-e.pdf, 19.

4 TRC, *Honouring the Truth, Reconciling for the Future*.

5 TRC, *Honouring the Truth, Reconciling for the Future*, 144.

6 Prime Minister of Canada, "Statement by Prime Minister on Release of the Final Report of the Truth and Reconciliation Commission," Government of Canada, December 15, 2015, https://www.pm.gc.ca/en/news/statements/2015/12/15/statement-prime-minister-release-final-report-truth-and-reconciliation.

7 Ailsa M. Watkinson, "Time to Remove Section 43 from the Criminal Code," *Regina Leader Post*, December 14, 2021, https://leaderpost.com/opinion/opinion-time-to-remove-section-43-from-the-criminal-code.

8 CHEO, "Joint Statement"; CHEO, "Rationale for Repeal."

repeal of s. 43, but in January 2025, Justin Trudeau resigned as prime minister and prorogued Parliament. Once Parliament is prorogued, all bills that were in progress are wiped off the parliamentary agenda. If a new bill is introduced, the whole process has to start over.

TRY AGAIN?

The interpretation of s. 7,[9] and in particular the phrase "in accordance with the principles of fundamental justice," has resulted in significant development of the law since the *Foundation* case. The arguments put forward by the Canadian Foundation for Children, Youth and the Law (CFCYL) proposing that s. 43 is "vague" and "overly broad" may hold sway if the case were heard today. Most certainly evidence of the harms associated with child physical punishment has grown exponentially over the past twenty years. Current research supports the position that there is no corrective value associated with corporal punishment.[10]

Once the Supreme Court of Canada has ruled on a case, there is no other recourse to appeal; however, recent developments on the interpretation of the *Charter* have raised the possibility that the Supreme Court could reconsider their decision in the *Foundation*[11] case, which attempted to find the use of child physical punishment unconstitutional. Since the *Foundation* case was decided in 2004, the Supreme Court of Canada has overridden three of its earlier cases by expanding on the interpretation and development of various sections of the *Charter*. In 2013, the Supreme Court reconsidered an earlier decision on the constitutionality of Canada's prostitution laws.[12] The second and third cases, both heard in 2015, dealt with assisted dying[13] and the right to strike.[14]

---

9 Section 7 of the *Charter* provides, "Everyone has the right to life, liberty and security of the person and the right not to be deprived thereof except in accordance with the principles of fundamental justice."

10 See chapter 7 for a full exploration of current research on the harms associated with child physical punishment.

11 *Canadian Foundation for Children, Youth and the Law v. Canada (Attorney General)*, [2004] 1 SCR 76.

12 *Canada (AG) v. Bedford*, [2013] 3 SCR 1101.

13 *Carter v. Canada (Attorney General)*, [2015] 1 SCR 331.

14 *Saskatchewan Federation of Labour v. Saskatchewan*, [2015] 1 SCR 245.

In 1990, the Supreme Court of Canda heard a case on the constitutionality of the *Criminal Code*'s provisions regarding prostitution. They ruled that these laws, making it an offence to run a bawdy house, live of the avails of prostitution, and communicate in public for the purpose of prostitution, were constitutional and did not violate the *Charter of Rights and Freedoms.*[15] Twenty-three years later, in 2013, the issue of the constitutionality of prostitution laws came before the Supreme Court again. This time the Court found the same provisions of the *Criminal Code* dealing with prostitution to be unconstitutional.[16]

The Supreme Court provided justification for revisiting previous decisions when "new legal issues are raised as a consequence of significant development in the law, or if there is a change in the circumstances or evidence that fundamentally shifts the parameters of the debate."[17] These same reasons for revisiting an earlier decision were drawn upon again in the 2015 case on assisted dying.[18] In 1993, Sue Rodriguez challenged the *Criminal Code* provisions that said anyone who aids a person to commit suicide is guilty of an indictable offence.[19] Ms. Rodriguez had amyotrophic lateral sclerosis, which caused her to lose the capacity to eat and breathe without medical interventions. When she could no longer enjoy her life, she wanted to choose when to end it. She based her case, in part, on s. 7, arguing that limiting her choice of when to die violated her personal autonomy and security. The majority of the Court at that time upheld the law. Over twenty years later, the Supreme Court found the same law to be a violation of s. 7 of the *Charter*, and thus the section of the *Criminal Code* prohibiting assisted deaths was ruled unconstitutional. And again, in 2015, the Supreme Court overruled its own 1987 decision[20] that found freedom of association, as provided for under s. 2 of the *Charter*, did not protect the right to collective bargaining or to strike. Instead, almost thirty years later, they affirmed the right to collective bargaining and the right to strike as being an essential part of freedom of association under s. 2 of the *Charter.*[21]

---

15 *Reference re ss. 193 and 195.1(1) of the Criminal Code (Man.)*, [1990] 1 SCR 1123.
16 *Canada (AG) v. Bedford*, [2013] 3 SCR 1101.
17 *Canada (AG) v. Bedford*, [2013] 3 SCR 1101, at ¶ 42.
18 *Carter v. Canada (AG)*, [2015] 1 SCR 331.
19 *Rodriguez v British Columbia (AG)*, [1993] 3 SCR 519.
20 *Reference re Public Service Employee Relations Act* (Alta.), [1987] 1 SCR 313.
21 *Saskatchewan Federation of Labour v. Saskatchewan*, [2015] 1 SCR 245.

Mark Carter, a legal scholar who has written extensively on s. 43 and corporal punishment, contends that the *Bedford* case provides an opportunity to reconsider the *Foundation* case.[22] In *Bedford*, the Supreme Court developed new criteria for determining "the principles of fundamental justice," an important consideration under s. 7 of the *Charter* and a section that was given extensive coverage in the *Foundation* decision. The CFCYL had argued that s. 43 was "vague" and "overly broad" and applied in a manner that differed among provinces and territories, exposing children to the possibility of harm and even injury.[23] The Court rejected the CFCYL's argument because, as noted in chapter 5, the Supreme Court undertook to "delineate a sphere of non-criminal conduct" as part of their decision that would allow those who use physical punishment on children and youth to know when they risk criminal sanctions.[24]

It was at this stage that Chief Justice McLachlin defined what is now known as the "zone of risk."[25] This undertaking happened within the writing of the decision and was roundly criticized by the minority on the Court, as well as by legal scholars.[26] It bears pointing out that the Chief Justice's rationale for setting up the limits on the scope of s. 43 was not to protect the rights of children but to provide those who use physical force on a child with guidelines as to when they might step into the "zone of risk" and face possible criminalizing. Carter describes this inversion of rights as "surreal," saying "it proceeded as if the parties who are most worthy of constitutional concern are the adults engaging in forceful conduct against children, rather than the children who are subject to that conduct."[27]

Carter also notes another possible ground for re-examination of the *Foundation* case. The Court in *Bedford* stated that the purpose of the legislation in question in a *Charter* challenge (in this case, s. 43 of the *Criminal Code*) is to be clearly identified as part of a s. 7 analysis. However, as Carter points out, "there has been remarkably little consideration of [s. 43's]

---

22 Carter, "Fundamentally Flawed," 1.

23 *Canadian Foundation for Children, Youth and the Law v. Canada (Attorney General)*, [2004] 1 SCR 76 (Factum of the Appellant (CFCYL)), at ¶ 82.

24 *Canadian Foundation for Children, Youth and the Law v. Canada (Attorney General)*, [2004] 1 SCR 76 (Factum of the Appellant (CFCYL)), at ¶ 19.

25 See chapter 5 from subhead "Zone of Risk."

26 See chapter 5 from subhead "Zone of Risk."

27 Carter, "Fundamentally Flawed," 97–98 and n. 43.

purpose." In cases involving s. 7, the Supreme Court said that if a law is found to limit the right to security of the person, courts are to identify the purpose or object of the law and then consider if there is a connection between the purpose and the limitation of rights.[28]

The Supreme Court said the purpose behind s. 43 was to "recognize that the force that it allows must have corrective value as determined most significantly by expert evidence."[29] Based on overwhelming expert evidence that shows there are no benefits to using physical punishment on children, Carter concludes: "There is, therefore, no connection between the limit that s. 43 imposes on children's rights to security of the person and the objective of the law."[30]

WHAT HAVE OTHER COUNTRIES DONE?

Currently, sixty-seven countries have banned all forms of child physical punishment in the home, schools, and other institutions.[31] These countries banned child physical punishment and instead placed positive statements regarding a child's right to security in their respective civil laws, such as family laws or human rights laws.[32] The effect being that within the civil law, the emphasis is on a child's right not to be subjected to physical punishment, rather than the criminal law that requires proof "beyond a reasonable doubt" and may criminally penalize parents. These changes resulted in an "overall prohibition on the use of corporal punishment against children by both parents and teachers."[33] Their experiences are worth considering in more detail.

Sweden

The first country to ban corporal punishment outright was Sweden. In 1957, Swedish legislators took what has been described as the "revolutionary

28 Carter, "Fundamentally Flawed," 104–05.
29 Carter, "Fundamentally Flawed," 108.
30 Carter, "Fundamentally Flawed," 109.
31 For a list of states prohibiting all corporal punishment of children, including in the home, see "Countdown to Universal Prohibition," End Corporal Punishment, https://endcorporalpunishment.org/countdown/.
32 Shmueli, "The Influence of the UN Convention," 189.
33 Shmueli, "Corporal Punishment in the Education System," 290.

step of removing from the *Penal Code* the corporal punishment defense to criminal assault,"[34] thus providing children with the same protection from assault as adults. In other words, the Swedish parliament repealed their equivalent to Canada's s. 43 of the *Criminal Code*. Later, in 1979, following a far-reaching study into the effects of child physical punishment that found it to be deleterious to a child's health and well-being, the Swedish parliament passed, by a vote of 259–6,[35] the following clear statement in the *Parental Code*:

> Children have the right to care, security and a good upbringing. Children are to be treated with respect for their person and individuality and may not be subjected to physical punishment or other injurious or humiliating treatment.[36]

Joan Durrant, a professor in the Department of Family Studies, University of Manitoba, has studied child corporal punishment and the Swedish ban for over forty years. In a study evaluating the impact of the Swedish ban, she reported that by placing the ban in the *Parents Code* (similar to our civic laws such as child and family legislation) rather than the *Penal Code* (similar to our *Criminal Code*) it carried no criminal penalty.

The objectives of the ban were threefold: first, it was hoped that it would bring about a change in attitude among Swedish families, leading to a decrease in the use of child corporal punishment; second, the ban would provide guidance on what are acceptable child-rearing practices, allowing professionals such as doctors, social workers, and child protection workers to have clear guidelines to inform parents that physical force on children is not permitted; and third, earlier detection of children at risk would allow for earlier intervention. A follow-up study found that support for child physical punishment dropped over the following decades from 53 percent in 1965 to 11 percent in the 1990s.[37]

Other studies found that in the 1960s almost all Swedish preschool children had been physically punished once or several times a year by

34 Bitensky, *Corporal Punishment of Children*, 154–55.
35 Bitensky, *Corporal Punishment of Children*, 155.
36 Janson et al., "Sweden: A 30-Year Ban," 247.
37 Durrant, "Evaluating the Success of Sweden's Corporal Punishment Ban," 435.

their parents, but by the 1970s the numbers indicated that less than half of children had been physically punished, and by 2000 the numbers fell to 13 to 14 percent.[38] Child abuse rates and child injuries have declined while reports of child assaults increased during this time. This is not surprising since parental practices considered "normal" at one time are now recognized as harmful and therefore are more likely to be reported as assault. The increase in reports of child abuse, as Janson and colleagues note, "does not indicate an actual increase in assaults on children; rather, it reflects a decreased tolerance of such assaults."[39]

While the *Parental Code* explicitly prohibits child physical punishment, it does not impose penalties—those are still outlined in the Swedish *Penal Code.* Assaults that meet the standard of "bodily injury, illness, or pain... or renders him or her powerless... shall be sentenced for assault"[40] under Sweden's *Penal Code.* The "aim of the law [*Parental Code*] was not to punish parents, but to raise awareness."[41] Cases of assault, under the *Penal Code,* are investigated by the police under the direction of the prosecutor. They work together to determine if it is in the "public interest" to prosecute the parents. They collaborate with social workers, health-care providers, and child psychologists to put the needs of the child first. As one Swedish prosecutor stated, "parents do not go to jail"; rather they are provided supports to ensure that the child is provided with "security and a good upbringing." Social Services are mandated to ensure children are protected from all forms of violence. Thus, even if a case has not met the threshold of being reported to the police, the children will receive help. Violence in the home—whether perpetrated against a parent, child, or both—is handled by the police, prosecutors, social workers, and health professionals in the same way.

Finland

Scandinavian countries have led the way in prohibiting child physical punishment, and they have all done it by including consistent positive statements in their relevant civil laws. For example, Finland, which followed Sweden's lead, becoming the second country to ban child physical

38 Janson et al., "Sweden: A 30-Year Ban," 250.
39 Janson et al., "Sweden: A 30-Year Ban," 251.
40 Janson et al., "Sweden: A 30-Year Ban," 247.
41 Janson et al., "Sweden: A 30-Year Ban," 248.

punishment in 1983, reformed its *Child Custody and Right of Access Act* with the addition of the following statement:

> A child shall be brought up in the spirit of understanding, security and love. He shall not be subdued, corporally punished or otherwise humiliated. His growth towards independence, responsibility and adulthood shall be encouraged, supported and assisted.[42]

In 1970, prior to the revisions to the *Act*, Finland removed the right of parents and others to use physical force on children from its *Penal Code*. Subsequent research has shown a decrease in violence, including corporal punishment, perpetrated against children. In a 1988 survey of almost 7,500 teenagers aged fifteen and sixteen, researchers found that 72 percent had encountered minor violence in the home, with more than 60 percent experiencing hair pulling and 25 percent being slapped.[43] A similar study, conducted in 2004 with 6,200 teenagers, found that 46 percent reported being physically punished by their parents at some point in their lives, but only 7 percent had been physically punished in the year preceding the study.[44]

It is clear that incidents of child physical punishment in Finland have been reduced over the past thirty years, but credit also belongs to other legal reforms that accompanied the ban on physical punishment. For example, the *Welfare Act* was amended to emphasize the human rights of children and consider the child's best interests, including their overall well-being. An extensive public education campaign also aided in the change in public attitude toward child physical punishment by making recommendations aimed at preventing domestic/family violence.

Germany

Germany banned child physical punishment in 2000 by amending their *Civil Code* to say, "Children have a right to be reared without violence."[45] At the time, a nationwide campaign took place "to publicize the new legislation, make the general public aware of the harmful consequences

42 Husa, "Finland Children's Right to Protection," 122.
43 Husa, "Finland Children's Right to Protection," 129.
44 Husa, "Finland Children's Right to Protection," 129.
45 Bussman, "Germany: Background and Legal Consequences," 135.

of violence, and promote a change of attitude towards a new model of non-violent childrearing characterised by respect and care for the child."[46] The events included media promotions, seminars, discussions, and even street parties.

Germany, like other countries, placed an emphasis on promoting "methods of therapy for avoiding family disputes or for treating them if they had already occurred."[47] The objective was to change the norm and thus avoid criminal sanctions by focusing on therapy and welfare services to provide programs for prevention and solutions to familial violence.[48]

Cyprus

Cyprus, another European country, has extended protection to children who are assaulted in their homes by including in their *Law Which Provides for the Prevention of Violence in the Family and Protection of Victims* (part of Cyprus's *Criminal Code*) a definition that defines violence in the family as "any unlawful act, omission or behaviour which results in the direct infliction of physical, sexual or mental injury to any member of the family."[49]

As Bitensky notes, the enjoining of child physical punishment within legislation aimed at preventing family violence also brought with it a provision allowing for the prosecution of family members who, if convicted, could be fined or incarcerated.[50] The Cyprus law imposes an even more stringent penalty on a family member who assaults another family member than it does on individuals convicted of assaulting someone outside the family, drawing no distinction between intimate partner violence and child corporal punishment. For example, a person convicted of common assault may face a fine and/or prison term of one year, but if the assaulted person is a family member, the convicted person faces a fine and/or a two-year prison term.[51] In addition to providing for criminal sanctions such as incarceration and fines, the Cyprus law "obliges the welfare services to give advice and mediation services to members of the family for the

46 Bussman, "Germany: Background and Legal Consequences," 137.
47 Shmueli, "Corporal Punishment in the Education System," 234.
48 Shmueli, "Corporal Punishment in the Education System," 241.
49 Shmueli, "Corporal Punishment in the Education System," 228.
50 Bitensky, *Corporal Punishment of Children*, 174.
51 Bitensky, *Corporal Punishment of Children*, 175.

prevention of the intra-familial disputes that have led or might lead to domestic violence."[52]

New Zealand

New Zealand became the first common law country in the world to ban child physical punishment.[53] Their ban was implemented through a Private Member's Bill. The PMB introduced in 2007 removed from the country's *Criminal Act* the defence for parents and others who assault children. Their *Criminal Act*, like Canada's *Criminal Code*, had its origins in English common law, and Canada shares the same legal history in the development of our criminal laws. New Zealand brought about their changes by amending the *Criminal Act*. Parliament repealed the previous section (s. 59) permitting child physical punishment and replaced it with the new *Crimes (Substitute Section 59) Amendment Act* 2007. The new *Act*, under subsection (1), acknowledges that parents are justified in using force if it is reasonable for preventing or minimizing harm to a child, preventing a child from engaging in disruptive behaviour, or performing normal tasks necessary for good care.[54] The key section of the new *Act* states: "Nothing in subsection (1) or in any rule of common law justifies the use of force for the purpose of correction."[55]

The wording was a compromise hammered out between the prime minister, the leader of the Opposition, and the member of Parliament who introduced the PMB. The compromise was seen to alleviate public anxiety over the criminalizing of parents for minor assaults, and it reiterated police discretion in determining what cases would be prosecuted.

---

52 Shmueli, "Corporal Punishment in the Education System," 228. Bitensky, *Corporal Punishment of Children*, 175, reported that in Austria the Supreme Court interpreted their ban on child physical punishment, which took place in 1989, to deny the continuation of parental custody to a father who used corporal punishment on his sons. The Court found that the father believed in strict discipline and expected his sons to show him respect and absolute obedience and "bear pain like men." The Court determined that his striking of his sons along with his authoritarian disposition violated Austria's ban and awarded custody of the sons to their mother.

53 Taylor et al., "New Zealand: The Achievements and Challenges of Prohibition," 182.

54 Taylor, et al., "New Zealand: The Achievements and Challenges of Prohibition," 182.

55 Taylor et al., "New Zealand: The Achievements and Challenges of Prohibition," 185.

CRITICS

Critics of the repeal of s. 43 have argued that if the defence were removed, there would be an increase in the criminalizing of parents. However, follow-up studies conducted in countries that have repealed their equivalent of s. 43 say this has not happened. In New Zealand, for example, following their prohibition and after five years of police monitoring, it was found that any prosecutions involved only extreme acts of violence such as causing injuries, kicking, and holding by the neck. None of these incidents led to prison sentences.[56] The authors note that instead, "police worked more closely with the child protection authority, diverting cases from the justice system to agencies that could respond supportively."[57] The limits on prosecutions is an important fact, substantiated in other countries,[58] as it was the fear of criminalizing parents that influenced the Supreme Court in Canada to maintain s. 43 of the *Criminal Code*. The Swedish experience has seen that parents are more likely to voluntarily seek support from outside services. Moreover, out of home placements were reduced in Sweden by one-third.[59]

OTHER CONSIDERATIONS TO BRING AN END TO CHILD PHYSICAL PUNISHMENT

Various initiatives and preventative measures are needed to bring about substantive change to the norms surrounding child physical punishment,[60] many of which could be implemented now. The perception that child

---

56 Heilmann et al., "Physical Punishment and Child Outcomes," 361.

57 Heilmann et al., "Physical Punishment and Child Outcomes," 361.

58 For an excellent overview of efforts to eliminate corporal punishment worldwide, see Durrant and Smith, eds., *Global Pathways to Abolishing Physical Punishment*; Bitensky, *Corporal Punishment of Children*.

59 Durrant, "Evaluating the Success of Sweden's Corporal Punishment Ban," 435.

60 Durrant et al., "Predicting Adults' Approval," 127–53; Naudin et al., "Physically Violent Parental Practices."

Homer Simpson, in the thirty-fifth season of *The Simpsons*, stated, "I don't do that anymore," referring to "throttling" his son, Bart, which had become a common scene and had been described as "a clear form of animated child abuse that was played for laughs." Sopan Deb, "Is Homer Simpson a Good Dad Now?," *New York Times*, November 7, 2023.

physical punishment is a normal part of child rearing is being contested and public opinion has evolved.[61] This requires public exposure and public messages regarding the harm caused to a child's development that follows them into later life, along with the commitment of governments, the public, and professionals to take the lead in promoting the fact children have rights.[62]

Public Education

Canada, as a signatory to many international human rights documents, is obliged to provide education on human rights. This obligation is consistently referred to in every major human rights document, including the *Universal Declaration of Human Rights* (article 26), the *International Covenant on Economic, Social and Cultural Rights* (article 13), the *Convention on the Elimination of All Forms of Discrimination Against Women* (article 10), the *International Convention on the Elimination of All Forms of Racial Discrimination*[63] (article 7), and the *Convention on the Rights of the Child* (article 29).

Provincial Departments of Education thus have the mandate therefore to ensure that their curriculum provides information that develops within the child a respect for and understanding of human rights. This includes knowledge on their rights and on their responsibility in upholding the rights of others. Within this framework comes a duty on the part of educators to provide students with an understanding of their rights to physical and mental integrity, including their right to be free from physical punishment. Research shows that children raised with corporal punishment display more aggressive tendencies toward others. This has important implications for their interactions with peers at schools as research shows a likelihood of bullying.[64]

Sweden, Finland, Germany, Cyprus, and other countries that have implemented a ban on corporal punishment have done so alongside a well-orchestrated public education initiative. The aim is to build knowledge on the impact of child physical punishment, and, to do this, countries have

---

61 Fréchette and Romano, "Change in Corporal Punishment over Time," 507–17.

62 See chapter 7 for a full discussion on the harms of child physical punishment.

63 The full texts of these United Nations human rights documents can be found at https://www.ohchr.org/en/core-international-human-rights-instruments-and-their-monitoring-bodies.

64 Statistics Canada, "Parenting Style and Children's Aggressive Behaviour"; Dussich and Maekoya, "Physical Child Harm and Bullying-Related Behaviors," 495.

undertaken educational programs designed to create "empathy for a ban on corporal punishment"[65] while affirming the "importance of protecting children's rights without irreparably harming the family unit in mild cases."[66]

The Government of Sweden undertook an extensive public education campaign, including printing information about the new law on milk cartons for families to read and discuss. Austrian schools teach children about their rights, including their right to be free of child physical punishment, and other departments provide a child helpline and pamphlets outlining the rights of children. These initiatives are consistent with the UN's *Convention on the Rights of the Child*, which calls on State parties to take appropriate measures to ensure children are protected from physical violence (article 19) and to undertake a public education campaign on the rights of children as stated in the CRC (article 42).

Family Violence

It is a curious fact that some *Domestic Violence Acts* do not consider a child, who is being struck in the home, to be a victim of domestic violence. This speaks to our propensity to compartmentalize violence against children as "discipline" or a "reprimand," whereas violence against adults is "assault."[67] In Saskatchewan, for example, *The Victims of Interpersonal Violence Act*[68] aids persons who experience domestic violence by, among other measures, removing the perpetrator from the home. The *Act* defines the victim as the "cohabitant who has been subjected to interpersonal violence by another cohabitant."[69] This implies it is violence between adults. The definition of "cohabitants" reinforces this interpretation as it is defined to mean people who have resided together, are the parents of children, and who have an ongoing relationship.[70] Children are protected from witnessing violence in most *Domestic Violence Acts* across the country, but they are not included in the *Act* as being protected from violence perpetrated against them by a family member, such as a parent.

---

65 Shmueli, "Corporal Punishment in the Education System," 293.
66 Shmueli, "Corporal Punishment in the Education System," 294.
67 Watkinson, "Physical Punishment in Childhood," 207.
68 *The Victims of Interpersonal Violence Act*, RSS 1994 as amended 2016.
69 *The Victims of Interpersonal Violence Act*, ibid. at s. 2(i), https://publications.saskatchewan.ca/#/products/929.
70 *The Victims of Interpersonal Violence Act*, ibid. at s. 2(a).

As noted earlier, Cyprus includes children in their law, which provides protection from family violence and imposes even harsher penalties on those who inflict harm on family members. This reinforces the position that violating vulnerable dependents is an especially egregious act.

Professionals

Professionals encounter and play a major role in the lives of children and their families. These include child protection workers, social workers, medical personnel, police, religious leaders, and teachers. When Sweden enacted their *Children and Parents Code* in 1979, one of the reasons behind its implementation was to give professionals guidance on what to provide to parents concerning acceptable child-rearing practices.[71]

While Canada has yet to pass legislation confirming that physical punishment is not permissible, we know that it is harmful to the well-being of children. It seems evident that professionals have a moral and professional duty to advise parents against the use of child physical punishment based on the evidence of the harm it causes and the rights of children to fair and respectful treatment. It is not unusual to take preventative measures when certain medicines or practices are shown to be harmful, and the same needs to be done for corporal punishment. For example, when a drug is found to have noxious side effects, the government does not hesitate to warn against its use or withdraw it altogether. Not everyone who smokes will die of lung cancer, but we have evidence that smoking increases the likelihood of lung cancer and, for this reason, the public is advised not to smoke. And so, it is imperative to do likewise when proffering professional advice concerning child physical punishment. It has noxious side effects, there are alternatives, and the proliferation of evidence shows it is bad for a child's well-being, now and later in life.

CHILD WELFARE

A national protocol is needed for child protection workers, social workers, all police (national and municipal), and others who work with

71 *Children and Parents Code of Sweden*, https://www.informationsverige.se/en/jag-har-fatt-uppehallstillstand/att-vara-foralder/rattigheter-och-skyldigheter.html. https://www.futurepolicy.org/rightsofchildren/swedens-children-and-parent-code-to-prohibit-all-corporal-punishment-and-other-humiliating-treatment-of-children.

family violence when dealing with child physical assault. Professor Tammy Landau, a criminologist, conducted a study into police responses to allegations of child assault.[72] Her study looked at police responses in the cities of Toronto, Winnipeg, and Timmons. She found a "dog's breakfast," with police handling of such cases varying widely. In Toronto, police laid charges in 40 percent of the cases; but in Winnipeg and Timmons, police laid charges in approximately 10 percent of the cases. Rural communities are often policed by the Royal Canadian Mounted Police, and based on the experiences of child protection workers, the way such cases are handled differs from one police detachment to another, and even, in some cases, in detachments located side by side.

Police, prosecutors, and judges have a great deal of discretion in dealing with cases as a means of avoiding criminalization such as those found in the *Youth Criminal Justice Act* (YCJA).[73] The YCJA provides opportunities within the criminal justice process to divert a case out of the justice system. The changes have brought about a dramatic decrease in incarceration rates for youth across Canada.[74] One such example is conferencing, which can be used in criminal and civil cases. The conferencing process is based on the principles of restorative justice, which aims to repair the harm done and heal the wounds caused by an action. The focus is on restoration of the victim rather than punishment for the violation of the law. Family conferences could be convened with the assistance of social workers, health workers, and child protection agencies to determine the harm, seek restitution, and consider what family supports are needed (parenting skills development, family support initiatives). As noted earlier, Cyprus's family violence law obliges the child welfare system to follow up with family members for mediation following an intra-family dispute. In a study conducted eighteen months after the Supreme Court decision on child physical punishment,

---

72 Landau, "Policing the Punishment," 121.

73 *Youth Criminal Justice Act*, S.C. 2002, c1.

74 The number of youth found guilty and sentenced to custody was down more than 50 percent in 2006–07 as compared to the year prior to the introduction of the *Youth Criminal Justice Act* in 2003. One of the major purposes of drafting a new YCJA was to decrease the high rate of youth incarceration. In addition, court cases prior to the introduction of the YCJA in 2003 compared to the period ending 2006–07 shows a 26 percent decrease in youth court cases in Canada. See Thomas, *Youth Court Statistics 2006/2007*; Green and Healy, *Tough on Kids.*

participants were asked what they needed to avoid using physical punishment on their children. The most common theme was "parental support."[75]

RELIGIOUS LEADERS

Religions for Peace, a nonprofit organization and international coalition of religious leaders, and UNICEF put forth a declaration on children and violence called the Kyoto Declaration.[76] The Kyoto Declaration came about following the release of the United Nations *Study on Violence Against Children*.[77] This UN study documented the violence perpetrated against children, saying it occurs in every country in the world in a variety of forms. Violence against children is deeply rooted in religious, economic, and cultural practices. Corporal punishment was identified as one of the most extensive forms of violence experienced by children.[78] The authors of the Kyoto Declaration acknowledge,

> Our religious communities have not fully upheld their obligation to protect our children from violence. Through omission, denial and silence, we have at times tolerated, perpetuated and ignored the reality of violence against children in homes, families, institutions and communities, and not actively confronted the suffering that this violence causes.[79]

The history of religion and its influence on the spread of corporal punishment has been well documented.[80] In Canada, as noted in the TRC's Calls to Action, religious institutions played a major role in the abuse of Indigenous children. Most of the churches involved in the establishment of residential schools have issued apologies for the intergenerational harms they have caused.[81]

The Kyoto Declaration affirmed that religious communities are uniquely positioned to speak up and address violence against children, and it urged

75 Watkinson, "Physical Punishment in Childhood."
76 UNICEF and Religions for Peace, "From Commitment to Action," 6.
77 Pinheiro, *World Report on Violence Against Children*.
78 Pinheiro, *World Report on Violence Against Children*.
79 UNICEF and Religions for Peace, "From Commitment to Action," 6.
80 See chapters 1 and 2.
81 See chapter 2, footnotes 95–101, and related text.

religious communities around the world to do so,[82] saying that "religious leaders can be powerful children's advocates." As follow-up to the Kyoto Declaration, they provided suggestions for action such as promoting discussions in religious communities and places of worship about children's rights, working with governments to promote children's rights in school curricula, and initiating campaigns for law reform to prohibit violence in the home and provide advice on positive parenting.[83]

A group of religious leaders and scholars in Canada, representing Anglicans, United Church, Methodists, and Presbyterian Churches along with Schools of Hebrew Scriptures and public health, pastoral care, and social work organizations, came together with a similar statement in support of the TRC's Call to Action 6.[84] The statement calls upon Christian churches to work with the government for the repeal of s. 43, to recognize the deep wounds caused by colonization, to actively address the disproportionate physical, spiritual, and emotional harms experienced by Indigenous children and youth, and to work with communities to protect children and develop healthy and non-violent approaches to discipline.[85]

Other religious organizations and leaders have taken very public stances to show their support for an end to violence against children. Archbishop Emeritus Desmond Tutu said, in 2006, "Violence begets violence that instils fear and misery, and I look forward to church communities working with other organisations to make progress towards ending all forms of violence against children."[86] The work and commitment of these religious leaders are an important and credible source to be called upon when working

---

82 UNICEF and Religions for Peace, "From Commitment to Action 6."

83 UNICEF and Religions for Peace, "From Commitment to Action 6," at 26–32.

84 MacDonald et al., "A Christian Theological Statement," 11.

85 MacDonald et al., "A Christian Theological Statement," 12. The ignatories of "A Christian Theological Statement" also asked the churches to endorse the *Joint Statement on Physical Punishment of Children and Youth*, online at http://www.cheo.on.ca/en/physicalpunishment. This statement is highly recommended as an up-to-date resource on research, political initiatives, positive discipline, and the rights of children. It has been endorsed by close to seven hundred organizations and even more distinguished Canadians.

86 Churches' Network for Non-Violence and Global Initiative to End All Corporal Punishment of Children, "Ending Corporal Punishment of Children—A Handbook for Worship and Gatherings," 2015, 3, https://jliflc.com/resources/ending-corporal-violence-against-children-a-handbook-for-worship-and-religious-gatherings/.

with governments, advocating, and counselling around family violence. The role of religious leaders in attempting to shift the norms away from an acceptance and tolerance for child physical punishment is vital.

ALTERNATIVES TO CORPORAL PUNISHMENT

Positive discipline resources are available,[87] and it has been shown that efforts to reduce child physical punishment through parental education and intervention techniques do work.[88] Positive discipline methods are those that focus on verbal interactions: explaining to a child why something is wrong; providing clear, age-appropriate, and firm rules; being consistent in what is considered appropriate behaviour; providing structure and predictability as well as age-appropriate and reasonable deprivation of privilege while bolstered by a warm and involved family environment.[89]

A Canadian study on a program offered across Canada and around the world called Positive Discipline in Everyday Parenting found that 95 percent of parents who took the parenting program reported a reduction in their approval of child physical punishment, and more than 80 percent believed that they would use physical punishment less often.[90] The program is grounded within the principles that positive discipline is non-violent, solution focused, respectful, and based on the best knowledge available about child development.

CONCLUSION

There are four important points to highlight in considering an end to the legal protection given to those who use physical punishment on children. The first obvious solution is to remove the defence to child physical

87 Durrant, *Positive Discipline in Everyday Parenting*. See also resources listed online at https://www.cheo.on.ca/en/about-us/physical-punishment.aspx; Durrant and Ensom, *Joint Statement on Physical Punishment of Children and Youth*; Fletcher, "Positive Parenting, Not Physical Punishment," 1339.

88 See for example current research discussed in Durrant and Ensom, "Physical Punishment of Children," 1373; Gershoff et al., "Promising Intervention Strategies," 9.

89 Sege and Siegel, "Effective Discipline to Raise Healthy Children," 1; Durrant and Ensom, "Physical Punishment of Children," 1373; Ma et al., "Corporal Punishment and Youth," 489.

90 Durrant et al., "Preventing Punitive Violence," 109.

punishment by repealing s. 43 of the *Criminal Code*. While many countries have initiated a ban on child physical punishment, those who had a criminal defence repealed it. These countries then used their civil or human rights laws to affirm a child's right to be free from physical punishment. By affirming a child's right to be free from violence in our civil laws, we lessen the fear of criminalizing parents, eliminate the often insurmountable obligation to prove guilt "beyond a reasonable doubt," and focus instead on the rights of the child.

Second, all provinces, territories, and most Indigenous communities have *Child and Family Services Acts* that provide direction on the role of governments and bands regarding the welfare of children. They generally include provisions for foster care placements, family services, and procedures for child welfare hearings and children in need of protection from maltreatment. As we have seen, all the countries that have banned child corporal punishment in all its forms have included in their civil laws positive statements affirming a child's right to care and guidance void of any physical punishment or humiliating treatment. These laws can be amended to include a strong supportive statement to explicitly state that children are entitled to care and security. This position can be affirmed within all provincial, territorial, and Indigenous child and family legislation, school acts, and child protection laws, along with a consistent, countrywide protocol on handling child protection cases. Concurrently, provinces could expand thier domestic violence laws to include protection of children from family violence. *Domestic Violence Acts* in Canada could be amended to make it clear that children in families are protected from assault in the same manner as cohabitants are protected.

Third, a prohibition on child physical punishment must be embedded within a social welfare support system such that it is made mandatory that services bolstered by trauma-informed care be provided to families facing violence.[91] These services may include restorative justice initiatives, parenting classes, family support, and positive discipline classes.

Finally, governments at all levels have an especially important role to play in funding and developing public education and media campaigns, working within their jurisdictions to ensure their education and child

---

91 Piotrowski, "ACEs and Trauma-Informed Care," 307–28; Nonomura et al., *Toward a Trauma- and Violence-Informed Research Ethics Module.*

protection legislation reflect the rights of the child.[92] All these initiatives must be supported by a publicly funded education campaign discussing the short- and long-term harms associated with child physical punishment embedded within a focus on children's rights. This requires the support of governments and their departments (including education departments, social services, and health), professional practitioners and their associations, and religious leaders.[93]

In the meantime, while we wait for the demise of s. 43, each one of these points can be undertaken now. Writing in 2019, Dr. Joan Durrant of the University of Manitoba, a leading international expert on the subject, put it succinctly: "Debates over corporal punishment's effectiveness have come to an end. No study has shown it to have long-term benefits, while many have demonstrated its substantial and wide-ranging risks."[94]

---

92 Durrant et al., "Predicting Adults' Approval," 127–53; Pinheiro, *World Report on Violence Against Children.* See Overarching Recommendations which calls upon governments to develop and implement legislation and policies on child protection including eliminating corporal punishment and other humiliating treatment in school and the home. https://docs.un.org/en/A/61/299 (p. 25–26); Sansone et al., *Understanding the Effects of Corporal Punishment on Children, Families and Communities.*

93 For example, the Government of Canada could consider, among other ideas, producing public announcements similar to its produced television vignettes drawing attention to elder abuse. The vignettes sent a clear message informing the public that there are various forms of elder abuse, it happens within families, it is harmful to senior citizens, and society has a role to play in stopping it.

94 Durrant, "Corporal Punishment," 18.

APPENDIX A

THE CANADIAN CHARTER OF RIGHTS AND FREEDOMS

Whereas Canada is founded upon principles that recognize the supremacy of God and the rule of law:

Guarantee of Rights and Freedoms

RIGHTS AND FREEDOMS IN CANADA

1. The Canadian Charter of Rights and Freedoms guarantees the rights and freedoms set out in it subject only to such reasonable limits prescribed by law as can be demonstrably justified in a free and democratic society.

Fundamental Freedoms

FUNDAMENTAL FREEDOMS

2. Everyone has the following fundamental freedoms:
   (a) freedom of conscience and religion;
   (b) freedom of thought, belief, opinion and expression, including freedom of the press and other media of communication;
   (c) freedom of peaceful assembly; and
   (d) freedom of association.

Democratic Rights

DEMOCRATIC RIGHTS OF CITIZENS

3. Every citizen of Canada has the right to vote in an election of members of the House of Commons or of a legislative assembly and to be qualified for membership therein.

MAXIMUM DURATION OF LEGISLATIVE BODIES

4. (1) No House of Commons and no legislative assembly shall continue for longer than five years from the date fixed for the return of the writs at a general election of its members.

CONTINUATION IN SPECIAL CIRCUMSTANCES

(2) In time of real or apprehended war, invasion or insurrection, a House of Commons may be continued by Parliament and a legislative assembly may be continued by the legislature beyond five years if such continuation is not opposed by the votes of more than one-third of the members of the House of Commons or the legislative assembly, as the case may be.

ANNUAL SITTING OF LEGISLATIVE BODIES

5. There shall be a sitting of Parliament and of each legislature at least once every twelve months.

Mobility Rights

MOBILITY OF CITIZENS

6. (1) Every citizen of Canada has the right to enter, remain in and leave Canada.

RIGHTS TO MOVE AND GAIN LIVELIHOOD

(2) Every citizen of Canada and every person who has the status of a permanent resident of Canada has the right
   (a) to move to and take up residence in any province; and
   (b) to pursue the gaining of a livelihood in any province.

LIMITATION

(3) The rights specified in subsection (2) are subject to

(c) any laws or practices of general application in force in a province other than those that discriminate among persons primarily on the basis of province of present or previous residence; and

(d) any laws providing for reasonable residency requirements as a qualification for the receipt of publicly provided social services.

AFFIRMATIVE ACTION PROGRAMS

(4) Subsections (2) and (3) do not preclude any law, program or activity that has as its object the amelioration in a province of conditions of individuals in that province who are socially or economically disadvantaged if the rate of employment in that province is below the rate of employment in Canada.

Legal Rights

LIFE, LIBERTY AND SECURITY OF PERSON

7. Everyone has the right to life, liberty and security of the person and the right not to be deprived thereof except in accordance with the principles of fundamental justice.

SEARCH OR SEIZURE

8. Everyone has the right to be secure against unreasonable search or seizure.

DETENTION OR IMPRISONMENT

9. Everyone has the right not to be arbitrarily detained or imprisoned.

ARREST OR DETENTION

10. Everyone has the right on arrest or detention

(a) to be informed promptly of the reasons therefor;

(b) to retain and instruct counsel without delay and to be informed of that right; and

(c) to have the validity of the detention determined by way of habeas corpus and to be released if the detention is not lawful.

PROCEEDINGS IN CRIMINAL AND PENAL MATTERS

11. Any persons charged with an offence has the right
    (a) to be informed without unreasonable delay of the specific offence;
    (b) to be tried within a reasonable time;
    (c) not to be compelled to be a witness in proceedings against that person in respect of the offence;
    (d) to be presumed innocent until proven guilty according to law in a fair and public hearing by an independent and impartial tribunal;
    (e) not to be denied reasonable bail without just cause;
    (f) except in the case of an offence under military law tried before a military tribunal, to the benefit of trial by jury where the maximum punishment for the offence is imprisonment for five years or a more severe punishment;
    (g) not to be found guilty on account of any act or omission unless, at the time of the act or omission, it constituted an offence under Canadian or international law or was criminal according to the general principles of law recognized by the community of nations;
    (h) if finally acquitted of the offence, not to be tried for it again and, if finally found guilty and punished for the offence, not to be tried or punished for it again; and
    (i) if found guilty of the offence and if the punishment for the offence has been varied between the time of commission and the time of sentencing, to the benefit of the lesser punishment.

TREATMENT OR PUNISHMENT

12. Everyone has the right not to be subjected to any cruel and unusual treatment or punishment.

SELF-INCRIMINATION

13. A witness who testifies in any proceedings has the right not to have any incriminating evidence so given used to incriminate that witness in any other proceedings, except in a prosecution for perjury or for the giving of contradictory evidence.

INTERPRETER

14. A party or witness in any proceedings who does not understand or speak the language in which the proceedings are conducted or who is deaf has the right to the assistance of an interpreter.

Equality Rights

EQUALITY BEFORE AND UNDER LAW AND EQUAL PROTECTION AND BENEFIT OF LAW

15. (1) Every individual is equal before and under the law and has the right to the equal protection and equal benefit of the law without discrimination and, in particular, without discrimination based on race, national or ethnic origin, colour, religion, sex, age or mental or physical disability.

AFFIRMATIVE ACTION PROGRAMS

(2) Subsection (1) does not preclude any law, program or activity that has as its object the amelioration of conditions of disadvantaged individuals or groups including those that are disadvantaged because of race, national or ethnic origin, colour, religion, sex, age or mental or physical disability.

Official Languages of Canada

OFFICIAL LANGUAGES OF CANADA

16. (1) English and French are the official languages of Canada and have equality of status and equal rights and privileges as to their use in all institutions of the Parliament and government of Canada.

OFFICIAL LANGUAGES OF NEW BRUNSWICK

(2) English and French are the official languages of New Brunswick and have equality of status and equal rights and privileges as to their use in all institutions of the legislature and government of New Brunswick.

ADVANCEMENT OF STATUS AND USE

(3) Nothing in this Charter limits the authority of Parliament or a legislature to advance the equality of status or use of English and

French.

ENGLISH AND FRENCH LINGUISTIC COMMUNITIES IN NEW BRUNSWICK

16.1(1) The English linguistic community and the French linguistic community in New Brunswick have equality of status and equal rights and privileges, including the right to distinct educational institutions and such distinct cultural institutions as are necessary for the preservation and promotion of those communities.

ROLE OF THE LEGISLATURE AND GOVERNMENT OF NEW BRUNSWICK

(2) The role of the legislature and government of New Brunswick to preserve and promote the status, rights and privileges referred to in subsection (1) is affirmed.

PROCEEDINGS OF PARLIAMENT

17. (1) Everyone has the right to use English or French in any debates and other proceedings of Parliament.

PROCEEDINGS OF NEW BRUNSWICK LEGISLATURE

(2) Everyone has the right to use English or French in any debates and other proceedings of the legislature of New Brunswick.

PARLIAMENTARY STATUTES AND RECORDS

18. (1) The statutes, records and journals of Parliament shall be printed and published in English and French and both language versions are equally authoritative.

NEW BRUNSWICK STATUTES AND RECORDS

(2) The statutes, records and journals of the legislature of New Brunswick shall be printed and published in English and French and both language versions are equally authoritative.

PROCEEDINGS IN COURTS ESTABLISHED BY PARLIAMENT

19. (1) Either English or French may be used by any person in, or in any pleading in or process issuing from, any court established by Parliament.

PROCEEDINGS IN NEW BRUNSWICK COURTS

(2) Either English or French may be used by any person in, or in any pleading in or process issuing from, any court of New Brunswick.

COMMUNICATIONS BY PUBLIC WITH FEDERAL INSTITUTIONS

20. (1) Any member of the public in Canada has the right to communicate with, and to receive available services from, any head or central office of an institution of the Parliament or government of Canada in English or French, and has the same right with respect to any other office of any such institution where

(a) there is a significant demand for communications with and services from that office in such language; or

(b) due to the nature of the office, it is reasonable that communications with and services from that office be available in both English and French.

COMMUNICATIONS BY PUBLIC WITH NEW BRUNSWICK INSTITUTIONS

(2) Any member of the public in New Brunswick has the right to communicate with, and to receive available services from, any office of an institution of the legislature or government of New Brunswick in English or French.

CONTINUATION OF EXISTING CONSTITUTIONAL PROVISIONS

21. Nothing in sections 16 to 20 abrogates or derogates from any right, privilege or obligation with respect to the English and French languages, or either of them, that exists or is continued by virtue of any other provision of the Constitution of Canada.

RIGHTS AND PRIVILEGES PRESERVED

22. Nothing in sections 16 to 20 abrogates or derogates from any legal or customary right or privilege acquired or enjoyed either before or after the coming into force of this Charter with respect to any language that is not English or French.

Minority Language Educational Rights

LANGUAGE OF INSTRUCTION

23. (1) Citizens of Canada
   (a) whose first language learned and still understood is that of the English or French linguistic minority population of the province in which they reside, or
   (b) who have received their primary school instruction in Canada in English or French and reside in a province where the language in which they received that instruction is the language of the English or French linguistic minority population of the province,

have the right to have their children receive primary and secondary school instruction in that language in that province.

CONTINUITY OF LANGUAGE INSTRUCTION

(2) Citizens of Canada of whom any child has received or is receiving primary or secondary school instruction in English or French in Canada, have the right to have all their children receive primary and secondary school instruction in the same language.

APPLICATION WHERE NUMBERS WARRANT

(3) The right of citizens of Canada under subsections (1) and (2) to have their children receive primary and secondary school instruction in the language of the English or French linguistic minority population of a province
   (c) applies wherever in the province the number of children of citizens who have such a right is sufficient to warrant the provision to them out of public funds of minority language instruction; and
   (d) includes, where the number of those children so warrants, the right to have them receive that instruction in minority language educational facilities provided out of public funds.

Enforcement

ENFORCEMENT OF GUARANTEED RIGHTS AND FREEDOMS

24. (1) Anyone whose rights or freedoms, as guaranteed by this Charter, have been infringed or denied may apply to a court of competent

jurisdiction to obtain such remedy as the court considers appropriate and just in the circumstances.

EXCLUSION OF EVIDENCE BRINGING ADMINISTRATION OF JUSTICE INTO DISREPUTE

(2) Where, in proceedings under subsection (1), a court concludes that evidence was obtained in a manner that infringed or denied any rights or freedoms guaranteed by this Charter, the evidence shall be excluded if it is established that, having regard to all the circumstances, the admission of it in the proceedings would bring the administration of justice into disrepute.

General

ABORIGINAL RIGHTS AND FREEDOMS NOT AFFECTED BY CHARTER

25. The guarantee in this Charter of certain rights and freedoms shall not be construed so as to abrogate or derogate from any aboriginal, treaty or other rights or freedoms that pertain to the aboriginal peoples of Canada including
    (a) any rights or freedoms that have been recognized by the Royal Proclamation of October 7, 1763; and
    (b) any rights or freedoms that now exist by way of land claims agreements or may be so acquired.

OTHER RIGHTS AND FREEDOMS NOT AFFECTED BY CHARTER

26. The guarantee in this Charter of certain rights and freedoms shall not be construed as denying the existence of any other rights or freedoms that exist in Canada.

MULTICULTURAL HERITAGE

27. This Charter shall be interpreted in a manner consistent with the preservation and enhancement of the multicultural heritage of Canadians.

RIGHTS GUARANTEED EQUALLY TO BOTH SEXES

28. Notwithstanding anything in this Charter, the rights and freedoms referred to in it are guaranteed equally to male and female persons.

RIGHTS RESPECTING CERTAIN SCHOOLS PRESERVED

29. Nothing in this Charter abrogates or derogates from any rights or privileges guaranteed by or under the Constitution of Canada in respect of denominational, separate or dissentient schools.

APPLICATION TO TERRITORIES AND TERRITORIAL AUTHORITIES

30. A reference in this Charter to a province or to the legislative assembly or legislature of a province shall be deemed to include a reference to the Yukon Territory and the Northwest Territories, or to the appropriate legislative authority thereof, as the case may be.

LEGISLATIVE POWERS NOT EXTENDED

31. Nothing in this Charter extends the legislative powers of any body or authority.

Application of Charter

APPLICATION OF CHARTER

32. (1) This Charter applies
   (a) to the Parliament and government of Canada in respect of all matters within the authority of Parliament including all matters relating to the Yukon Territory and Northwest Territories; and
   (b) to the legislature and government of each province in respect of all matters within the authority of the legislature of each province.

EXCEPTION

(2) Notwithstanding subsection (1), section 15 shall not have effect until three years after this section comes into force.

EXCEPTION WHERE EXPRESS DECLARATION

33. (1) Parliament or the legislature of a province may expressly declare in an Act of Parliament or of the legislature, as the case may be, that the Act or a provision thereof shall operate notwithstanding a provision included in section 2 or sections 7 to 15 of this Charter.

OPERATION OF EXCEPTION

(2) An Act or a provision of an Act in respect of which a declaration made under this section is in effect shall have such operation as it would have but for the provision of this Charter referred to in the declaration.

FIVE YEAR LIMITATION

(3) A declaration made under subsection (1) shall cease to have effect five years after it comes into force or on such earlier date as may be specified in the declaration.

RE-ENACTMENT

(4) Parliament or a legislature of a province may re-enact a declaration made under subsection (1).

FIVE YEAR LIMITATION

(5) Subsection (3) applies in respect of a re-enactment made under subsection (4).

Citation

CITATION

34. This Part may be cited as the Canadian Charter of Rights and Freedoms.

APPENDIX B

UNITED NATIONS CONVENTION ON THE RIGHTS OF THE CHILD

ARTICLES 1–41

Adopted and opened for signature, ratification and accession by General Assembly resolution 44/25 of 20 November 1989. Entry into force 2 September 1990, in accordance with article 49.

PREAMBLE

The States Parties to the present Convention,

Considering that, in accordance with the principles proclaimed in the Charter of the United Nations, recognition of the inherent dignity and of the equal and inalienable rights of all members of the human family is the foundation of freedom, justice and peace in the world,

Bearing in mind that the peoples of the United Nations have, in the Charter, reaffirmed their faith in fundamental human rights and in the dignity and worth of the human person, and have determined to promote social progress and better standards of life in larger freedom,

Recognizing that the United Nations has, in the Universal Declaration of Human Rights and in the International Covenants on Human Rights, proclaimed and agreed that everyone is entitled to all the rights and freedoms set forth therein, without distinction of any kind, such as race, colour, sex, language, religion, political or other opinion, national or social origin, property, birth or other status,

Recalling that, in the Universal Declaration of Human Rights, the United Nations has proclaimed that childhood is entitled to special care and assistance,

Convinced that the family, as the fundamental group of society and the natural environment for the growth and well-being of all its members and particularly children, should be afforded the necessary protection and assistance so that it can fully assume its responsibilities within the community,

Recognizing that the child, for the full and harmonious development of his or her personality, should grow up in a family environment, in an atmosphere of happiness, love and understanding,

Considering that the child should be fully prepared to live an individual life in society, and brought up in the spirit of the ideals proclaimed in the Charter of the United Nations, and in particular in the spirit of peace, dignity, tolerance, freedom, equality and solidarity,

Bearing in mind that the need to extend particular care to the child has been stated in the Geneva Declaration of the Rights of the Child of 1924 and in the Declaration of the Rights of the Child adopted by the General Assembly on 20 November 1959 and recognized in the Universal Declaration of Human Rights, in the International Covenant on Civil and Political Rights (in particular in articles 23 and 24), in the International Covenant on Economic, Social and Cultural Rights (in particular in article 10) and in the statutes and relevant instruments of specialized agencies and international organizations concerned with the welfare of children,

Bearing in mind that, as indicated in the Declaration of the Rights of the Child, "the child, by reason of his physical and mental immaturity, needs special safeguards and care, including appropriate legal protection, before as well as after birth,"

Recalling the provisions of the Declaration on Social and Legal Principles relating to the Protection and Welfare of Children, with Special Reference to Foster Placement and Adoption Nationally and Internationally; the United Nations Standard Minimum Rules for the Administration of Juvenile Justice (The Beijing Rules); and the Declaration on the Protection of Women and Children in Emergency and Armed Conflict, Recognizing that, in all countries in the world, there are children living in exceptionally difficult conditions, and that such children need special consideration,

Taking due account of the importance of the traditions and cultural values of each people for the protection and harmonious development of the child, Recognizing the importance of international co-operation for improving the living conditions of children in every country, in particular in the developing countries,

Have agreed as follows:

PART I

Article 1

For the purposes of the present Convention, a child means every human being below the age of eighteen years unless under the law applicable to the child, majority is attained earlier.

Article 2

1. States Parties shall respect and ensure the rights set forth in the present Convention to each child within their jurisdiction without discrimination of any kind, irrespective of the child's or his or her parent's or legal guardian's race, colour, sex, language, religion, political or other opinion, national, ethnic or social origin, property, disability, birth or other status.
2. States Parties shall take all appropriate measures to ensure that the child is protected against all forms of discrimination or punishment on the basis of the status, activities, expressed opinions, or beliefs of the child's parents, legal guardians, or family members.

Article 3

1. In all actions concerning children, whether undertaken by public or private social welfare institutions, courts of law, administrative authorities or legislative bodies, the best interests of the child shall be a primary consideration.
2. States Parties undertake to ensure the child such protection and care as is necessary for his or her well-being, taking into account

the rights and duties of his or her parents, legal guardians, or other individuals legally responsible for him or her, and, to this end, shall take all appropriate legislative and administrative measures.

3. States Parties shall ensure that the institutions, services and facilities responsible for the care or protection of children shall conform with the standards established by competent authorities, particularly in the areas of safety, health, in the number and suitability of their staff, as well as competent supervision.

Article 4

States Parties shall undertake all appropriate legislative, administrative, and other measures for the implementation of the rights recognized in the present Convention. With regard to economic, social and cultural rights, States Parties shall undertake such measures to the maximum extent of their available resources and, where needed, within the framework of international co-operation.

Article 5

States Parties shall respect the responsibilities, rights and duties of parents or, where applicable, the members of the extended family or community as provided for by local custom, legal guardians or other persons legally responsible for the child, to provide, in a manner consistent with the evolving capacities of the child, appropriate direction and guidance in the exercise by the child of the rights recognized in the present Convention.

Article 6

1. States Parties recognize that every child has the inherent right to life.
2. States Parties shall ensure to the maximum extent possible the survival and development of the child.

Article 7

1. The child shall be registered immediately after birth and shall have the right from birth to a name, the right to acquire a nationality and, as far as possible, the right to know and be cared for by his or her parents.
2. States Parties shall ensure the implementation of these rights in accordance with their national law and their obligations under the

relevant international instruments in this field, in particular where the child would otherwise be stateless.

Article 8

1. States Parties undertake to respect the right of the child to preserve his or her identity, including nationality, name and family relations as recognized by law without unlawful interference.
2. Where a child is illegally deprived of some or all of the elements of his or her identity, States Parties shall provide appropriate assistance and protection, with a view to re-establishing speedily his or her identity.

Article 9

1. States Parties shall ensure that a child shall not be separated from his or her parents against their will, except when competent authorities subject to judicial review determine, in accordance with applicable law and procedures, that such separation is necessary for the best interests of the child. Such determination may be necessary in a particular case such as one involving abuse or neglect of the child by the parents, or one where the parents are living separately and a decision must be made as to the child's place of residence.
2. In any proceedings pursuant to paragraph 1 of the present article, all interested parties shall be given an opportunity to participate in the proceedings and make their views known.
3. States Parties shall respect the right of the child who is separated from one or both parents to maintain personal relations and direct contact with both parents on a regular basis, except if it is contrary to the child's best interests.
4. Where such separation results from any action initiated by a State Party, such as the detention, imprisonment, exile, deportation or death (including death arising from any cause while the person is in the custody of the State) of one or both parents or of the child, that State Party shall, upon request, provide the parents, the child or, if appropriate, another member of the family with the essential information concerning the whereabouts of the absent member(s) of the family unless the provision of the information would be detrimental to the well-being of the child. States Parties shall

further ensure that the submission of such a request shall of itself entail no adverse consequences for the person(s) concerned.

Article 10

1. In accordance with the obligation of States Parties under article 9, paragraph 1, applications by a child or his or her parents to enter or leave a State Party for the purpose of family reunification shall be dealt with by States Parties in a positive, humane and expeditious manner. States Parties shall further ensure that the submission of such a request shall entail no adverse consequences for the applicants and for the members of their family.
2. A child whose parents reside in different States shall have the right to maintain on a regular basis, save in exceptional circumstances personal relations and direct contacts with both parents. Towards that end and in accordance with the obligation of States Parties under article 9, paragraph 1, States Parties shall respect the right of the child and his or her parents to leave any country, including their own, and to enter their own country. The right to leave any country shall be subject only to such restrictions as are prescribed by law and which are necessary to protect the national security, public order (ordre public), public health or morals or the rights and freedoms of others and are consistent with the other rights recognized in the present Convention.

Article 11

1. States Parties shall take measures to combat the illicit transfer and non-return of children abroad.
2. To this end, States Parties shall promote the conclusion of bilateral or multilateral agreements or accession to existing agreements.

Article 12

1. States Parties shall assure to the child who is capable of forming his or her own views the right to express those views freely in all matters affecting the child, the views of the child being given due weight in accordance with the age and maturity of the child.
2. For this purpose, the child shall in particular be provided the opportunity to be heard in any judicial and administrative

proceedings affecting the child, either directly, or through a representative or an appropriate body, in a manner consistent with the procedural rules of national law.

Article 13

1. The child shall have the right to freedom of expression; this right shall include freedom to seek, receive and impart information and ideas of all kinds, regardless of frontiers, either orally, in writing or in print, in the form of art, or through any other media of the child's choice.
2. The exercise of this right may be subject to certain restrictions, but these shall only be such as are provided by law and are necessary:
   (a) For respect of the rights or reputations of others; or
   (b) For the protection of national security or of public order (ordre public), or of public health or morals.

Article 14

1. States Parties shall respect the right of the child to freedom of thought, conscience and religion.
2. States Parties shall respect the rights and duties of the parents and, when applicable, legal guardians, to provide direction to the child in the exercise of his or her right in a manner consistent with the evolving capacities of the child.
3. Freedom to manifest one's religion or beliefs may be subject only to such limitations as are prescribed by law and are necessary to protect public safety, order, health or morals, or the fundamental rights and freedoms of others.

Article 15

1. States Parties recognize the rights of the child to freedom of association and to freedom of peaceful assembly.
2. No restrictions may be placed on the exercise of these rights other than those imposed in conformity with the law and which are necessary in a democratic society in the interests of national security or public safety, public order (ordre public), the protection of public health or morals or the protection of the rights and freedoms of others.

Article 16

1. No child shall be subjected to arbitrary or unlawful interference with his or her privacy, family, home or correspondence, nor to unlawful attacks on his or her honour and reputation.
2. The child has the right to the protection of the law against such interference or attacks.

Article 17

States Parties recognize the important function performed by the mass media and shall ensure that the child has access to information and material from a diversity of national and international sources, especially those aimed at the promotion of his or her social, spiritual and moral well-being and physical and mental health.

To this end, States Parties shall:

(a) Encourage the mass media to disseminate information and material of social and cultural benefit to the child and in accordance with the spirit of article 29;

(b) Encourage international co-operation in the production, exchange and dissemination of such information and material from a diversity of cultural, national and international sources;

(c) Encourage the production and dissemination of children's books;

(d) Encourage the mass media to have particular regard to the linguistic needs of the child who belongs to a minority group or who is indigenous;

(e) Encourage the development of appropriate guidelines for the protection of the child from information and material injurious to his or her well-being, bearing in mind the provisions of articles 13 and 18.

Article 18

1. States Parties shall use their best efforts to ensure recognition of the principle that both parents have common responsibilities for the upbringing and development of the child. Parents or, as the case may be, legal guardians, have the primary responsibility for the

upbringing and development of the child. The best interests of the child will be their basic concern.

2. For the purpose of guaranteeing and promoting the rights set forth in the present Convention, States Parties shall render appropriate assistance to parents and legal guardians in the performance of their child-rearing responsibilities and shall ensure the development of institutions, facilities and services for the care of children.
3. States Parties shall take all appropriate measures to ensure that children of working parents have the right to benefit from child-care services and facilities for which they are eligible.

Article 19

1. States Parties shall take all appropriate legislative, administrative, social and educational measures to protect the child from all forms of physical or mental violence, injury or abuse, neglect or negligent treatment, maltreatment or exploitation, including sexual abuse, while in the care of parent(s), legal guardian(s) or any other person who has the care of the child.
2. Such protective measures should, as appropriate, include effective procedures for the establishment of social programmes to provide necessary support for the child and for those who have the care of the child, as well as for other forms of prevention and for identification, reporting, referral, investigation, treatment and follow-up of instances of child maltreatment described heretofore, and, as appropriate, for judicial involvement.

Article 20

1. A child temporarily or permanently deprived of his or her family environment, or in whose own best interests cannot be allowed to remain in that environment, shall be entitled to special protection and assistance provided by the State.
2. States Parties shall in accordance with their national laws ensure alternative care for such a child.
3. Such care could include, inter alia, foster placement, kafalah of Islamic law, adoption or if necessary placement in suitable institutions for the care of children. When considering solutions,

due regard shall be paid to the desirability of continuity in a child's upbringing and to the child's ethnic, religious, cultural and linguistic background.

Article 21

States Parties that recognize and/or permit the system of adoption shall ensure that the best interests of the child shall be the paramount consideration and they shall:

(a) Ensure that the adoption of a child is authorized only by competent authorities who determine, in accordance with applicable law and procedures and on the basis of all pertinent and reliable information, that the adoption is permissible in view of the child's status concerning parents, relatives and legal guardians and that, if required, the persons concerned have given their informed consent to the adoption on the basis of such counselling as may be necessary;

(b) Recognize that inter-country adoption may be considered as an alternative means of child's care, if the child cannot be placed in a foster or an adoptive family or cannot in any suitable manner be cared for in the child's country of origin;

(c) Ensure that the child concerned by inter-country adoption enjoys safeguards and standards equivalent to those existing in the case of national adoption;

(d) Take all appropriate measures to ensure that, in inter-country adoption, the placement does not result in improper financial gain for those involved in it;

(e) Promote, where appropriate, the objectives of the present article by concluding bilateral or multilateral arrangements or agreements, and endeavour, within this framework, to ensure that the placement of the child in another country is carried out by competent authorities or organs.

Article 22

1. States Parties shall take appropriate measures to ensure that a child who is seeking refugee status or who is considered a refugee in accordance with applicable international or domestic law and

procedures shall, whether unaccompanied or accompanied by his or her parents or by any other person, receive appropriate protection and humanitarian assistance in the enjoyment of applicable rights set forth in the present Convention and in other international human rights or humanitarian instruments to which the said States are Parties.

2. For this purpose, States Parties shall provide, as they consider appropriate, co-operation in any efforts by the United Nations and other competent intergovernmental organizations or non-governmental organizations co-operating with the United Nations to protect and assist such a child and to trace the parents or other members of the family of any refugee child in order to obtain information necessary for reunification with his or her family. In cases where no parents or other members of the family can be found, the child shall be accorded the same protection as any other child permanently or temporarily deprived of his or her family environment for any reason, as set forth in the present Convention.

Article 23

1. States Parties recognize that a mentally or physically disabled child should enjoy a full and decent life, in conditions which ensure dignity, promote self-reliance and facilitate the child's active participation in the community.
2. States Parties recognize the right of the disabled child to special care and shall encourage and ensure the extension, subject to available resources, to the eligible child and those responsible for his or her care, of assistance for which application is made and which is appropriate to the child's condition and to the circumstances of the parents or others caring for the child.
3. Recognizing the special needs of a disabled child, assistance extended in accordance with paragraph 2 of the present article shall be provided free of charge, whenever possible, taking into account the financial resources of the parents or others caring for the child, and shall be designed to ensure that the disabled child has effective access to and receives education, training, health care services, rehabilitation services, preparation for employment and recreation opportunities in a manner conducive to the child's achieving the

fullest possible social integration and individual development, including his or her cultural and spiritual development.

4. States Parties shall promote, in the spirit of international cooperation, the exchange of appropriate information in the field of preventive health care and of medical, psychological and functional treatment of disabled children, including dissemination of and access to information concerning methods of rehabilitation, education and vocational services, with the aim of enabling States Parties to improve their capabilities and skills and to widen their experience in these areas. In this regard, particular account shall be taken of the needs of developing countries.

Article 24

1. States Parties recognize the right of the child to the enjoyment of the highest attainable standard of health and to facilities for the treatment of illness and rehabilitation of health. States Parties shall strive to ensure that no child is deprived of his or her right of access to such health care services.
2. States Parties shall pursue full implementation of this right and, in particular, shall take appropriate measures:
   (a) To diminish infant and child mortality;
   (b) To ensure the provision of necessary medical assistance and health care to all children with emphasis on the development of primary health care;
   (c) To combat disease and malnutrition, including within the framework of primary health care, through, inter alia, the application of readily available technology and through the provision of adequate nutritious foods and clean drinking-water, taking into consideration the dangers and risks of environmental pollution;
   (d) To ensure appropriate pre-natal and post-natal health care for mothers;
   (e) To ensure that all segments of society, in particular parents and children, are informed, have access to education and are supported in the use of basic knowledge of child health and nutrition, the advantages of breastfeeding, hygiene and environmental sanitation and the prevention of accidents;

(f) To develop preventive health care, guidance for parents and family planning education and services.

3. States Parties shall take all effective and appropriate measures with a view to abolishing traditional practices prejudicial to the health of children.
4. States Parties undertake to promote and encourage international co-operation with a view to achieving progressively the full realization of the right recognized in the present article. In this regard, particular account shall be taken of the needs of developing countries.

Article 25

States Parties recognize the right of a child who has been placed by the competent authorities for the purposes of care, protection or treatment of his or her physical or mental health, to a periodic review of the treatment provided to the child and all other circumstances relevant to his or her placement.

Article 26

1. States Parties shall recognize for every child the right to benefit from social security, including social insurance, and shall take the necessary measures to achieve the full realization of this right in accordance with their national law.
2. The benefits should, where appropriate, be granted, taking into account the resources and the circumstances of the child and persons having responsibility for the maintenance of the child, as well as any other consideration relevant to an application for benefits made by or on behalf of the child.

Article 27

1. States Parties recognize the right of every child to a standard of living adequate for the child's physical, mental, spiritual, moral and social development.
2. The parent(s) or others responsible for the child have the primary responsibility to secure, within their abilities and financial capacities, the conditions of living necessary for the child's development.

3. States Parties, in accordance with national conditions and within their means, shall take appropriate measures to assist parents and others responsible for the child to implement this right and shall in case of need provide material assistance and support programmes, particularly with regard to nutrition, clothing and housing.
4. States Parties shall take all appropriate measures to secure the recovery of maintenance for the child from the parents or other persons having financial responsibility for the child, both within the State Party and from abroad. In particular, where the person having financial responsibility for the child lives in a State different from that of the child, States Parties shall promote the accession to international agreements or the conclusion of such agreements, as well as the making of other appropriate arrangements.

Article 28

1. States Parties recognize the right of the child to education, and with a view to achieving this right progressively and on the basis of equal opportunity, they shall, in particular:
    (a) Make primary education compulsory and available free to all;
    (b) Encourage the development of different forms of secondary education, including general and vocational education, make them available and accessible to every child, and take appropriate measures such as the introduction of free education and offering financial assistance in case of need;
    (c) Make higher education accessible to all on the basis of capacity by every appropriate means;
    (d) Make educational and vocational information and guidance available and accessible to all children;
    (e) Take measures to encourage regular attendance at schools and the reduction of drop-out rates.
2. States Parties shall take all appropriate measures to ensure that school discipline is administered in a manner consistent with the child's human dignity and in conformity with the present Convention.
3. States Parties shall promote and encourage international cooperation in matters relating to education, in particular with a view to contributing to the elimination of ignorance and illiteracy throughout the world and facilitating access

to scientific and technical knowledge and modern teaching methods. In this regard, particular account shall be taken of the needs of developing countries.

Article 29

1. States Parties agree that the education of the child shall be directed to:
    (a) The development of the child's personality, talents and mental and physical abilities to their fullest potential;
    (b) The development of respect for human rights and fundamental freedoms, and for the principles enshrined in the Charter of the United Nations;
    (c) The development of respect for the child's parents, his or her own cultural identity, language and values, for the national values of the country in which the child is living, the country from which he or she may originate, and for civilizations different from his or her own;
    (d) The preparation of the child for responsible life in a free society, in the spirit of understanding, peace, tolerance, equality of sexes, and friendship among all peoples, ethnic, national and religious groups and persons of indigenous origin;
    (e) The development of respect for the natural environment.
2. No part of the present article or article 28 shall be construed so as to interfere with the liberty of individuals and bodies to establish and direct educational institutions, subject always to the observance of the principle set forth in paragraph 1 of the present article and to the requirements that the education given in such institutions shall conform to such minimum standards as may be laid down by the State.

Article 30

In those States in which ethnic, religious or linguistic minorities or persons of indigenous origin exist, a child belonging to such a minority or who is indigenous shall not be denied the right, in community with other members of his or her group, to enjoy his or her own culture, to profess and practise his or her own religion, or to use his or her own language.

Article 31

1. States Parties recognize the right of the child to rest and leisure, to engage in play and recreational activities appropriate to the age of the child and to participate freely in cultural life and the arts.
2. States Parties shall respect and promote the right of the child to participate fully in cultural and artistic life and shall encourage the provision of appropriate and equal opportunities for cultural, artistic, recreational and leisure activity.

Article 32

1. States Parties recognize the right of the child to be protected from economic exploitation and from performing any work that is likely to be hazardous or to interfere with the child's education, or to be harmful to the child's health or physical, mental, spiritual, moral or social development.
2. States Parties shall take legislative, administrative, social and educational measures to ensure the implementation of the present article. To this end, and having regard to the relevant provisions of other international instruments, States Parties shall in particular:
    (a) Provide for a minimum age or minimum ages for admission to employment;
    (b) Provide for appropriate regulation of the hours and conditions of employment;
    (c) Provide for appropriate penalties or other sanctions to ensure the effective enforcement of the present article.

Article 33

States Parties shall take all appropriate measures, including legislative, administrative, social and educational measures, to protect children from the illicit use of narcotic drugs and psychotropic substances as defined in the relevant international treaties, and to prevent the use of children in the illicit production and trafficking of such substances.

Article 34

States Parties undertake to protect the child from all forms of sexual exploitation and sexual abuse. For these purposes, States Parties shall in particular take all appropriate national, bilateral and multilateral measures to prevent:

(a) The inducement or coercion of a child to engage in any unlawful sexual activity;
(b) The exploitative use of children in prostitution or other unlawful sexual practices;
(c) The exploitative use of children in pornographic performances and materials.

Article 35

States Parties shall take all appropriate national, bilateral and multilateral measures to prevent the abduction of, the sale of or traffic in children for any purpose or in any form.

Article 36

States Parties shall protect the child against all other forms of exploitation prejudicial to any aspects of the child's welfare.

Article 37

States Parties shall ensure that:

(a) No child shall be subjected to torture or other cruel, inhuman or degrading treatment or punishment. Neither capital punishment nor life imprisonment without possibility of release shall be imposed for offences committed by persons below eighteen years of age;
(b) No child shall be deprived of his or her liberty unlawfully or arbitrarily. The arrest, detention or imprisonment of a child shall be in conformity with the law and shall be used only as a measure of last resort and for the shortest appropriate period of time;
(c) Every child deprived of liberty shall be treated with humanity and respect for the inherent dignity of the human person, and in a manner which takes into account the needs of persons of his or her age. In particular, every child deprived of liberty shall be separated from adults unless it is considered in the child's best interest not to do so and shall have the right to maintain contact with his

or her family through correspondence and visits, save in exceptional circumstances;

(a) Every child deprived of his or her liberty shall have the right to prompt access to legal and other appropriate assistance, as well as the right to challenge the legality of the deprivation of his or her liberty before a court or other competent, independent and impartial authority, and to a prompt decision on any such action.

Article 38

1. States Parties undertake to respect and to ensure respect for rules of international humanitarian law applicable to them in armed conflicts which are relevant to the child.
2. States Parties shall take all feasible measures to ensure that persons who have not attained the age of fifteen years do not take a direct part in hostilities.
3. States Parties shall refrain from recruiting any person who has not attained the age of fifteen years into their armed forces. In recruiting among those persons who have attained the age of fifteen years but who have not attained the age of eighteen years, States Parties shall endeavour to give priority to those who are oldest.
4. In accordance with their obligations under international humanitarian law to protect the civilian population in armed conflicts, States Parties shall take all feasible measures to ensure protection and care of children who are affected by an armed conflict.

Article 39

States Parties shall take all appropriate measures to promote physical and psychological recovery and social reintegration of a child victim of: any form of neglect, exploitation, or abuse; torture or any other form of cruel, inhuman or degrading treatment or punishment; or armed conflicts. Such recovery and reintegration shall take place in an environment which fosters the health, self-respect and dignity of the child.

Article 40

1. States Parties recognize the right of every child alleged as, accused of, or recognized as having infringed the penal law to be treated

in a manner consistent with the promotion of the child's sense of dignity and worth, which reinforces the child's respect for the human rights and fundamental freedoms of others and which takes into account the child's age and the desirability of promoting the child's reintegration and the child's assuming a constructive role in society.

2. To this end, and having regard to the relevant provisions of international instruments, States Parties shall, in particular, ensure that:
   (a) No child shall be alleged as, be accused of, or recognized as having infringed the penal law by reason of acts or omissions that were not prohibited by national or international law at the time they were committed;
   (b) Every child alleged as or accused of having infringed the penal law has at least the following guarantees:
      (i) To be presumed innocent until proven guilty according to law;
      (ii) To be informed promptly and directly of the charges against him or her, and, if appropriate, through his or her parents or legal guardians, and to have legal or other appropriate assistance in the preparation and presentation of his or her defence;
      (iii) To have the matter determined without delay by a competent, independent and impartial authority or judicial body in a fair hearing according to law, in the presence of legal or other appropriate assistance and, unless it is considered not to be in the best interest of the child, in particular, taking into account his or her age or situation, his or her parents or legal guardians;
      (iv) Not to be compelled to give testimony or to confess guilt; to examine or have examined adverse witnesses and to obtain the participation and examination of witnesses on his or her behalf under conditions of equality;
      (v) If considered to have infringed the penal law, to have this decision and any measures imposed

in consequence thereof reviewed by a higher competent, independent and impartial authority or judicial body according to law;

(vi) To have the free assistance of an interpreter if the child cannot understand or speak the language used;

(vii) To have his or her privacy fully respected at all stages of the proceedings.

3. States Parties shall seek to promote the establishment of laws, procedures, authorities and institutions specifically applicable to children alleged as, accused of, or recognized as having infringed the penal law, and, in particular:

(a) The establishment of a minimum age below which children shall be presumed not to have the capacity to infringe the penal law;

(b) Whenever appropriate and desirable, measures for dealing with such children without resorting to judicial proceedings, providing that human rights and legal safeguards are fully respected. 4. A variety of dispositions, such as care, guidance and supervision orders; counselling; probation; foster care; education and vocational training programmes and other alternatives to institutional care shall be available to ensure that children are dealt with in a manner appropriate to their well-being and proportionate both to their circumstances and the offence.

Article 41

Nothing in the present Convention shall affect any provisions which are more conducive to the realization of the rights of the child and which may be contained in:

(c) The law of a State party; or

(d) International law in force for that State.

BIBLIOGRAPHY

Afifi, Tracie O. “Considerations for Expanding the Definition of ACES.” In *Adverse Childhood Experiences: Using Evidence to Advance Research, Practice, Policy, and Prevention*, edited by Gordon J.G. Asmundson and Tracie O. Afifi. Elsevier, 2020.

Afifi, Tracy O., Derek Ford, Elizabeth T. Gershoff, et al. “Spanking and Adult Mental Health Impairment: The Case for the Designation of Spanking as an Adverse Childhood Experience.” *Child Abuse & Neglect* 71 (2017): 24–31. https://doi.org/10.1016/j.chiabu.2017.01.014.

Afifi, Tracie O., Janique Fortier, Jitender Sareen, and Tamara Taillieu. “Associations of Harsh Physical Punishment and Child Maltreatment in Childhood with Antisocial Behaviors in Adulthood.” *JAMA Network Open* 2, no. 1 (2019): e187374. https://doi.org/10.1001/jamanetworkopen.2018.7374.

Afifi, Tracie O., Natalie P. Mota, Patricia Dasiewicz, Harriet L. MacMillan, and Jitender Sareen. “Physical Punishment and Mental Disorders: Results from a Nationally Representative US Sample.” *Pediatrics* 130, no. 2 (2012): 184–92. https://doi.org/10.1542/peds.2011–2947.

Afifi, Tracie O., Samantha Salmon, Ashley Stewart-Tufescu, et al. “Associations Between Spanking Beliefs and Reported Spanking Among Adolescents-Parent/Caregiver Dyads in a Canadian Sample.” *BMC Public Health* 22, no. 493 (2022). https://doi.org/10.1186/s12889-022-12856-z.

Alaggia, Ramona, and Cathy Vine, eds. *Cruel but Not Unusual: Violence in Canadian Families.* Wilfrid Laurier University Press, 2006.

Anand, Sanjeev. “Reasonable Chastisement: A Critique of the Supreme Court of Canada’s Decision in the ‘Spanking’ Case.” *Alberta Law Review* 41, no. 4 (2004): 871–78. https://canlii.ca/t/2d7z.

Anda, Robert F., Maxia Dong, David W. Brown, et al. "The Relationship of Adverse Childhood Experiences to a History of Premature Death of Family Members." *BMC Public Health* 9, no. 106 (2009). https://doi.org/10.1186/1471-2458-9-106.

Andero, Abraham A., and Allen Stewart. "Issue of Corporal Punishment: Re-Examined." *Journal of Instructional Psychology* 29, no 2 (2002): 90–97.

Antwi-Boasiako, Kofi, Barbara Fallon, Bryn King, Nico Trocmé, and John Fluke. "Understanding the Overrepresentation of Black Children in Ontario's Child Welfare System: Perspectives from Child Welfare Workers and Community Service Providers," *Child Abuse & Neglect* 123 (2022): 105425. https://doi.org/10.1016/j.chiabu.2021.105425.

Archard, David. *Children: Rights and Childhood.* 3rd ed. Routledge, 2015.

Asmundson, Gordon J.G., and Tracie O. Afifi, eds. *Adverse Childhood Experiences: Using Evidence to Advance Research, Practice, Policy, and Prevention.* Elsevier, 2020.

Bagnell, Kenneth. *The Little Immigrants: The Orphans Who Came to Canada.* Dundurn Press, 2001.

Bala, Nicholas, Michael Kim Zapf, R. James Williams, Robin Vogl, and Joseph P. Hornick, eds. *Canadian Child Welfare Law: Children, Families and the State.* 2nd ed. Thompson Educational Publishing, 2004.

Baumrind, Diana, Robert E. Larzelere, and Philip A. Cowan. "Ordinary Physical Punishment: Is It Harmful? Comment on Gershoff." *Psychological Bulletin* 128, no. 4 (2002): 580–89. https://doi.org/10.1037/0033-2909.128.4.580.

Berlin, Lisa J., Jean M. Ispa, Mark A. Fine, et al. "Correlates and Consequences of Spanking and Verbal Punishment for Low-Income White, African American, and Mexican American Toddlers." *Child Development* 80, no. 5 (2009): 1403–20. https://doi.org/10.1111/j.1467-8624.2009.01341.x.

Bitensky, Susan H. *Corporal Punishment of Children: A Human Rights Violation.* Transnational Publishers, 2006.

Blackstone, William. *Commentaries on the Laws of England 1705–1769*, vol. 1. 15th ed. London, 1809.

Bomysoad, Rachel N., and Lori A. Francis. "Adverse Childhood Experiences and Mental Health Conditions Among Adolescents." *Journal of Adolescent Health* 67, no. 6 (2020): 868–70.

Bonnie, Nicole, and Keishia Facey. *Ontario Incidence Study of Reported Child Abuse and Neglect 2018: Understanding the Over-Representation of Black Children in Ontario Child Services.* Child Welfare Research Portal, 2022. https://www.oacas.org/wp-content/uploads/2022/06/Black-Children-in-Care-OIS-Report-2022-Final.pdf.

Bouvier, Rita. "remembering Charlie." In *nakamowin'sa for the seasons.* Thistledown Press, 2015.

Brown, Alan S., George W. Holden, and Rose Ashraf. "Spank, Slap or Hit? How Labels Alter Perceptions of Child Discipline." *Psychology of Violence* 8, no. 1 (2018): 1–9. https://doi.org/10.1037/vio0000080.

Burt, S. Alexandra, D. Angus Clark, Elizabeth T. Gershoff, Kelly L. Klump, and Luke W. Hyde. "Twin Differences in Harsh Parenting Predict Youth's Antisocial Behavior." *Psychological Science* 32, no. 3 (2021): 395–409. https://doi.org/10.1177/0956797620968532.

Bussman, Kai-D. "Germany: Background and Legal Consequences of the Right to Be Raised Without Violence." In *Global Pathways to Abolishing Physical Punishment: Realizing Children's Rights*, edited by Joan E. Durrant and Anne B. Smith. Routledge, 2011.

Butler, Samuel. "Part II, Canto I." *Hudibras, in Three Parts, Written in the Time of the Late Wars.* Project Gutenberg. Text scanned from edition published in 1805. http://www.gutenberg.org/ebooks/4937.

Canada Family Action. "About Us: Over 20 Years of Getting Results for Canadian Families." https://www.familyaction.ca/about-us/.

Canadian Charter of Rights and Freedoms, as enacted by *Canada Act, 1982*, (UK), 1982 c.11.

Canadian Press. "'I Am Deeply Sorry': Full Text of Residential School Apology from Pope Francis." *CBC News*, July 25, 2022. https://www.cbc.ca/news/canada/edmonton/pope-francis-maskwacis-apology-full-text-1.6531341.

Carter, Mark. "Constitutional Validity of the Corporal Punishment Defence in Canada: A Critical Analysis of Canadian Foundation for Children, Youth and the Law versus Canada (Attorney General)." *International Journal of Victimology* 12, no. 2 (2005): 189–211. https://www.ojp.gov/ncjrs/virtual-library/abstracts/constitutional-validity-corporal-punishment-defence-canada-critical.

Carter, Mark. "Fundamentally Flawed: The Arbitrariness of the Corporal Punishment Defence." *Manitoba Law Journal* 44, no. 4 (2021). https://doi.org/10.29173/mlj1285.

CBC News. "British PM Apologizes to 'Home Children.'" February 24, 2010. http://www.cbc.ca/world/story/2010/02/24/britain-home-children-apology.html.

CBC News. "Pope Francis Apologizes for Forced Assimilation of Indigenous Children at Residential Schools." July 25, 2022. https://www.cbc.ca/news/canada/edmonton/edmonton-pope-alberta-apology-1.6530947.

Centre of Excellence for Child Welfare. "About Us." https://cwrp.ca/about-us.

Chapman, Pamela A. "The Politics of Judging: Section 1 of the *Charter of Rights and Freedoms*." *Osgoode Hall Law Journal* 24, no. 4 (1986): 867–96. https://doi.org/10.60082/2817-5069.1854.

Child and Family Services Act, RSS. 1989–90, c. C-7.2.

Children's Protection Act, S.O. 1893, c. 45.

Clément, Marie Ève, and Claire Chamberland. "Physical Violence and Psychological Aggression Towards Children: Five-Year Trends in Practices and Attitudes from Two Populations Surveys." *Child Abuse & Neglect* 31, no. 9 (2007): 1001–11. https://doi.org/10.1016/j.chiabu.2007.04.005.

CHEO. "Rationale for Repeal of Section 43 of Canada's Criminal Code." March 2023. http://js-advocacy.ca/pdf/JS_repeal_43_rationale_EN.pdf.

CHEO. "Joint Statement on Physical Punishment of Children and Youth." About Us: Advocacy—Physical Punishment. https://www.cheo.on.ca/en/about-us/physical-punishment.aspx.

Collins, Vicky. "Children Reject Smacking." *Herald*, February 21, 2002.

Committee on the Rights of the Child. "Concluding Observations on the Combined Third and Fourth Periodic Report of Canada, Adopted by the Committee at Its Sixty-First Session (17 September–5 October 2012) " CRC/C/Can/CO/3–4, 45. October 5, 2012.

Committee on the Rights of the Child. CRC/C/15/Add.215. October 27, 2003.

Committee on the Rights of the Child. *Report Adopted by the Committee at Its 209th Meeting on January 1995*, Eighth Session, CRC/C/38. January 1995.

Committee on the Rights of the Child. "Sixty First Session: Concluding Observations: Canada." CRC.C/CAN/CO/3–4. October 5, 2012.

Condon, Richard. *Inuit Youth: Growth and Change in the Canadian Arctic*. Rutgers University Press, 1988.

Convention on the Rights of the Child, (1989), UN Doc. A/RES/44/25 (1989).

Criminal Code of Canada, RSC 1985, c. C-46. https://laws-lois.justice.gc.ca/eng/acts/c-46/.

Cuartas, Jorge. "The Effect of Spanking on Early Social/Emotional Skills." *Child Development* 93, no. 1 (2021): 180–93. https://doi.org/10.1111/cdev.13646.

Cuartas, Jorge, Dana Charles McCoy, Andrew Grogan-Kaylor, and Elizabeth Gershoff. "Physical Punishment as a Predictor of Early Cognitive Development: Evidence from Econometric Approaches." *Developmental Psychology* 56, no. 11 (2020): 2013–26. https://doi.org/10.1037/dev0001114.

Cuartas, Jorge, David G. Weissman, Margaret A. Sheridan, Liliana Lengua, and Katie A. McLaughlin. "Corporal Punishment and Elevated Neural Response to Threat in Children." *Child Development* 92, no. 3 (2021): 821–32. https://doi.org/10.1111/cdev.13565.

CYC. "Prohibition of Corporal Punishment: An International Overview." CYC-Net, February 2006. https://cyc-net.org/cyc-online/cycol-0206-article19.html.

Daiute, Colette. "The Rights of Children, the Rights of Nations: Developmental Theory and the Politics of Children's Rights." *Journal of Social Issues* 64, no. 4 (2008): 701–23. https://doi.org/10.1111/j.1540-4560.2008.00585.x.

Daschuk, James. *Clearing the Plains: Disease, Politics of Starvation, and the Loss of Aboriginal Life.* University of Regina Press, 2013.

Davin, Nicholas Flood. *Report on Industrial Schools for Indians and Half-Breeds.* Ottawa, 1879.

Davison Hunter, James. *Culture Wars: The Struggle to Define America.* Basic Books, 1991.

deMause, Lloyd, ed. *The History of Childhood.* Souvenir Press, 1976.

Dickson, Courtney, and Bridgette Watson. "Remains of 215 Children Found Buried at Former B.C. Residential School, First Nation Says." *CBC News*, May 21, 2021. https://www.cbc.ca/news/canada/british-columbia/tk-eml%C3%BAps-te-secw%C3%A9pemc-215-children-former-kamloops-indian-residential-school-1.6043778.

Dobson, James. *Dare to Discipline.* Tyndale House Publishers, 1988.

Donnelly, Michael. "Putting Corporal Punishment of Children in Historical Perspective." In *Corporal Punishment of Children in Theoretical Perspective*, edited by Michael Donnelly and Murray A. Straus. Yale University Press, 2005.

Dornstauder, Frank, and David Macknak. "100 Years of Child Welfare in Saskatchewan: A Survey." Saskatchewan Association of Social Workers, 2009. http://www.sasw.ca/CW/100-ChildWelfarePaper.pdf.

Douglas, Emily M., and Murray A. Straus. "Assault and Injury of Dating Partners by University Students in 19 Countries and Its Relation to Corporal Punishment Experienced as a Child." *European Journal of Criminology* 3, no. 3 (2006): 293–318. https://doi.org/10.1177/1477370806065584.

Durrant, Joan E. "Corporal Punishment: A Violation of the Rights of the Child." In *A Question of Commitment: Children's Rights in Canada*, edited by R. Brian Howe and Katherine Covell. Wilfrid Laurier University Press, 2007.

Durrant, Joan E. "Corporal Punishment and the Law in Global Perspective." In *The Oxford Handbook of Children and the Law*, edited by James G. Dwyer. Oxford University Press, 2020.

Durrant, Joan E. "The Empirical Rationale for Eliminating Physical Punishment." In *Global Pathways to Abolishing Physical Punishment:*

Realizing Children's Rights, edited by Joan E. Durrant and Anne B. Smith. Routledge, 2011.

Durrant, Joan E. "Evaluating the Success of Sweden's Corporal Punishment Ban." *Child Abuse & Neglect* 23, no. 5 (1999): 435–48. https://doi.org/10.1016/s0145-2134(99)00021-6.

Durrant, Joan E. *Positive Discipline in Everyday Parenting*. 4th ed. Save the Children, 2021. http://js-advocacy.ca/pdf/JS_Positive_Discipline_English_4th_edition.pdf.

Durrant, Joan E., and Anne B. Smith, eds. *Global Pathways to Abolishing Physical Punishment: Realizing Children's Rights*. Routledge, 2011.

Durrant, Joan E., and Ron Ensom. *Joint Statement on Physical Punishment of Children and Youth*. Coalition on Physical Punishment of Children and Youth, 2004. http://js-advocacy.ca/pdf/joint_statement_e.pdf.

Durrant, Joan E., and Ron Ensom. "Physical Punishment of Children: Lessons from 20 Years of Research." *Canadian Medical Association Journal* 184, no. 12 (2012): 1373–77. https://doi.org/10.1503/cmaj.101314.

Durrant, Joan E., and Ron Ensom. "Twenty-Five Years of Physical Punishment Research: What Have We Learned?" *Journal of the Korean Academy of Child and Adolescent Psychiatry* 28, no. 1 (2017): 20–24. https://doi.org/10.5765/jkacap.2017.28.1.20.

Durrant, Joan E., Ashley Stewart-Tufescu, and Tracie O. Afifi. "Recognizing the Child's Right to Protection from Physical Violence: An Update on Progress and a Call to Action." *Child Abuse & Neglect* 110, Pt. 1 (2020): 104297. https://doi.org/10.1016/j.chiabu.2019.104297.

Durrant, Joan E., Dominique Pierre Plateau, Christine Ateah, et al. "Preventing Punitive Violence: Preliminary Data on the Positive Discipline in Everyday Parenting (PDEP) Program." *Canadian Journal of Community Mental Health* 33, no. 2 (2014): 109–25. https://doi.org/10.7870/cjcmh-2014-018.

Durrant, Joan E., Elif Acar, Justin McNeil, Ailsa M. Watkinson, and Anne McGillivray. "Predicting Adults' Approval of Physical Punishment from Their Perceptions of Their Childhood Experiences." *International Journal of Child, Youth & Family Studies* 8, no. 3/4 (2017): 127–53. https://doi.org/10.18357/ijcyfs83/4201718074.

Durrant, Joan E., et al. "'It Didn't Do Me Any Harm': Explaining the Intergenerational Transmission of Approval of Child Physical Punishment in Canada." *International Journal of Victimology* (forthcoming).

Durrant, Joan E., Nadine Sigvaldason, and Lisa Bednar. "What Did the Canadian Public Learn from the 2004 Supreme Court Decision on

Physical Punishment?" *International Journal of Children's Rights* 16 (2008): 229–47.

Durrant, Joan E., Nico Trocmé, Barbara Fallon, Cheryl Milne, and Tara Black. "Protection of Children from Physical Maltreatment in Canada: An Evaluation of the Supreme Court's Definition of Reasonable Force." *Journal of Aggression, Maltreatment & Trauma* 18, no. 1 (2009): 64–87. https://doi.org/10.1080/10926770802610640.

Durrant, Joan E., Nico Trocmé, Barbara Fallon, Tara Black, and Della Knoke. "Punitive Violence Against Children in Canada." *CECW Information*, no. 41E (2006). https://cwrp.ca/sites/default/files/publications/en/PunitiveViolence41E.pdf.

Dussich, John P.J., and Chie Maekoya. "Physical Child Harm and Bullying-Related Behaviors: A Comparative Study in Japan, South Africa and the United States." *International Journal of Offender Therapy and Comparative Criminology* 51, no. 5 (2007): 495–509. https://doi.org/10.1177/0306624X06298463.

Ellison, Christopher G., and Matt Bradshaw. "Religious Beliefs, Sociopolitical Ideology, and Attitudes Toward Corporal Punishment." *Journal of Family Issues* 30, no. 3 (2009): 320–40. https://doi.org/10.1177/0192513X08326331.

Ember, Carol R., and Melvin Ember. "Explaining Corporal Punishment of Children: A Cross-Cultural Study." *American Anthropologist* 107, no. 4 (2005): 609–19. https://www.jstor.org/stable/3567379.

Eneas, Bryan. "Sask. First Nation Announces Discovery of 751 Unmarked Graves Near Former Residential School." *CBC News*, June 24, 2021. https://www.cbc.ca/news/canada/saskatchewan/cowessess-marieval-indian-residential-school-news-1.6078375.

Ensom, Ron. "Submission to the Standing Committee on Justice and Human Rights, House of Commons." Ensom & Associates, April 14, 2014.

Fallon, Barbara, Nico Trocmé, Tara Black, et al. "Denouncing the Continued Overrepresentation of First Nations Children in Canadian Child Welfare: Findings from the First Nations/Canadian Incidence Study of Reported Child Abuse and Neglect—2019." Assembly of First Nations, 2019. https://cwrp.ca/publications/denouncing-continued-overrepresentation-first-nations-children-canadian-child-welfare.

Faraday, Fay, Margaret Denike, and M. Kate Stephenson, eds. *Making Equality Rights Real: Securing Substantive Equality under the Charter*. Irwin Law, 2006.

Felitti, Vincent J., Robert F. Anda, Dale Nordenberg, et al. "Relationship of Childhood Abuse and Household Dysfunction to Many of the Leading Causes of Death in Adults: The Adverse Childhood Experiences (ACE)

Study." *American Journal of Preventative Medicine* 14, no. 4 (1998): 245–58. https://doi.org/10.1016/s0749-3797(98)00017-8.

Fletcher, John. "Positive Parenting, Not Physical Punishment." *Canadian Medical Association Journal* 184, no. 12 (2012): 1339. https://doi.org/10.1503/cmaj.121070.

Fortier, Janique, Ashley Stewart-Tufesco, Tracie O. Afifi, et al. "Associations Between Lifetime Spanking/Slapping and Adolescent Physical and Mental Health and Behavioral Outcomes." *Canadian Journal of Psychiatry* 67, no. 4 (2022): 280–88. https://doi.org/10.1177/07067437211000632.

Fortin, Jane. *Children's Rights and the Developing Law*. 3rd ed. Cambridge University Press, 2009.

Fournier, Suzanne, and Ernie Crey. *Stolen from Our Embrace: The Abduction of First Nations Children and the Restoration of Aboriginal Communities*. Douglas & McIntyre, 1997.

Fréchette, Sabrina, and Elisa Romano. "Change in Corporal Punishment Over Time in a Representative Sample of Canadian Parents." *Journal of Family Psychology* 29, no. 4 (2015): 507–17. http://dx.doi.org/10.1037/fam0000104.

Fryer, Sara, and Marlisa Tiedemann. "Bill C-92: An Act Respecting First Nations, Inuit and Métis Children, Youth and Families." Legislative Summary. November 7, 2019. https://lop.parl.ca/staticfiles/PublicWebsite/Home/ResearchPublications/LegislativeSummaries/PDF/42-1/42-1-c92-e.pdf.

Fuller, Jason M. "The Science and Statistics Behind Spanking Suggest That Laws Allowing Corporal Punishment Are in the Best Interests of the Child." *Akron Law Review* 42, no. 243 (2009): 243–74. https://ideaexchange.uakron.edu/cgi/viewcontent.cgi?article=1192&context=akronlawreview.

Garbarino, James. "Corporal Punishment in Ecological Perspective." In *Corporal Punishment of Children in Theoretical Perspective*, edited by Michael Donnelly and Murray A. Straus. Yale University Press, 2005.

Gershoff, Elizabeth T. "Corporal Punishment by Parents and Associated Child Behaviors and Experiences: A Meta-Analytic and Theoretical Review." *Psychological Bulletin* 128, no. 4 (2002): 529–79. http://dx.doi.org/10.1037/0033-2909.128.4.539.

Gershoff, Elizabeth T. "More Harm Than Good: A Summary of Scientific Research on the Intended and Unintended Effects of Corporal Punishment on Children." *Law and Contemporary Problems* 73, no. 2 (2010): 31–56. https://pmc.ncbi.nlm.nih.gov/articles/pmc8386132.

Gershoff, Elizabeth T., and Andrew Grogan-Kaylor. "Spanking and Child Outcomes: Old Controversies and New Meta-Analyses." *Journal of Family Psychology* 30, no. 4 (2016). 453–69. https://doi.org/10.1037/fam0000191.

Gershoff, Elizabeth T., Shawna J. Lee, and Joan E. Durrant. "Promising Intervention Strategies to Reduce Parents' Use of Physical Punishment." *Child Abuse & Neglect* 71 (2017): 9–23. https://doi.org/10.1016/j.chiabu.2017.01.017.

Gracia, Enrique, and Juan Herrero. "Beliefs in the Necessity of Corporal Punishment of Children and Public Perceptions of Child Physical Abuse as a Social Problem." *Child Abuse & Neglect* 32, no. 11 (2008): 1058–62. https://doi.org/10.1016/j.chiabu.2008.05.004.

Green, Ross Gordon, and Kearney Healy. *Tough on Kids: Rethinking Approaches to Youth Justice*. Purich Publishing, 2003.

Greven, Philip. *Spare the Child: The Religious Roots of Punishment and the Psychological Impact of Physical Abuse*. Alfred A. Nephew, 1991.

Grogan-Kaylor, Andrew. "The Effect of Corporal Punishment on Antisocial Behavior in Children." *Social Work Research* 28, no. 3 (2004): 153–62. https://doi.org/10.1093/swr/28.3.153.

Gunter, Lorne. "Kill the Court Challenges Program." *National Post*, September 8, 2006. https://www.pressreader.com/canada/national-post-latest-edition/20060908/281788509540028?srsltid=AfmBOop62AJybO_UecboKQJJUjj9kCo7lBVNb27x82jc7hd5EwMgybGA.

Hammarberg, Thomas. "The UN *Convention on the Rights of the Child*—and How to Make It Work." *Human Rights Quarterly* 12, no. 1 (1990): 97–105.

Heilmann, Anja, Anita Mehay, Richard G. Watt, et al. "Physical Punishment and Child Outcomes: A Narrative Review of Prospective Studies." *Lancet* 398, no. 10297 (2021): 355–64. https://doi.org/10.1016/S0140-6736(21)00582-1.

Heywood, Colin. *A History of Childhood: Children and Childhood in the West from Medieval to Modern Times*. Polity Press, 2001.

Howe, R. Brian, and Katherine Covell, eds. *A Question of Commitment: Children's Rights in Canada*. Wilfrid Laurier University Press, 2007.

Husa, Sari. "Finland Children's Right to Protection." In *Global Pathways to Abolishing Physical Punishment: Realizing Children's Rights*, edited by Joan E. Durrant and Anne B. Smith. Routledge, 2011.

INAC File 1/25-1Vol. 15, L. Vankoughnet to Sir John A. Macdonald. August 26, 1887.

Indian Act, RSC, (1985). c I-5.

International NGO Council on Violence Against Children. *Violating Children's Rights: Harmful Practices Based on Tradition, Culture, Religion or Superstition*. 2012. https://resourcecentre.savethechildren.net/pdf/7212.pdf.

Jack, Susan, Catharine Munn, Chiachen Cheng, and Harriet MacMillan. *Child Maltreatment in Canada: Overview Paper*. National Clearinghouse on Family Violence, Public Health Agency of Canada, 2006. https://www.

canada.ca/content/dam/phac-aspc/migration/phac-aspc/sfv-avf/sources/nfnts/nfnts-2006-maltr/assets/pdf/nfnts-2006-maltr-eng.pdf.

Jaffee, Sara R., and Cindy W. Christian. "The Biological Embedding of Child Abuse and Neglect: Implications for Policy and Practice." *Society for Research in Child Development* 28, no. 1 (2014). https://www.srcd.org/sites/default/files/file-attachments/spr_28_1_newfinal.pdf.

Janson, Staffan, Bodil Langberg, and Birgitta Svensson. "Sweden: A 30-Year Ban on Physical Punishment of Children." In *Global Pathways to Abolishing Physical Punishment: Realizing Children's Rights*, edited by Joan E. Durrant and Anne B. Smith. Routledge, 2011.

Joel-Hanson, Michael. "John Olubobokun Guilty of Assaulting Former Christian School Students with a Paddle." *Saskatoon Star Phoenix*, July 21, 2025. https://thestarphoenix.com/news/local-news/john-olubobokun-guilty-of-assaulting-former-christian-school-students-with-paddle

Kempe, C. Henry, Frederic N. Silverman, Brandt F. Steele, William Droegemueller, and Henry K. Silver. "The Battered-Child Syndrome." *Journal of American Medical Association* 181, no. 1 (1962): 17–24.

Landau, Tammy. "Policing the Punishment: Charging Practices Under Canada's Corporal Punishment Laws." *International Review of Victimology* 12, no. 2 (2005): 121–38. https://doi.org/10.1177/026975800501200202.

Lansford, Jennifer E., and Kenneth A. Dodge. "Cultural Norms for Adult Corporal Punishment of Children and Societal Rates of Endorsement and Use of Violence." *Parenting: Science and Practice* 8, no. 3 (2008): 257–70. https://doi.org/10.1080/15295190802204843.

Larzelere, Robert E., and Diana Baumrind. "Are Spanking Injunctions Scientifically Supported?" *Law and Contemporary Problems* 73, no. 2 (2010): 57–87. https://scholarship.law.duke.edu/cgi/viewcontent.cgi?article=1566&context=lcp.

Larzelere, Robert E., Ronald B. Cox Jr., and Gail L. Smith. "Do Nonphysical Punishments Reduce Antisocial Behavior More Than Spanking? A Comparison Using the Strongest Previous Causal Evidence Against Spanking." *BMC Pediatrics* 10, no. 1 (2010). https://doi.org/10.1186/1471-2431-10-10.

Larzelere, Robert E., Marjorie Lindner Gunnoe, and Christopher J. Ferguson. "Improving Causal Inferences in Meta-Analyses of Longitudinal Studies: Spanking as an Illustration." *Child Development* 89, no. 6 (2018): 2038–50. https://doi.org/10.1111/cdev.13097.

Latimer, Kendall, and Jessie Anton, "Sask. Christian School Coach Who Sexually Exploited, Assaulted Teen Taken Into Custody Ahead of

Sentencing." *CBC News*, January 4, 2024. https://www.cbc.ca/news/canada/saskatoon/aaron-benneweis-sentencing-arguments-legacy-christian-academy-1.7073564

Law Commission of Canada. *What Is a Crime? Challenges and Alternatives.* Government of Canada, 2003. https://www.canada.ca/content/dam/lcc-cdc/documents/lcc-archives-discussion-papers/JL2-21-2003E.pdf.

Lyman, Richard B. "Barbarism and Religion: Late Roman and Early Medieval Childhood." In *The History of Childhood*, edited by Lloyd deMause. Souvenir Press, 1976.

Ma, Julie, Yoonsun Han, Andrew Grogan-Kaylor, Jorge Delva, and Marcela Castillo. "Corporal Punishment and Youth Externalizing Behavior in Santiago, Chile." *Child Abuse & Neglect* 4, no. 36 (2012): 481–90. https://doi.org/10.1016/j.chiabu.2012.03.006.

MacDonald, Mark Bishop, Bishop Riscylla Walsh Shaw, Dr. John H. Young, et al. "A Christian Theological Statement in Support of the Truth and Reconciliation Commission's' Call to Action 6." In *Decolonizing Discipline: Children, Corporal Punishment, Christian Theologies, and Reconciliation*, edited by Valerie E. Michaelson and Joan E. Durrant. University of Manitoba Press, 2020. https://doi.org/10.1515/9780887558672-004.

Maclean's. "Spare the Rod, Spoil the Child?" March 10, 1997. https://www.corpun.com/casc9703.htm.

Mandelbaum, David G. *The Plains Cree: An Ethnographic, Historical, and Comparative Study*. Canadian Plains Research Center, 1979.

Manuel, Arthur, and Grand Chief Ronald M. Derrickson. *Unsettling Canada: A National Wake-Up Call.* Between the Lines, 2015.

Manuel, George, and Michael Posluns. *The Fourth World: An Indian Reality.* Collier-Macmillan Canada, 1974.

Massetti, Greta M., Karen Hughes, Mark A. Bellis, and James Mercy. "Global Perspective on ACES." In *Adverse Childhood Experiences: Using Evidence to Advance Research, Practice, Policy and Prevention*, edited by Gordon J. G. Asmundson and Tracie O. Afifi. Elsevier, 2020. https://doi.org/10.1016/B978-0-12-816065-7.00011-2.

McAdam, Bre. "Assault Charges Withdrawn Against Saskatoon Legacy Christian Employee." *Saskatoon Star Phoenix*, November 18, 2024. https://thestarphoenix.com/news/crime/assault-charge-withdrawn-against-saskatoon-legacy-christian-employee.

McAdam, Bre. "Former Christian School Principal Convicted of One of Four Historical Assault Charges." *Saskatoon Star Phoenix*, May 22, 2025. https://thestarphoenix.com/news/crime/duff-friesen-verdict.

McAdam, Bre. "Olubobokun Denies Paddling Nine Students While Director of Saskatoon Private Christian School." *Saskatoon Star Phoenix*, March 11, 2025. https://thestarphoenix.com/news/crime/olubobokun-denies-paddling-nine-students-while-director-of-saskatoon-private-christian-school.

McAdam, Sylvia (Saysewahum). *Nationhood Interrupted: Revitalizing nêhiyaw Legal Systems.* Purich Publishing, 2015.

McDonald, Marci. *The Armageddon Factor: The Rise of Christian Nationalism in Canada.* Random House Canada, 2010.

McEwen, Bruce S. "Understanding the Potency of Stressful Early Life Experiences on Brain and Body Function." *Metabolism: Clinical and Experimental* 57, no. 2 (2008): S11–S15. https://doi.org/10.1016/j.metabol.2008.07.006.

McGillivray, Anne. "Child Physical Assault: Law, Equality and Intervention." *Manitoba Law Journal* 30, no. 2 (2004): 133–70.

McGillivray, Anne. "'He'll Learn It on His Body': Disciplining Childhood in Canadian Law." *International Journal of Children's Rights* 5, no. 2 (1998): 193–242. https://doi.org/10.1163/15718189720493627.

McGillivray, Anne. "Nowhere to Stand: Correction by Force in the Supreme Court of Canada." In *Children and the Law: Essays in Honour of Professor Nicholas Bala*, edited by Sanjeev Anand. Irwin Law, 2011.

McGillivray, Anne, and Joan E. Durrant. "Child Corporal Punishment: Violence, Law and Rights." In *Cruel but Not Unusual: Violence in Canadian Families*, edited by Ramona Alaggia and Cathy Vine. Wilfrid Laurier University Press, 2006.

McGillivray, Anne, and Cheryl Milne. "Canada: The Rocky Road of Repeal." In *Global Pathways to Abolishing Physical Punishment: Realizing Children's Rights*, edited by Joan E. Durrant and Anne B. Smith. Routledge, 2011.

McIntyre, Sheila. "Answering the Siren Call of Abstract Formalism with the Subjects and Verbs of Domination." In *Making Equality Rights Real: Securing Substantive Equality Under the Charter*, edited by Fay Faraday, Margaret Denike, and M. Kate Stephenson. Irwin Law, 2006.

Mersky, J.P., J. Topitzes, and A.J. Reynolds. "Impacts of Adverse Childhood Experiences on Health, Mental Health, and Substance Use in Early Adulthood: A Cohort Study of an Urban, Minority Sample in the U.S." *Child Abuse & Neglect* 37, no. 11 (2013): 917–25. https://doi.org/10.1016/j.chiabu.2013.07.011.

Michaelson, Valerie E. "Lies That Have Shaped Us: Racism, Violence and Ageism in Canadian Churches." In *Decolonizing Discipline: Children, Corporal Punishment, Christian Theologies, and Reconciliation*, edited by

Valerie E. Michaelson and Joan E. Durrant. University of Manitoba Press, 2020. https://doi.org/10.1515/9780887558672-008.

Miller, Alice. *For Your Own Good: Hidden Cruelty in Child Rearing and the Root of Violence.* Translated by Hildegarde Hannum and Hunter Hannum. Farrar, Straus and Giroux, 1990.

Miller, J.R. *Shingwauk's Vision: A History of Native Residential Schools.* University of Toronto Press, 1996.

Milloy, John S. *A National Crime: The Canadian Government and the Residential School System, 1879 to 1986.* University of Manitoba Press, 1999.

Milne, Cheryl. *A Brief Submitted to the Standing Committee on Justice and Human Rights House of Commons: Regarding Bill C-273, an Act to Amend the Criminal Code of Canada.* David Asper Centre for Constitutional Rights.

Mohr, Wanda K., Theodore A. Petti, and Brian D. Mohr. "Adverse Effects Associated with Physical Restraint." *The Canadian Journal of Psychiatry* 48, no. 5 (2003): 330–37. https://doi.org/10.1177/070674370304800509.

Moogk, Peter N. "Les Petits Sauvages: The Children of Eighteenth-Century New France." In *Histories of Canadian Children and Youth*, edited by Nancy Janovicek and Joy Parr. Oxford University Press, 2003.

Morrow, William S. "What Do We Do with Proverbs?" In *Decolonizing Discipline: Children, Corporal Punishment, Christian Theologies, and Reconciliation*, edited by Valerie E. Michaelson and Joan E. Durrant. University of Manitoba Press, 2020. https://doi.org/10.1515/9780887558672-011.

Mosoff, Judith, and Isabel Grant. "Upholding Corporal Punishment: For Whose Benefit?" *Manitoba Law Journal* 31, no. 1 (2005): 177. https://doi.org/10.29173/mlj735.

Mulvaney, Matthew K., and Carolyn J. Mebert. "Parental Corporal Punishment Predicts Behavior Problems in Early Childhood." *Journal of Family Psychology* 21, no. 3 (2007): 389–97. https://doi.org/10.1037/0893-3200.21.3.389.

NACRG 10, Vol. 7185, File 1/25-1-7-1, D.C. Scott to Hon. Charles Stewart, October 31, 1927.

Naudin, Caroline, Veronica Gatti, Kossi B. Kounou, et al. "Physically Violent Parental Practices: A Cross-Cultural Study in Cameroon, Switzerland, and Togo." *Journal of Child & Adolescent Trauma* 16 (2023): 959–71. https://doi.org/10.1007/s40653-023-00564-8.

Newell, Peter. "The Human Rights Imperative to Eliminate Physical Punishment." In *Global Pathways to Abolishing Physical Punishment: Realizing Children's Rights*, edited by Joan E. Durrant and Anne B. Smith. Routledge, 2011.

New York Society for the Prevention of Cruelty to Children. "About the NYSPCC: History." http://www.nyspcc.org/about-the-new-york-society-for-the-prevention-of-cruelty-to-children/history/.

Nicholson, Alastair. "Choose to Hug, Not Hit." *Family Court Review* 46, no. 1 (2007): 11–36. https://doi.org/10.1111/j.1744-1617.2007.00180.x.

Nock, David. *A Victorian Missionary and Canadian Indian Policy: Cultural Synthesis vs Cultural Replacement.* Wilfrid Laurier University Press, 1988.

Nonomura, Robert, Crystal Giesbrecht, Tania Jivraj, et al. *Toward a Trauma- and Violence-Informed Research Ethics Module: Considerations and Recommendations.* Centre for Research & Education on Violence Against Women & Children, Western University, 2020. https://www.kh-cdc.ca/en/resources/reports/Grey-Report---English.pdf.

Ouimet, Roger. *Report of the Canadian Committee on Corrections: Toward Unity: Criminal Justice and Corrections.* Queen's Printer, 1969. https://publications.gc.ca/site/eng/9.905520/publication.html.

Parker, Roy. *Uprooted: The Shipment of Poor Children to Canada, 1867–1917.* Policy Press, 2008.

Parr, Joy. *Labouring Children: British Immigrant Apprentices to Canada, 1869–1924.* University of Toronto Press, 1994.

Pinheiro, Paulo S. *World Report on Violence Against Children.* United Nations Secretary-General's Study on Violence Against Children, 2006.

Piotrowski, Caroline C. "ACEs and Trauma-Informed Care." In *Adverse Childhood Experiences: Using Evidence to Advance Research, Practice, Policy and Prevention*, edited by Gordon J.G. Asmundson and Tracie O. Afifi. Elsevier, 2020.

Pollock, Linda A. *Forgotten Children: Parent Child Relations from 1500–1900.* Cambridge University Press, 1983.

Price Cohen, Cynthia, Stuart N. Hart, and Susan M. Kosloske. "The UN *Convention on the Rights of the Child*: Developing an Information Model to Computerize the Monitoring of Treaty Compliance." *Human Rights Quarterly* 14, no. 2 (1992): 216–31. https://doi.org/10.2307/762425.

Radbill, Samuel X. "Children in a World of Violence: A History of Child Abuse." In *The Battered Child*, edited by Ray E. Helfer and Ruth S. Kempe. University of Chicago Press, 1986.

Reference re Same-Sex Marriage, [2004] 3 SCR 698.

Rooke, Patricia T., and R.L. Schnell. *Discarding the Asylum: From Child Rescue to the Welfare State in English-Canada (1800–1950).* University Press of America, 1983.

Royal Commission on Aboriginal Peoples. *Report of the Royal Commission on Aboriginal Peoples.* Vol. 1, *Looking Forward, Looking Back.* Ministry of Supply and Services, 1996.

Royal Commission on Aboriginal Peoples. *Report of the Royal Commission on Aboriginal Peoples.* Vol. 3, *Gathering Strength.* Ministry of Supply and Services, 1996.

Rubin Stiffman, Arlene. "Physical and Sexual Abuse in Runaway Youths." *Child Abuse & Neglect* 13, no. 3 (1989): 417–26.

Rustad, Michael, and Thomas Koenig. "The Supreme Court and Junk Social Science: Selective Distortions in Amicus Briefs." *North Carolina Law Review* 72, no. 1 (1993): 91–162.

Ryder, Bruce, Cidalia C. Faria, and Emily Lawrence. "What's *Law* Good For? An Empirical Overview of *Charter* Equality Rights Decisions." *Supreme Court Law Review* 24 (2004). https://doi.org/10.60082/2563-8505.1050.

Ryley Scott, George. *The History of Corporal Punishment: A Survey of Flagellation in Its Historical Anthropological and Sociological Aspects.* T. Werner Laurie, 1938/1954.

Saller, Richard P. *Patriarchy, Property and Death in the Roman Family.* Cambridge University Press, 1994.

Sansone, G., B. Fallon, A. Vandermorris, A. Zuzino, and C. Milne. *Understanding the Effects of Corporal Punishment on Children, Families and Communities and Implications for Legal Reform in Canada.* Policy Bench, Fraser Mustard Institute of Human Development, University of Toronto.

Saskatchewan Provincial Child Abuse Protocol. 2023. Ministry of Social Services, 2023. https://pubsaskdev.blob.core.windows.net/pubsask-prod/18812/Sask%252BChild%252BAbuse%252BProtocol_June%252B2024.pdf.

Sege, Robert D., and Benjamin S. Siegel. "Effective Discipline to Raise Healthy Children." *Pediatrics* 142, no. 6 (2018): e20183112. https://doi.org/10.1542/peds.2018-3112.

Sheffler, Julia L., Ian Stanley, and Natalie Sachs-Ericsson. "ACEs and Mental Health Outcomes." In *Adverse Childhood Experiences: Using Evidence to Advance Research, Practice, Policy and Prevention,* edited by Gordon J.G. Asmundson and Tracie O. Afifi. Elsevier, 2020. https://doi.org/10.1016/B978-0-12-816065-7.00004-5.

Shelman, Eric A., and Stephen Lazoritz. *The Mary Ellen Wilson Child Abuse Case and the Beginning of Children's Rights in 19th Century America.* McFarland & Company, 2005.

Shmueli, Benjamin. "Corporal Punishment in the Education System Versus Corporal Punishment by Parents: A Comparative View." *Law and*

Contemporary Problems 73 (2010): 281–320. https://scholarship.law.duke.edu/lcp/vol73/iss2/11.

Shmueli, Benjamin. "The Influence of the UN Convention on the Rights of the Child on Corporal Punishment—A Comparative Look." *Oregon Review of International Law* 10 (2008): 189. https://ssrn.com/abstract=1514367.

Shonkoff, Jack P., and Andrew S. Garner. "The Lifelong Effects of Early Childhood Adversity and Toxic Stress." *Pediatrics* 129, no. 1 (2012): e232–e246. https://doi.org/10.1542/peds.2011-2663.

Smandych, Russell, and Anne McGillivray. "Images of Aboriginal Childhood." In *Empire and Others: British Encounters with Indigenous Peoples, 1600–1850*, edited by Martin Daunton and Rick Halpern. University of Pennsylvania Press, 1999.

Smith, Anne B., and Joan E. Durrant. "Introduction to the Global Movement to Ban Physical Punishment of Children." In *Global Pathways to Abolishing Physical Punishment: Realizing Children's Rights*, edited by Joan E. Durrant and Anne B. Smith. Routledge, 2011.

Statistics Canada. "Family Violence in Canada: A Statistical Profile." Canada Centre for Justice Studies, Ministry of Industry, 2011.

Statistics Canada. "Parenting Style and Children's Aggressive Behaviour." *The Daily*, October 25, 2004. http://www150.statcan.gc.ca/daily-quotidien/041025/d041025b-eng.htm.

Statistics Canada. "Victims of Police-Reported Family and Intimate Partner Violence in Canada, 2021." *The Daily*, October 19, 2022. https://www150.statcan.gc.ca/n1/daily-quotidien/221019/dq221019c-eng.html.

Stefanovich, Olivia. "Doctor Who Blew Whistle on Atrocities of Residential Schools Honoured in Ottawa." *CBC News*, September 30, 2022. https://www.cbc.ca/news/politics/peter-bryce-plaque-ottawa-national-truth-reconciliation-1.6599608.

Straus, Murray A., and Denise A. Donnelly. *Beating the Devil Out of Them: Corporal Punishment in American Families*. Lexington Press, 1994.

Straus, Murray A., and Denise A. Donnelly. *Beating the Devil Out of Them: Corporal Punishment in American Families and Its Effect on Children*. 2nd ed. Transaction Publishers, 2001.

Straus, Murray A., and E.M. Douglas. "Research on Spanking by Parents: Implications for Public Policy." *Family Psychologist: Bulletin of the Division of Family Psychology* 43, no. 24 (2008): 18–20.

Straus, Murray A., and Mallie J. Paschall. "Corporal Punishment by Mothers and Development of Children's Cognitive Ability: A Longitudinal Study of Two Nationally Representative Age Cohorts." *Journal of*

Aggression, Maltreatment & Trauma 18, no. 5 (2009): 459–83. http://dx.doi.org/10.1080/10926770903035168.

Stuart, Don. *Canadian Criminal Law: A Treatise*. 7th ed. Carswell, 2014.

Sykes, Katie. "Bambi Meets Godzilla: Children's and Parents' Rights in *Canadian Foundation for Children, Youth and the Law v. Canada*." *McGill Law Journal* 51, no 1 (2006). https://ssrn.com/abstract=2003948.

Tait, Caroline L. *Fetal Alcohol Syndrome Among Aboriginal People in Canada: Review and Analysis of the Intergenerational Links to Residential Schools*. Aboriginal Healing Foundation, 2003.

Taylor, Catherine A., Jennifer A. Manganello, Shawna J. Lee, and Janet C. Rice. "Mothers' Spanking of 3-Year-Old Children and Subsequent Risk of Children's Aggressive Behaviour." *Pediatrics* 125, no. 5 (2010): e1057–e1065. https://doi.org/10.1542/peds.2009-2678.

Taylor, Nicola, Beth Wood, and Anne B. Smith, "New Zealand: The Achievements and Challenges of Prohibition." In *Global Pathways to Abolishing Physical Punishment: Realizing Children's Rights*, edited by Joan E. Durrant and Anne B. Smith. Routledge, 2011.

Thomas, Jennifer. "Youth Court Statistics, 2006/2007." *Juristat* 28, no. 4 (2009). http://www.statcan.gc.ca/pub/85-002-x/2008004/article/10568-eng.htm#n15.

Tonmyr, Lil, Ben Mathews, Margot E. Shields, Wendy E. Hovdestad, and Tracie O. Afifi. "Does Mandatory Reporting Legislation Increase Contact with Child Protection?—A Legal Doctrinal Review and an Analytical Examination." *BMC Public Health* 18, no. 1021 (2018). https://bmcpublichealth.biomedcentral.com/articles/10.1186/s12889-018-5864-0.

Toronto Public Health. *National Survey of Canadians' Knowledge of the Law on Physical Punishment of Children (Section 43 of the Criminal Code of Canada)*. 2007. http://www.toronto.ca/health/ssl_index.html.

Trocmé, Nico, and David Wolfe. *Child Maltreatment in Canada: Selected Results from the Canadian Incidence Study of Reported Child Abuse and Neglect*. Minister of Public Works and Government Services Canada, 2001.

Trocmé, Nico, Barbara Fallon, Bruce MacLaurin, et al. *Canadian Incidence Study of Reported Child Abuse and Neglect: Final Report*. Health Canada, 2010.

Trocmé, Nico, Barbara Fallon, Bruce MacLaurin, et al. *Canadian Incidence Study of Reported Child Abuse and Neglect 2003: Major Findings*. Minister of Public Works and Government Services Canada, 2005.

Trocmé, Nico, Barbara Fallon, Bruce MacLaurin, et al. *Canadian Incidence Study of Reported Child Abuse and Neglect—2008: Major Findings*. Public Health Agency of Canada, 2010. http://www.phac-aspc.gc.ca/cm-vee/public-eng.php. https://cwrp.ca/sites/default/files/publications/CIS-2008-rprt-eng.pdf.

Truth and Reconciliation Commission of Canada. *Honouring the Truth, Reconciling for the Future: Summary of the Final Report of the Truth and Reconciliation Commission of Canada.* 2015. http://publications.gc.ca/collections/collection_2015/trc/IR4-7-2015-eng.pdf.

Turner, Heather A., and David Finkelhor. "Corporal Punishment as a Stressor Among Youth." *Journal of Marriage and Family* 58, no. 1 (1996): 155–66. https://doi.org/10.2307/353384.

Turner, Susan M. *Something to Cry About: An Argument Against Corporal Punishment of Children in Canada.* Wilfrid Laurier University Press, 2002.

UNCRC (United Nations Committee on the Rights of the Child). *General Comment No. 8: The Right of the Child to Protection from Corporal Punishment and Other Cruel or Degrading Forms of Punishment (Articles 19, 28(2) and 37, Inter Alia).* CRC/C/GC/8, June 2, 2006.

UNICEF. *Hidden in Plain Sight: A Statistical Analysis of Violence Against Children.* United Nation Children's Fund, Division of Data, Research and Policy, 2014. https://data.unicef.org/wp-content/uploads/2015/12/VR-full-report_Final-LR-3_2_15_189.pdf.

UNICEF and Religions for Peace. "From Commitment to Action: What Religious Communities Can Do to Eliminate Violence Against Children." February 2010. https://reliefweb.int/report/world/commitment-action-what-religious-communities-can-do-eliminate-violence-against-children.

United Nations. *Convention on the Rights of the Child.* Can. T.S. 1992 no. 3, art. 3(1).

United Nations. "Goal 16: Promote Peaceful and Inclusive Societies for Sustainable Development, Provide Access to Justice for All and Build Effective, Accountable and Inclusive Institutions at All Levels." Department of Economic and Social Affairs: Sustainable Development. https://sustainabledevelopment.un.org/sdg16.

United Nations. "The 17 Goals." Department of Economic and Social Affairs: Sustainable Development. https://sustainabledevelopment.un.org/?menu=1300.

United Nations High Commissioner for Human Rights. *Report of the Special Rapporteur of the Commission on Human Rights on the Question of Torture and Other Cruel, Inhuman, or Degrading Treatment or Punishment.* A/57/173, July 2, 2002.

United Nations Human Rights Commission. "Concluding Observations on the Sixth Periodic Report of Canada," CCPR/C/CAN/6, Aug 13, 2015. https://docs.un.org/en/CCPR/C/CAN/CO/6

US General Accounting Office. *Mental Health: Improper Restraint or Seclusion*

Use Places People at Risk. GAO publication HEHS-99-176, 1999. https://www.gao.gov/products/hehs-99-176.

Van Stolk, Mary. *The Battered Child in Canada*. McClelland & Stewart, 1978.

Veerman, Philip E. *The Rights of the Child and the Changing Image of Childhood*. Martinus Nijhoff Publishers, 1992.

Vittrup, Brigitte, and George W. Holden. "Children's Assessment of Corporal Punishment and Other Disciplinary Practices: The Role of Age, Race, SES, and Exposure to Spanking." *Journal of Applied Developmental Psychology* 31 (2010): 211–20. https://doi.org/10.1016/j.appdev.2009.11.003.

Vohito, Sonia. "Africa: Growing Momentum Towards the Prohibition of Corporal Punishment." In *Global Pathways to Abolishing Physical Punishment: Realizing Children's Rights*, edited by Joan E. Durrant and Anne B. Smith. Routledge, 2011.

Warick, Jason. "Abuse Allegations from Students at Private Sask. Christian School Are '100% True' Says Former Top Official." *CBC News*, August 11, 2022. https://www.cbc.ca/news/canada/saskatoon/christian-school-allegations-true-says-former-official-1.6547525.

Warick, Jason. "Exorcisms, Violent Discipline and Other Abuse Alleged by Former Students of Private Sask. Christian School." *CBC News*, August 2, 2022. https://www.cbc.ca/news/canada/saskatoon/abuse-alleged-former-students-of-private-christian-school-1.6532329.

Warick, Jason. "List of Students Alleging Abuse at Sask. Christian School Growing Rapidly." *CBC News*, August 5, 2022. https://www.cbc.ca/news/canada/saskatoon/saskatoon-legacy-christian-centre-academy-more-allegations-of-abuse-1.6541710.

Warick, Jason. "Tax-Subsidized Fight Irks MP: Vellacott Wants to End Federal Program That Will Pay for Woman's Battle Against Corporal Punishment." *Saskatoon Star Phoenix*, December 24, 1997.

Watkinson, Ailsa M. "Children Still Unprotected from Violence." *Saskatoon Star Phoenix*, May 11, 1995, A11.

Watkinson, Ailsa M. "Corporal Punishment: Apply the Charter, Spare the Child." *Canadian School Executive* 8, no. 5 (1988): 15–21.

Watkinson, Ailsa M. "Corporal Punishment and Education: Oh Canada! Spare Us!" In *The Courts, the Charter, and the Schools: The Impact of the Charter of Rights and Freedoms on Educational Policy and Practice, 1982–2007*, edited by Michael Manley-Casimir and Kirsten Manley-Casimir. University of Toronto Press, 2009.

Watkinson, Ailsa M. *Education, Student Rights and the Charter*. Purich Publishing, 1999.

Watkinson, Ailsa M. "Physical Punishment in Childhood: A Human Rights and Child Protection Issue." In *Passion for Action in Child and Family Services: Voices from the Prairies*, edited by Sharon McKay, Don Fuchs, and Ivan Brown. Canadian Plains Research Center, University of Regina, 2009.

Watkinson, Ailsa M. "Prohibiting Corporal Punishment: In the Name of the Charter, the Child and Societal Values." In *The Management of Values: Organizational and Educational Issues*, edited by Samuel Natale. University Press of America, 1998.

Watkinson, Ailsa M., and Letnie Rock. "A Comparative Study of the Attitudes of Graduating Bachelor of Social Work Students in Barbados and Canada Towards Child Physical Punishment." *Journal of Human Rights and Social Work* 4 (2019): 192–200. https://doi.org/10.1007/s41134-019-00094-0.

Wickstrom, Allan. "Name Change Cannot Erase Saskatoon Christian School's Legacy." Letter to *Regina Leader Post*, September 24, 2024. https://leaderpost.com/opinion/letters/letters-legacy-of-valour-academy-cannot-be-erased-with-a-name-change.

Wilson, Jeffery. *Wilson on Children and the Law*. Butterworths Law, 1978.

Winfield, Nicole. "Indigenous Leaders Hope Vatican's Repudiation of Oppressive Colonial Concepts Leads to Real Change." *CBC News*, March 30, 2023. https://www.cbc.ca/news/canada/vatican-reject-discovery-doctrine-indigenous-demands-1.6795728.

Young, John H. "'On Sparing the Rod and Spoiling the Child': Preaching on Call to Action 6 and the Repeal of Section 43 of the Criminal Code." In *Decolonizing Discipline: Children, Corporal Punishment, Christian Theologies, and Reconciliation*, edited by Valerie E. Michaelson and Joan E. Durrant. University of Manitoba Press, 2020. https://doi.org/10.1515/9780887558672-020.

Youth Criminal Justice Act, S.C. 2002. c1.

Court Cases

Alberta v. Hutterian Brethren of Wilson Colony, [2009] 2 SCR 567.

Andrews v. Law Society of British Columbia, [1989] 1 SCR 143.

Canada (Attorney General) v. Bedford, [2013] 3 SCR 1101.

Canadian Foundation for Children, Youth and the Law v. Canada (Attorney General), (2000) 188 DLR (4th) 718 (Ont. Sup. Ct.).

Canadian Foundation for Children, Youth and the Law v. Canada (Attorney General), (2002), 207 DLR (4th) 632 (Ont. CA).

Canadian Foundation for Children, Youth and the Law v. Canada (Attorney General), [2004] 1 SCR 76.

Carter v. Canada (Attorney General), [2015] 1 SCR 331.

Dagenais v. Canadian Broadcasting Corp., [1994] 3 SCR 835.
Egan v. Canada, [1995] 2 SCR 513.
Granovsky v. Canada (M.E.I.), [2001] 1 SCR 703.
Grayned v. City of Rockford, 408 U.S. 104 (1972) at 108–09 (USSC).
Irwin Toy Ltd. v. Quebec, [1989] 1 SCR 927.
Jones v. The Queen, [1986] 2 SCR 284.
Law v. Canada (Minister of Employment and Immigration), [1999] 1 SCR 497.
Miron v. Trudel, [1995] 2 SCR 418.
New Brunswick (Minister of Health and Community Services) v. G.(J.), [1999] 3 SCR 46.
Ogg-Moss v. The Queen, [1984] 2 SCR 173.
Pearlman v. Manitoba Law Society Judicial Committee, [1991] 2 SCR 869.
R. v. A. (M.), [2011] ONCJ 91.
R. v. Bell, [2001] OJ No. 1820 (Sup. Ct.).
R. v. Big M Drug Mart, [1985] 1 SCR 295.
R. v. Catellier, [2011] MBQB 77.
R. v. Demelo, [2009] OJ No. 2387 (CtJ).
R. v. Edwards Books and Art Ltd., [1986] 2 SCR 713.
R. v. Fitzpatrick, [2012] N.J. No. 19 (Prov. Ct.) per Porter J.
R. v. Gervin, [2012] MBQB 44.
R. v. Haberstock, (1970) 1 CCC (2d) 433 (Sask. CA).
R. v. Halcrow, [1993] BCJ No. 1227 (BCCA).
R. v. James, [1998] OJ No. 1438 (Ont. CJ) per Weagant J.
R. v. Kapp, [2008] 2 SCR 483.
R. v. Lifchus, [1997] 3 SCR 320.
R. v. McGrath, [2021] CanLii 7914 (NL), at para. 2.
R. v. Malmo-Levine, [2003] 3 SCR 571.
R. v. Morro, [2009] ABPC 114.
R. v. Nova Scotia Pharmaceutical Society, [1992] 1 SCR 606.
R. v. Oakes, [1986] 65 N.R. 87.
R. v. Peterson, [1995], 98 CCC (3d) 253 (Ont. CJ (Prov. Div.)).
R. v. Smith, [1987] 1 SCR 1045 at 1074.
R.W.D.S.U. v. Dolphin Delivery Ltd., [1986] 2 SCR 573.
Rodriguez v. British Columbia (Attorney General), [1993] 3 SCR 519.
Saskatchewan Federation of Labour v. Saskatchewan, [2015] 1 SCR 245.
Slaight Communications Inc. v. Davidson, [1989] 1 SCR 1038.
Trinity Western University v. British Columbia College of Teachers, [2001] 1 SCR 772.
Winnipeg Child and Family Services v. K.L.W., [2000] 2 SCR 519.
Withler v. Canada (Attorney General), [2011] 1 SCR 396.

INDEX

Ailsa M. Watkinson is Professor Emerita of Social Work, University of Regina, and a human rights advocate. She is the mother of three sons and grandmother to two grandchildren. She lives in Saskatoon, Saskatchewan.